劉毅老師回答同學的問題

1. **問：** 我國中英文很好，上了高一以後，我對英文就沒興趣了。為什麼我讀不下課本？

   答： 課文多改編自外國文章，有的單字已經過時，現在外國人都少用，如三民版第一冊的nuttiness (古怪)，moutza (灰燼)，這些艱深少用的單字，使你受盡挫折。你背了難的單字，反而忽略了常用的單字。

2. **問：** 我該怎麼樣增加英文程度？

   答： 高中課本和大學入學考試範圍是7000字，□要把7000字背得滾瓜爛熟，看到少數超出範圍□□ □不會害怕。因為一篇文章中，你不會的□□ □□深的單字混在一起，你當然學習起□□

3. **問：** 7000字我背不下來□□

   答： 英文一字多義，沒有□□□□ 所以我們編了「用會話背7000字」、□□□□個單字」、「時速破百單字快速記憶」，用□□暖你迅速背下來。

4. **問：** 我背了7000字，不會用怎麼辦？

   答： 「用會話背7000字」就是讓你背完馬上會用。如你背了：

   Holy cow! （天啊！）
   What a ***coincidence***! （真巧！）
   I wasn't ***expecting*** you. （我沒想到會遇見你。）

你就會 *holy, coincidence, expect,* 全部是7000字範圍內的單字。更棒的是，每句都在5個字以內，容易背，可主動說出。背的句子說出來、寫出來，都有信心。你一旦會說英文，就開始對學習英文有興趣了。有興趣的課程，學起來不累。

5. 問： 我要如何增強閱讀能力？

　答： 我們有出版以7000字為範圍的升大學叢書。如：
「7000字克漏字測驗詳解」、
「7000字文意選填詳解」、
「7000字閱讀測驗詳解」、
「7000字學測試題詳解」。
不一定要等到高三，從高一就要開始讀。

6. 問： 為什麼一定要讀以7000字為範圍的閱讀測驗？報章雜誌和課本的文章，不是都超出範圍嗎？

　答： 英文單字無限多，做了100份試題還是有80幾個生字，唯有題目在7000字範圍內，把常用的單字背熟，才會越做越有信心，才會進步。背熟後，再看報章雜誌和課本，就輕鬆了，碰到一些超出範圍的單字，不會影響到你的閱讀。

7. 問：我可不可以做歷屆試題？

　答：大考中心在歷屆試題花了很大工夫，你可參照我們的「歷屆學測英文試題詳解」，附有勘誤表及出題來源，即使那麼重要的考試，仍然有錯誤，那一般的試題更不用說。

8. 問：我如何在月期考中得高分？

答：把課本熟讀是必要條件，另外百分之五十
課外，如建中，包含聽力測驗(20%)、字
彙與片語(5%)、綜合測驗(25%)、文法選擇
(5%)、文意選填(5%)、閱讀測驗(5%)、文
意字彙(25%)需要拼字，翻譯(10%)，沒有
經過訓練，英文再好，也很難高分。
除了背單字以外，平常就要練習各種題型。
「學習」有出版「高中英語聽力測驗」及
「高中英語聽力測驗進階」。課外太多，
最好的準備方式，就是大量閱讀以7000字
為範圍的書。

9. 問：我要讀課本，又要背「高中常用7000字」，該怎麼兼
顧？

答：你可參加全國各單位舉辦的「高中英文單
字大賽」，以考試為目標來激勵自己背單
字，「背單字、領獎金，是人生美好的事」
比賽成績有助於你進入理想大學。

10. 問：還有什麼其他比賽？

答：有「英文演講比賽」和「英文作文比賽」，報名參加，
接受挑戰，只要參加就是勝利者，成功得到榮譽，失
敗得到經驗。不斷參加，能督促你學英文。

11. 問： 我英文學那麼久，見到外國人不會說話怎麼辦？

答： 學校考課本，你又讀不下去，該怎麼辦呢？我們現在新研發的「用演講背7000字」，將課本內容改編成短篇演講稿，共27句，同學背了，會演講、會寫作文，也會說話。

下面是改編自「高一龍騰版第二冊第二課」的演講稿，你背完之後，不僅會讀課本，對你的身心都有幫助。

How to Beat the Blues
（如何克服憂鬱）

Ladies and gentlemen.	各位先生，各位女士。
Boys and girls.	各位男孩和女孩。
Teacher and students.	老師和同學們。
Have you ever felt down?	你有沒有曾經感到沮喪？
Do you have pressure at school?	在學校上學有沒有壓力？
Let me tell you how to beat the blues.	讓我來告訴你如何克服憂鬱。
First, exercise is a great start.	首先，運動是很好的開始。
Physical activities are the way.	運動就對了。
Jog, bicycle, or take a brisk walk daily.	要每天慢跑、騎腳踏車，或快走。
Second, eat fruits and vegetables.	第二，要吃蔬菜和水果。
Don't consume junk food.	不要吃垃圾食物。
Don't drink too much tea or coffee.	不要喝太多茶或咖啡。
Third, take a few deep breaths.	第三，做幾個深呼吸。
Controlled breathing can lower your blood pressure.	控制呼吸可降低你的血壓。
It will lighten your mood.	它能使你心情變輕鬆。
Fourth, get a proper amount of sunlight.	第四，要適度曬太陽。
It helps a lot when you are moody.	你心情不好時，會對你很有幫助。
It costs you nothing but does you good.	它不花一分錢，但對你有益。

TEST 1

【命題範圍：「高中生必背 4500 字」
p.1-10，abandon～anxious】

Directions: *Choose the one word that best completes the sentence.*

1. Jim and Jack became _____ while working together in a restaurant.
   (A) announced   (B) allowed
   (C) adapted   (D) acquainted   (　　)

2. Solar panels _____ sunlight and turn it into electricity.
   (A) admit   (B) absorb
   (C) amuse   (D) amaze   (　　)

3. Many cafes in this neighborhood offer free Internet _____.
   (A) accent   (B) accident
   (C) access   (D) accuracy   (　　)

4. Betty made a doctor's appointment for her _____ physical exam.
   (A) absolute   (B) annual
   (C) acceptable   (D) acid   (　　)

5. The hikers were _____ not to stray too far from the main trail.
   (A) advised   (B) afforded
   (C) annoyed   (D) accompanied   (　　)

6. The captain ordered his crew to _____ the ship as water flooded the lower decks.
   (A) abandon   (B) accomplish
   (C) analyze   (D) anger   (　　)

7. Over the last three years, the museum has _____ more than a dozen priceless works of art.
   (A) acquired   (B) accused
   (C) adjusted   (D) addressed   (　　)

8. Mr. Jackson takes medication to treat his _____ and depression.
   - (A) ability
   - (B) agency
   - (C) anxiety
   - (D) advertisement
   ( )

9. The university announced an _____ project to build a solar farm.
   - (A) anxious
   - (B) alive
   - (C) ambitious
   - (D) ancient
   ( )

10. The blood samples have been sent away for _____.
    - (A) angle
    - (B) almond
    - (C) amazement
    - (D) analysis
    ( )

11. The remote village lacks _____ sanitation facilities; thus, diseases run rampant.
    - (A) abstract
    - (B) adequate
    - (C) absent
    - (D) academic
    ( )

12. Unable to have children of their own, the couple decided to _____ a boy from Japan.
    - (A) ache
    - (B) achieve
    - (C) adopt
    - (D) admire
    ( )

13. Ted hosted a party in celebration of the 10th _____ of the day he moved to Taiwan.
    - (A) anniversary
    - (B) action
    - (C) accountant
    - (D) acre
    ( )

14. Disabled people are excited by the potential benefits of using _____ technologies at home.
    - (A) afraid
    - (B) alike
    - (C) active
    - (D) advanced
    ( )

15. Though most alligators are not _____, they will attack if threatened or cornered.
    - (A) accidental
    - (B) aggressive
    - (C) additional
    - (D) admirable
    ( )

TEST 1 詳解

1. (**D**) Jim and Jack became <u>acquainted</u> while working together in a
restaurant. 吉姆和傑克是在餐廳一起工作時<u>認識</u>的。
　　(A) announce³〔əˈnaʊns〕v. 宣布
　　(B) allow¹〔əˈlaʊ〕v. 允許
　　(C) adapt⁴〔əˈdæpt〕v. 適應；改編
　　(D) ***acquaint***⁴〔əˈkwent〕v. 使認識；使熟悉

2. (**B**) Solar panels <u>absorb</u> sunlight and turn it into electricity.
太陽能板會<u>吸收</u>陽光，並把它轉換成電。
　　(A) admit³〔ədˈmɪt〕v. 承認
　　(B) ***absorb***⁴〔əbˈsɔrb〕v. 吸收
　　(C) amuse⁴〔əˈmjuz〕v. 娛樂
　　(D) amaze³〔əˈmez〕v. 使驚訝
　　＊solar⁴〔ˈsolɚ〕adj. 太陽的　　panel⁴〔ˈpænl〕n. 鑲板；金屬板
　　turn～into 使～變成　　electricity³〔ɪˌlɛkˈtrɪsətɪ〕n. 電

3. (**C**) Many cafés in this neighborhood offer free Internet <u>access</u>.
這附近的許多咖啡廳都提供免費<u>使用</u>網路。
　　(A) accent⁴〔ˈæksn̩t〕n. 口音
　　(B) accident³〔ˈæksədn̩t〕n. 意外
　　(C) ***access***⁴〔ˈæksɛs〕n. 接近或使用權
　　(D) accuracy⁴〔ˈækjərəsɪ〕n. 準確
　　＊café²〔kəˈfe〕n. 咖啡廳　　neighborhood³〔ˈnebɚˌhud〕n. 鄰近地區
　　offer²〔ˈɔfɚ〕v. 提供　　free¹〔fri〕adj. 免費的
　　Internet⁴〔ˈɪntɚˌnɛt〕n. 網際網路

4. (**B**) Betty made a doctor's appointment for her <u>annual</u> physical exam.
貝蒂跟醫生預約，要做<u>一年一度的</u>健康檢查。
　　(A) absolute⁴〔ˈæbsəˌlut〕adj. 絕對的
　　(B) ***annual***⁴〔ˈænjuəl〕adj. 一年一度的
　　(C) acceptable³〔əkˈsɛptəbl̩〕adj. 可接受的
　　(D) acid⁴〔ˈæsɪd〕adj. 酸的

appointment⁴〔ə'pɔɪntmənt〕n. 約會；約診

physical exam 身體檢查；健康檢查（= *check-up⁵*）

5. (**A**) The hikers were <u>advised</u> not to stray too far from the main trail.
那些健行者被<u>勸告</u>，不要偏離主要的道路太遠。

    (A) ***advise³*** 〔əd'vaɪz〕*v.* 勸告

    (B) afford³〔ə'fɔrd〕*v.* 負擔得起

    (C) annoy⁴〔ə'nɔɪ〕*v.* 使心煩

    (D) accompany⁴〔ə'kʌmpənɪ〕*v.* 陪伴

    hike³〔'haɪkə〕n. 健行者   stray⁵〔stre〕*v.* 離開；誤入歧途

    main²〔men〕*adj.* 主要的   trail³〔trel〕*n.* 小路；小徑

6. (**A**) The captain ordered his crew to <u>abandon</u> the ship as water flooded the
lower decks. 船長命令全體船員<u>棄船</u>，因為水已經淹到較低層的甲板。

    (A) ***abandon⁴*** 〔ə'bændn̩〕*v.* 拋棄

    (B) accomplish⁴〔ə'kɑmplɪʃ〕*v.* 完成

    (C) analyze⁴〔'ænl̩,aɪz〕*v.* 分析

    (D) anger¹〔'æŋgə〕*v.* 激怒

    captain²〔'kæptn̩〕n. 船長   crew³〔kru〕*n.* 全體船員

    flood²〔flʌd〕*v.* 使氾濫；使淹沒   deck³〔dɛk〕*n.* 甲板

7. (**A**) Over the last three years, the museum has <u>acquired</u> more than a
dozen priceless works of art.
在過去三年內，這家博物館已經<u>獲得</u>超過十二件的無價藝術品。

    (A) ***acquire⁴*** 〔ə'kwaɪr〕*v.* 獲得

    (B) accuse⁴〔ə'kjuz〕*v.* 控告

    (C) adjust⁴〔ə'dʒʌst〕*v.* 調整

    (D) address¹〔ə'drɛs〕*v.* 向⋯講話

    dozen¹〔'dʌzn̩〕n. 一打；十二個

    priceless⁵〔'praɪslɪs〕*adj.* 無價的   work¹〔wɜk〕*n.* 作品

8. (**C**) Mr. Jackson takes medication to treat his <u>anxiety</u> and depression.
傑克森先生服藥治療他的<u>焦慮</u>和憂鬱。

    (A) ability²〔ə'bɪlətɪ〕*n.* 能力

    (B) agency⁴〔'edʒənsɪ〕*n.* 代辦處

(C) *anxiety* [4] 〔 æŋ'zaɪətɪ 〕 *n.* 焦慮

(D) advertisement [3] 〔ˌædvə'taɪzmənt 〕 *n.* 廣告

*take [1] 〔 tek 〕 *v.* 服用　　treat [5,2] 〔 trit 〕 *v.* 治療

depression [4] 〔 dɪ'prɛʃən 〕 *n.* 憂鬱

9. (**C**) The university announced an <u>ambitious</u> project to build a solar farm.
   那所大學宣布一個<u>耗資巨大的</u>計劃，要建造一座太陽能農場。

   (A) anxious [4] 〔'æŋkʃəs 〕 *adj.* 焦慮的

   (B) alive [2] 〔 ə'laɪv 〕 *adj.* 活的

   (C) *ambitious* [4] 〔 æm'bɪʃəs 〕 *adj.* 有野心的；有抱負的；費力的；耗資的

   (D) ancient [2] 〔'enʃənt 〕 *adj.* 古代的

   *project [2] 〔'pradʒɛkt 〕 *n.* 計劃　　*solar farm* 太陽能農場

10. (**D**) The blood samples have been sent away for <u>analysis</u>.
    血液的樣本已經被送去做<u>分析</u>。

    (A) angle [3] 〔'æŋgl̩ 〕 *n.* 角度　　(B) almond [2] 〔'æmənd 〕 *n.* 杏仁

    (C) amazement [3] 〔 ə'mezmənt 〕 *n.* 驚訝

    (D) *analysis* [4] 〔 ə'næləsɪs 〕 *n.* 分析

    *blood [1] 〔 blʌd 〕 *n.* 血液　　sample [2] 〔'sæmpl̩ 〕 *n.* 樣本

11. (**B**) The remote village lacks <u>adequate</u> sanitation facilities; thus, diseases
    run rampant. 那個偏遠的村莊缺乏<u>足夠的</u>衛生設施；因此疾病很猖獗。

    (A) abstract [4] 〔'æbstrækt 〕 *adj.* 抽象的

    (B) *adequate* [4] 〔'ædəkwɪt 〕 *adj.* 足夠的

    (C) absent [2] 〔'æbsn̩t 〕 *adj.* 缺席的

    (D) academic [4] 〔ˌækə'dɛmɪk 〕 *adj.* 學術的

    *remote [3] 〔 rɪ'mot 〕 *adj.* 遍僻的；遙遠的　　village [2] 〔'vɪlɪdʒ 〕 *n.* 村莊
    lack [1] 〔 læk 〕 *v.* 缺乏　　sanitation [6] 〔ˌsændə'teʃən 〕 *n.* 衛生
    facilities [4] 〔 fə'sɪlətɪz 〕 *n. pl.* 設施　　thus [1] 〔 ðʌs 〕 *adv.* 因此
    run [1] 〔 rʌn 〕 *v.* 蔓延
    rampant 〔'ræmpənt 〕 *adj.* (疫病) 猖獗的；流行的

12. (**C**) Unable to have children of their own, the couple decided to <u>adopt</u> a
    boy from Japan.
    那對夫妻因爲無法生自己的小孩，所以決定從日本<u>領養</u>一個男孩。

(A) ache [3] 〔 ek 〕 v. 疼痛

(B) achieve [3] 〔 ə'tʃiv 〕 v. 達到

(C) *adopt* [3] 〔 ə'dɑpt 〕 v. 領養；採用

(D) admire [3] 〔 əd'maɪr 〕 v. 欽佩；讚賞

* *be unable to V.* 無法…　　　couple [2] 〔 'kʌpḷ 〕 n. 夫婦

13. (**A**) Ted hosted a party in celebration of the 10th <u>anniversary</u> of the day he moved to Taiwan.

泰德主辦一場派對，以慶祝他搬到台灣十<u>週年紀念</u>。

(A) *anniversary* [4] 〔 ˌænə'vɝsərɪ 〕 n. 週年紀念

(B) action [1] 〔 'ækʃən 〕 n. 行動

(C) accountant [4] 〔 ə'kaʊntənt 〕 n. 會計（師）

(D) acre [4] 〔 'ekɚ 〕 n. 英畝

* host [2,4] 〔 host 〕 v. 主辦　　celebration [4] 〔 ˌsɛlə'breʃən 〕 n. 慶祝
  in celebration of 爲了慶祝

14. (**D**) Disabled people are excited by the potential benefits of using <u>advanced</u> technologies at home.

殘障的人因爲在家使用<u>先進科技</u>可能會有的好處而感到興奮。

(A) afraid [1] 〔 ə'fred 〕 adj. 害怕的

(B) alike [2] 〔 ə'laɪk 〕 adj. 相像的

(C) active [2] 〔 'æktɪv 〕 adj. 活躍的

(D) *advanced* [3] 〔 əd'vænst 〕 adj. 先進的

* disabled [6] 〔 dɪs'ebḷd 〕 adj. 殘障的　　potential [5] 〔 pə'tɛnʃəl 〕 adj. 可能的
  benefit [3] 〔 'bɛnəfɪt 〕 n. 利益；好處

15. (**B**) Though most alligators are not <u>aggressive</u>, they will attack if threatened or cornered.　雖然大部份的短吻鱷是沒<u>有攻擊性的</u>，但如果受到威脅或被逼到角落，還是會展開攻擊。

(A) accidental [4] 〔 ˌæksə'dɛntḷ 〕 adj. 意外的

(B) *aggressive* [4] 〔 ə'grɛsɪv 〕 adj. 有攻擊性的

(C) additional [3] 〔 ə'dɪʃənḷ 〕 adj. 額外的

(D) admirable [4] 〔 'ædmərəbḷ 〕 adj. 令人欽佩的

* alligator [5] 〔 'æləˌgetɚ 〕 n. 短吻鱷　　attack [2] 〔 ə'tæk 〕 v. 攻擊
  threaten [3] 〔 'θrɛtṇ 〕 v. 威脅　　corner [2] 〔 'kɔrnɚ 〕 v. 把…逼到角落

TEST 2

【命題範圍：「高中生必背 4500 字」
p.11-20，anybody～barrel】

Directions: Choose the one word that best completes the sentence.

1. The singer's mistake was _____ to everyone in the audience.
   (A) appropriate　　　　(B) automatic
   (C) artistic　　　　　(D) apparent　　　　　(　)

2. Students _____ in the courtyard before and after classes.
   (A) assure　　　　　(B) arise
   (C) apologize　　　　(D) assemble　　　　　(　)

3. Please _____ a copy of your resume to the job application form.
   (A) attach　　　　　(B) attend
   (C) attack　　　　　(D) attract　　　　　(　)

4. James will _____ to read three books this month.
   (A) await　　　　　(B) avoid
   (C) bake　　　　　　(D) attempt　　　　　(　)

5. These shoes are _____ in four colors: blue, gray, brown, and black.
   (A) awkward　　　　(B) available
   (C) ashamed　　　　(D) awake　　　　　(　)

6. Exercise can help stimulate a person's _____ if he is not inclined to eat.
   (A) aspect　　　　　(B) apartment
   (C) appetite　　　　(D) apology　　　　　(　)

7. His early years were spent in Italy where he learned to _____ various types of coffee.
   (A) argue　　　　　(B) appreciate
   (C) arrest　　　　　(D) arouse　　　　　(　)

8. She was not _____ that the money was missing.
   (A) awful   (B) bankrupt
   (C) average   (D) aware   (   )

9. The man slipped on the wet floor but quickly regained his _____.
   (A) bacon   (B) bamboo
   (C) balance   (D) baggage   (   )

10. The poor family can hardly afford the _____ necessities to survive.
   (A) asleep   (B) bare
   (C) artistic   (D) artificial   (   )

11. Red cherry shrimp will thrive in the same conditions as many common _____ fish.
   (A) aquarium   (B) arch
   (C) armchair   (D) army   (   )

12. In Western culture, the color white is _____ with purity and innocence.
   (A) assisted   (B) assumed
   (C) associated   (D) assigned   (   )

13. Boys and girls with _____ ability are usually encouraged to participate in sports.
   (A) atomic   (B) athletic
   (C) attractive   (D) bald   (   )

14. Mr. Miller does not have the _____ to approve changes to the budget.
   (A) barrel   (B) attraction
   (C) authority   (D) atmosphere   (   )

15. Dr. Jenkins has won a number of _____ for his research in medicine.
   (A) awards   (B) backpacks
   (C) balloons   (D) arrows   (   )

TEST 2 詳解

1. (**D**) The singer's mistake was <u>apparent</u> to everyone in the audience.
　　 每個聽眾都<u>明白</u>那歌手犯了一個錯。
　　 (A) appropriate [4] 〔 ə'propriɪt 〕 *adj.* 適當的
　　 (B) automatic [3] 〔 ,ɔtə'mætɪk 〕 *adj.* 自動的
　　 (C) artistic [4] 〔 ar'tɪstɪk 〕 *adj.* 藝術的
　　 (D) ***apparent*** [3] 〔 ə'pærənt 〕 *adj.* 明顯的；明白的
　　 ＊mistake [1] 〔 mə'stek 〕 *n.* 錯誤
　　　 audience [3] 〔 'ɔdɪəns 〕 *n.* 聽眾；觀眾

2. (**D**) Students <u>assemble</u> in the courtyard before and after classes.
　　 學生們在上課前和下課後會在中庭<u>集合</u>。
　　 (A) assure [4] 〔 ə'ʃur 〕 *v.* 向 (人) 保證；使安心
　　 (B) arise [4] 〔 ə'raɪz 〕 *v.* 出現；發生
　　 (C) apologize [4] 〔 ə'palə,dʒaɪz 〕 *v.* 道歉
　　 (D) ***assemble*** [4] 〔 ə'sɛmbl̩ 〕 *v.* 聚集；集合
　　 ＊courtyard [5] 〔 'kɔrt,jard 〕 *n.* 中庭；庭院

3. (**A**) Please <u>attach</u> a copy of your resume to the job application form.
　　 請在工作申請表上<u>附</u>上一份你的履歷。
　　 (A) ***attach*** [4] 〔 ə'tætʃ 〕 *v.* 黏；附著；添加 < *to* >
　　 (B) attend [2] 〔 ə'tɛnd 〕 *v.* 參加；出席
　　 (C) attack [2] 〔 ə'tæk 〕 *v.* 攻擊
　　 (D) attract [3] 〔 ə'trækt 〕 *v.* 吸引
　　 ＊copy [2] 〔 'kapɪ 〕 *n.* 一份　　 resume [5] 〔 'rɛzu,me 〕 *n.* 履歷
　　　 application [4] 〔 ,æplə'keʃən 〕 *n.* 申請　　 form [2] 〔 fɔrm 〕 *n.* 表格

4. (**D**) James will <u>attempt</u> to read three books this month.
　　 詹姆士這個月會<u>嘗試</u>讀三本書。
　　 (A) await [4] 〔 ə'wet 〕 *v.* 等待
　　 (B) avoid [2] 〔 ə'vɔɪd 〕 *v.* 避免
　　 (C) bake [2] 〔 bek 〕 *v.* 烘焙
　　 (D) ***attempt*** [3] 〔 ə'tɛmpt 〕 *v.* 嘗試

5. (**B**) These shoes are <u>available</u> in four colors: blue, gray, brown, and black.

這鞋子<u>有</u>四種顏色：藍色、灰色、褐色，和黑色。

(A) awkward⁴ 〔 ˋɔkwəd 〕 *adj.* 笨拙的

(B) ***available***³ 〔 əˋveləbḷ 〕 *adj.* 可取得的；可買得到的

(C) ashamed⁴ 〔 əˋʃemd 〕 *adj.* 感到羞恥的 < *of* >

(D) awake³ 〔 əˋwek 〕 *adj.* 醒著的

* gray¹ 〔 gre 〕 *n.* 灰色　　brown¹ 〔 braun 〕 *n.* 褐色

6. (**C**) Exercise can help stimulate a person's <u>appetite</u> if he is not inclined to eat. 如果沒有食慾，運動可以刺激一個人的<u>胃口</u>。

(A) aspect⁴ 〔 ˋæspɛkt 〕 *n.* 方面

(B) apartment² 〔 əˋpɑrtmənt 〕 *n.* 公寓

(C) ***appetite***² 〔 ˋæpəˌtaɪt 〕 *n.* 食慾；胃口

(D) apology⁴ 〔 əˋpɑlədʒɪ 〕 *n.* 道歉

* exercise² 〔 ˋɛksɚˌsaɪz 〕 *n.* 運動　　stimulate⁶ 〔 ˋstɪmjəˌlet 〕 *v.* 刺激
  inclined⁶ 〔 ɪnˋklaɪnd 〕 *adj.* 想要…的

7. (**B**) His early years were spent in Italy where he learned to <u>appreciate</u> various types of coffee.

他早年在義大利度過，在那裡他學會<u>品味</u>各種類型的咖啡。

(A) argue² 〔 ˋɑrgju 〕 *v.* 爭論

(B) ***appreciate***³ 〔 əˋpriʃɪˌet 〕 *v.* 感激；欣賞；品味

(C) arrest² 〔 əˋrɛst 〕 *v.* 逮捕

(D) arouse⁴ 〔 əˋrauz 〕 *v.* 喚醒；激發

* various³ 〔 ˋvɛrɪəs 〕 *adj.* 各種的

8. (**D**) She was not <u>aware</u> that the money was missing.

她沒<u>有察覺到</u>錢不見了。

(A) awful³ 〔 ˋɔful 〕 *adj.* 很糟的；可怕的

(B) bankrupt⁴ 〔 ˋbæŋkrʌpt 〕 *adj.* 破產的

(C) average³ 〔 ˋævərɪdʒ 〕 *adj.* 平均的；一般的

(D) ***aware***³ 〔 əˋwɛr 〕 *adj.* 知道的；察覺到的 < *of* >

* missing³ 〔 ˋmɪsɪŋ 〕 *adj.* 不見的；下落不明的

9. (**C**) The man slipped on the wet floor but quickly regained his <u>balance</u>.
男士在潮濕的地板滑倒，但是很快就恢復<u>平衡</u>。

    (A) bacon³ (ˈbekən) *n.* 培根
    (B) bamboo² (bæmˈbu) *n.* 竹子
    (C) ***balance***³ (ˈbæləns) *n.* 平衡
    (D) baggage³ (ˈbægɪdʒ) *n.* 行李

    * slip² (slɪp) *v.* 滑倒   regain² (rɪˈgen) *v.* 恢復；重回

10. (**B**) The poor family can hardly afford the <u>bare</u> necessities to survive.
那貧窮的家庭幾乎買不起<u>最起碼的</u>生活必需品以生存。

    (A) asleep² (əˈslip) *adj.* 睡著的
    (B) ***bare***³ (bɛr) *adj.* 赤裸的；最少限度的；勉強的
        bare necessities 基本生活必需品
    (C) artistic⁴ (arˈtɪstɪk) *adj.* 藝術的
    (D) artificial⁴ (ˌartəˈfɪʃəl) *adj.* 人造的

    * hardly² (ˈhardlɪ) *adv.* 幾乎不   afford³ (əˈford) *v.* 買得起；負擔
    necessity³ (nəˈsɛsətɪ) *n.* 必需品   survive² (səˈvaɪv) *v.* 生存

11. (**A**) Red cherry shrimp will thrive in the same conditions as many
common <u>aquarium</u> fish.
櫻花蝦的生長環境和很多一般<u>水族箱</u>養殖的魚一樣。

    (A) ***aquarium***³ (əˈkwɛrɪəm) *n.* 水族館；水族箱
    (B) arch⁴ (artʃ) *n.* 拱門；拱形
    (C) armchair² (ˈarmˌtʃɛr) *n.* 扶椅
    (D) army¹ (ˈarmɪ) *n.* 軍隊

    * cherry³ (ˈtʃɛrɪ) *adj.* 櫻桃色的   shrimp² (ʃrɪmp) *n.* 小蝦
    red cherry shrimp 玫瑰蝦；櫻花蝦
    thrive⁶ (θraɪv) *v.* 茁壯；成長
    conditions³ (kənˈdɪʃənz) *n. pl.* 環境；條件
    common¹ (ˈkamən) *adj.* 一般的

12. (**C**) In Western culture, the color white is <u>associated</u> with purity and
innocence. 在西方文化，白色和純潔天眞<u>聯想</u>在一起。

    (A) assist³ (əˈsɪst) *v.* 幫助

(B) assume [4] 〔ə'sum〕 v. 假定;認為

(C) *associate* [4] 〔ə'soʃɪ,et〕 v. 聯想;使有關
be associated with 和…聯想在一起;和…有關

(D) assign [4] 〔ə'saɪn〕 v. 分配

*Western [2] 〔'wɛstən〕 adj. 西洋的;西方的
culture [2] 〔'kʌltʃə〕 n. 文化　　purity [6] 〔'pjʊrətɪ〕 n. 純潔
innocence [4] 〔'ɪnəsṇs〕 n. 天眞;單純

13. (**B**) Boys and girls with athletic ability are usually encouraged to
participate in sports.
有運動能力的男孩女孩通常被鼓勵去參加體育競賽。

(A) atomic [4] 〔ə'tɑmɪk〕 adj. 原子的

(B) *athletic* [4] 〔æθ'lɛtɪk〕 adj. 運動的

(C) attractive [3] 〔ə'træktɪv〕 adj. 吸引人的

(D) bald [4] 〔bɔld〕 adj. 禿頭的

*ability [2] 〔ə'bɪlətɪ〕 n. 能力　　encourage [2] 〔ɪn'kɝɪdʒ〕 v. 鼓勵
participate [3] 〔pɑr'tɪsə,pet〕 v. 參加 < in >

14. (**C**) Mr. Miller does not have the authority to approve changes to the
budget. 米勒先生沒有權限批准預算的變更。

(A) barrel [3] 〔'bærəl〕 n. 桶;一桶的量

(B) attraction [4] 〔ə'trækʃən〕 n. 吸引力

(C) *authority* [4] 〔ɔ'θɔrətɪ〕 n. 權威;權限

(D) atmosphere [4] 〔'ætməs,fɪr〕 n. 大氣;氣氛

*approve [3] 〔ə'pruv〕 v. 批准　　budget [3] 〔'bʌdʒɪt〕 n. 預算

15. (**A**) Dr. Jenkins has won a number of awards for his research in
medicine. 詹金斯醫生已經獲得了幾個醫學研究的獎。

(A) *award* [3] 〔ə'wɔrd〕 n. 獎

(B) backpack [4] 〔'bæk,pæk〕 n. 背包

(C) balloon [1] 〔bə'lun〕 n. 氣球

(D) arrow [2] 〔'æro〕 n. 箭

*Dr. [2] 〔'dɑktə〕 n. 醫生 (= *Doctor*)　　*a number of* 一些
research [4] 〔'risɝtʃ〕 n. 研究　　medicine [2] 〔'mɛdəsṇ〕 n. 醫學

TEST 3

【命題範圍：「高中生必背 4500 字」
p.21-30，barrier～buzz】

Directions: *Choose the one word that best completes the sentence.*

1. Lack of education can be a _____ to success.
   - (A) barrier
   - (B) branch
   - (C) basin
   - (D) basket   (   )

2. The cell phone's _____ is low and needs to be recharged.
   - (A) bath
   - (B) battery
   - (C) bay
   - (D) beak   (   )

3. The mother couldn't _____ to see her child cry.
   - (A) beg
   - (B) beat
   - (C) bear
   - (D) behave   (   )

4. The artist stared at the _____ canvas, wondering what to paint.
   - (A) brave
   - (B) brutal
   - (C) blank
   - (D) bloody   (   )

5. Roger began to _____ when he realized his mistake.
   - (A) blush
   - (B) blow
   - (C) blink
   - (D) boast   (   )

6. The field trip to the art museum was of great _____ to the students.
   - (A) block
   - (B) belief
   - (C) bench
   - (D) benefit   (   )

7. For his book report, John chose a _____ of the famous composer Mozart.
   - (A) biography
   - (B) beast
   - (C) brake
   - (D) blade   (   )

8. Julie is a social butterfly who _____ from one group to another.
   (A) bothers
   (B) bows
   (C) bounces
   (D) borrows ( )

9. The company has an annual operating _____ of 10 million euros.
   (A) budget
   (B) buffet
   (C) brook
   (D) battle ( )

10. The _____ of organizing the party fell on Lucy.
    (A) brush
    (B) burden
    (C) bulb
    (D) bush ( )

11. There are five elements of taste perception: salty, sour, _____, sweet and umami.
    (A) basic
    (B) bitter
    (C) bright
    (D) bold ( )

12. His dream lover smiled at him and he thought his heart might _____.
    (A) bury
    (B) bump
    (C) burst
    (D) broadcast ( )

13. Hanami is a traditional custom of enjoying the beauty of flower _____.
    (A) blankets
    (B) blessings
    (C) blouses
    (D) blossoms ( )

14. They snuck across the _____ into Mexico during the early hours of June 7th.
    (A) bookcase
    (B) border
    (C) bond
    (D) biscuit ( )

15. Victor is a _____ musician, but he lacks the discipline to become a master.
    (A) brief
    (B) broad
    (C) bony
    (D) brilliant ( )

TEST 3 詳解

1. (**A**) Lack of education can be a <u>barrier</u> to success.
   欠缺教育可能會<u>阻礙</u>成功。
   - (A) ***barrier*** [4] ﹝ˈbærɪɚ﹞ *n.* 阻礙；障礙
   - (B) branch [2] ﹝bræntʃ﹞ *n.* 樹枝；分公司
   - (C) basin [4] ﹝ˈbesn̩﹞ *n.* 盆地；水盆
   - (D) basket [1] ﹝ˈbæskɪt﹞ *n.* 籃子
   * lack [1] ﹝læk﹞ *n.* 缺乏　　education [2] ﹝ˌɛdʒəˈkeʃən﹞ *n.* 教育
   　success [2] ﹝səkˈsɛs﹞ *n.* 成功

2. (**B**) The cell phone's <u>battery</u> is low and needs to be recharged.
   這手機<u>電池</u>快沒電了，需要再充電。
   - (A) bath [1] ﹝bæθ﹞ *n.* 洗澡；沐浴
   - (B) ***battery*** [4] ﹝ˈbætərɪ﹞ *n.* 電池
   - (C) bay [3] ﹝be﹞ *n.* 海灣
   - (D) beak [4] ﹝bik﹞ *n.* 鳥嘴
   * ***cell phone*** 手機　　recharge [2] ﹝riˈtʃɑrdʒ﹞ *v.* 再充電

3. (**C**) The mother couldn't <u>bear</u> to see her child cry.
   那母親無法<u>忍受</u>看她的孩子哭。
   - (A) beg [2] ﹝bɛg﹞ *v.* 乞求
   - (B) beat [1] ﹝bit﹞ *v.* 打；打敗
   - (C) ***bear*** [2,1] ﹝bɛr﹞ *v.* 忍受
   - (D) behave [3] ﹝bɪˈhev﹞ *v.* 行為舉止

4. (**C**) The artist stared at the <u>blank</u> canvas, wondering what to paint.
   那藝術家凝視著<u>空白的</u>畫布，想著要畫什麼。
   - (A) brave [1] ﹝brev﹞ *adj.* 勇敢的
   - (B) brutal [4] ﹝ˈbrutl̩﹞ *adj.* 殘忍的
   - (C) ***blank*** [2] ﹝blæŋk﹞ *adj.* 空白的
   - (D) bloody [2] ﹝ˈblʌdɪ﹞ *adj.* 血腥的
   * stare [3] ﹝stɛr﹞ *v.* 注視；凝視 < at >　　canvas [6] ﹝ˈkænvəs﹞ *n.* 畫布
   　wonder [2] ﹝ˈwʌndɚ﹞ *v.* 想知道；盤算

5. (**A**) Roger began to <u>blush</u> when he realized his mistake.
當他認知到他的錯，羅傑<u>臉紅</u>了起來。

    (A) ***blush*** [4] 〔 blʌʃ 〕 *v.* 臉紅

    (B) blow [1] 〔 blo 〕 *v.* 吹

    (C) blink [4] 〔 blɪŋk 〕 *v.* 眨眼

    (D) boast [4] 〔 bost 〕 *v.* 自誇；以擁有…自豪

    *realize [2] 〔 ˈriəˌlaɪz 〕 *v.* 了解；認知

6. (**D**) The field trip to the art museum was of great <u>benefit</u> to the
students. 校外教學去美術館對學生很有<u>益處</u>。

    (A) block [1] 〔 blɑk 〕 *n.* 街區

    (B) belief [2] 〔 bəˈlif 〕 *n.* 信念

    (C) bench [2] 〔 bɛntʃ 〕 *n.* 長椅

    (D) ***benefit*** [3] 〔 ˈbɛnəfɪt 〕 *n.* 利益；好處

    field trip 校外教學   art [1] 〔 ɑrt 〕 *n.* 藝術

    museum [2] 〔 mjuˈziəm 〕 *n.* 博物館；美術館

7. (**A**) For his book report, John chose a <u>biography</u> of the famous
composer Mozart.
約翰選了知名作曲家莫札特的一本<u>傳記</u>來寫讀書心得。

    (A) ***biography*** [4] 〔 baɪˈɑgrəfɪ 〕 *n.* 傳記

    (B) beast [3] 〔 bist 〕 *n.* 野獸

    (C) brake [3] 〔 brek 〕 *n.* 煞車

    (D) blade [4] 〔 bled 〕 *n.* 刀鋒

    *report [1] 〔 rɪˈport 〕 *n.* 報告   famous [2] 〔 ˈfeməs 〕 *adj.* 知名的

    composer [4] 〔 kəmˈpozɚ 〕 *n.* 作曲家

    Mozart 〔 ˈmozɑrt 〕 *n.* 莫札特

8. (**C**) Julie is a social butterfly who <u>bounces</u> from one group to another.
朱莉是個交際花，<u>輕快地</u>從一群人<u>跑跳</u>到另一群人中。

    (A) bother [2] 〔 ˈbɑðɚ 〕 *v.* 打擾

    (B) bow [2] 〔 baʊ 〕 *v.* 鞠躬

    (C) ***bounce*** [4] 〔 baʊns 〕 *v.* 反彈；蹦蹦跳跳地走；急促地動

    (D) borrow [2] 〔 ˈbaro 〕 *v.* 借（入）

＊social² 〔'soʃəl 〕 *adj.* 社會的；社交的

butterfly¹ 〔'bʌtə,flaɪ 〕 *n.* 蝴蝶　　***social butterfly*** 交際花

9. (**A**) The company has an annual operating <u>budget</u> of 10 million euros.

這家公司每年的營運<u>預算</u>是一千萬歐元。

(A) ***budget***³ 〔'bʌdʒɪt 〕 *n.* 預算

(B) buffet³ 〔 bʌ'fe 〕 *n.* 自助餐

(C) brook³ 〔 brʊk 〕 *n.* 小溪

(D) battle² 〔'bætḷ 〕 *n.* 戰役

＊annual⁴ 〔'ænjʊəl 〕 *adj.* 一年的；每年的

operating² 〔'apə,retɪŋ 〕 *adj.* 經營的；營運的

euro 〔'jʊro 〕 *n.* 歐元

10. (**B**) The <u>burden</u> of organizing the party fell on Lucy.

籌畫派對的<u>重擔</u>由露西負責。

(A) brush² 〔 brʌʃ 〕 *n.* 刷子

(B) ***burden***³ 〔'bɝdṇ 〕 *n.* 負擔；責任

(C) bulb³ 〔 bʌlb 〕 *n.* 燈泡；球根

(D) bush³ 〔 bʊʃ 〕 *n.* 灌木叢

＊organize² 〔'ɔrgən,aɪz 〕 *v.* 組織；籌畫

fall on　（工作）落在；由…負責

11. (**B**) There are five elements of taste perception: salty, sour, <u>bitter</u>, sweet

and umami.　味覺有五個元素：鹹、酸、苦、甜、鮮。

(A) basic¹ 〔'besɪk 〕 *adj.* 基本的

(B) ***bitter***² 〔'bɪtə 〕 *adj.* 苦的

(C) bright¹ 〔 braɪt 〕 *adj.* 明亮的

(D) bold³ 〔 bold 〕 *adj.* 大膽的

＊element² 〔'ɛləmənt 〕 *n.* 元素　　taste¹ 〔 test 〕 *n.* 味覺

perception⁶ 〔 pə'sɛpʃən 〕 *n.* 知覺；感受

salty² 〔'sɔltɪ 〕 *adj.* 鹹的　　sour¹ 〔 saʊr 〕 *adj.* 酸的

sweet¹ 〔 swit 〕 *adj.* 甜的　　umami 〔 u'mɑmɪ 〕 *n.* 鮮味

12. (**C**) His dream lover smiled at him and he thought his heart might <u>burst</u>.

他的夢中情人對他笑，他覺得他的心臟要爆裂了。

(A) bury³〔'bɛrɪ〕v. 埋；埋葬

(B) bump³〔bʌmp〕v. 撞上

(C) **burst²**〔bɝst〕v. 爆破

(D) broadcast²〔'brɔd،kæst〕v. 廣播

dream lover 夢中情人

13. (**D**) Hanami is a traditional custom of enjoying the beauty of flower blossoms. 花見是個傳統習俗，欣賞<u>花</u>開的美。

(A) blanket³〔'blæŋkɪt〕n. 毯子

(B) blessing⁴〔'blɛsɪŋ〕n. 恩賜；幸福

(C) blouse³〔blaʊz〕n. 女用上衣

(D) *blossom⁴*〔'blɑsəm〕n. 花

*hanami〔hɑ'nɑmɪ〕n.（日文）花見；賞花

traditional²〔trə'dɪʃənl̩〕adj. 傳統的　　custom²〔'kʌstəm〕n. 習俗

14. (**B**) They snuck across the <u>border</u> into Mexico during the early hours of June 7th.

他們在六月七日凌晨的時候，偷偷跨過<u>國境</u>進入墨西哥。

(A) bookcase¹〔'bʊk،kes〕n. 書櫃

(B) *border²*〔'bɔrdɚ〕n. 邊界；國境

(C) bond²〔bɑnd〕n. 束縛；關係

(D) biscuit³〔'bɪskɪt〕n. 餅乾

*snuck⁵〔snʌk〕v. 偷偷溜走；潛行【sneak 的過去式】

Mexico〔'mɛksɪ،ko〕n. 墨西哥　　hours¹〔aʊrz〕n. pl. 時間

15. (**D**) Victor is a <u>brilliant</u> musician, but he lacks the discipline to become a master. 維克是個<u>才華洋溢的</u>音樂家，但是他缺乏成為大師的訓練。

(A) brief²〔brif〕adj. 簡短的

(B) broad²〔brɔd〕adj. 寬的

(C) bony²〔'bonɪ〕adj. 骨瘦如柴的

(D) *brilliant³*〔'brɪljənt〕adj. 燦爛的；才華洋溢的

*musician²〔mju'zɪʃən〕n. 音樂家

discipline⁴〔'dɪsəplɪn〕n. 訓練

master¹〔'mæstɚ〕n. 師傅；大師

TEST 4

【命題範圍：「高中生必背 4500 字」
p.31-40，cabbage～coarse】

Directions: Choose the one word that best completes the sentence.

1. The highlight of his trip to Egypt was riding a _____ in the desert.
   (A) channel　　　　　　(B) cabin
   (C) camel　　　　　　 (D) calculation　　　　　(　)

2. The escaped prisoners have been _____ after three days on the run.
   (A) captured　　　　　(B) ceased
   (C) cherished　　　　　(D) calculated　　　　　(　)

3. Susan accepted my _____ to a game of chess.
   (A) centimeter　　　　(B) characteristic
   (C) challenge　　　　　(D) cabinet　　　　　　(　)

4. The weeds are _____ the plants in my garden.
   (A) chewing　　　　　(B) casting
   (C) choking　　　　　 (D) camping　　　　　　(　)

5. She began exercising daily to improve her blood _____.
   (A) cafeteria　　　　　(B) calorie
   (C) circulation　　　　(D) citizen　　　　　　(　)

6. Joe felt that none of the _____ for president was qualified, so he didn't vote.
   (A) canoes　　　　　　(B) candidates
   (C) campuses　　　　　(D) candles　　　　　　(　)

7. The theater has reached its full _____; therefore, no more tickets will be sold.
   (A) calendar　　　　　(B) cable
   (C) capacity　　　　　(D) cap　　　　　　　　(　)

8. The teacher attempted to _____ the essay question.
 (A) clarify   (B) clash
 (C) cheat   (D) chase   ( )

9. She studied _____ dance at an academy in Paris.
 (A) coarse   (B) classical
 (C) cloudy   (D) calm   ( )

10. The books in the library are _____ by subject.
 (A) clipped   (B) celebrated
 (C) classified   (D) clothed   ( )

11. Kevin has no coordination; he's too _____ to play basketball.
 (A) civil   (B) chilly
 (C) clumsy   (D) circular   ( )

12. Buenos Aires, Argentina, is considered the business _____ of South America.
 (A) capitalist   (B) captain
 (C) charity   (D) capital   ( )

13. He struck up a _____ conversation with the passenger sitting to his right.
 (A) casual   (B) capable
 (C) ceramic   (D) central   ( )

14. The restaurant doesn't _____ for delivery when the order is more than $25.
 (A) chat   (B) charge
 (C) cheer   (D) chop   ( )

15. The poor villagers are actually quite _____ despite their awful circumstances.
 (A) childlike   (B) changeable
 (C) cheerful   (D) chief   ( )

TEST 4 詳解

1. (**C**) The highlight of his trip to Egypt was riding a <u>camel</u> in the desert.
他去埃及旅行最精彩的部分，是在沙漠騎<u>駱駝</u>。
   - (A) channel³ ﹝'tʃænḷ﹞ *n.* 頻道；海峽
   - (B) cabin³ ﹝'kæbɪn﹞ *n.* 小木屋；機艙
   - (C) ***camel***¹ ﹝'kæmḷ﹞ *n.* 駱駝
   - (D) calculation⁴ ﹝,kælkjə'leʃən﹞ *n.* 計算
   - *highlight⁶ ﹝'haɪ,laɪt﹞ *n.* 重點；最精彩的部分
     Egypt ﹝'idʒɪpt﹞ *n.* 埃及　　desert² ﹝'dɛzət﹞ *n.* 沙漠

2. (**A**) The escaped prisoners have been <u>captured</u> after three days on the
run. 那逃脫的囚犯奔逃三天後被<u>抓到</u>了。
   - (A) ***capture***³ ﹝'kæptʃə﹞ *v.* 抓住
   - (B) cease⁴ ﹝sis﹞ *v.* 停止
   - (C) cherish⁴ ﹝'tʃɛrɪʃ﹞ *v.* 珍惜
   - (D) calculate⁴ ﹝'kælkjə,let﹞ *v.* 計算
   - *escape³ ﹝ə'skep﹞ *v.* 逃脫　　prisoner² ﹝'prɪznə﹞ *n.* 囚犯
     on the run 奔逃；躲藏（= *trying to avoid being caught*）

3. (**C**) Susan accepted my <u>challenge</u> to a game of chess.
蘇珊接受我一場西洋棋比賽的<u>挑戰</u>。
   - (A) centimeter³ ﹝'sɛntə,mitə﹞ *n.* 公分
   - (B) characteristic⁴ ﹝,kærɪktə'rɪstɪk﹞ *n.* 特性
   - (C) ***challenge***³ ﹝'tʃælɪndʒ﹞ *n.* 挑戰
   - (D) cabinet⁴ ﹝'kæbənɪt﹞ *n.* 櫥櫃
   - *accept² ﹝ək'sɛpt﹞ *v.* 接受　　chess² ﹝tʃɛs﹞ *n.* 西洋棋

4. (**C**) The weeds are <u>choking</u> the plants in my garden.
雜草要<u>使</u>我花園的植物<u>枯死</u>了。
   - (A) chew³ ﹝tʃu﹞ *v.* 嚼　　　　(B) cast³ ﹝kæsto﹞ *v.* 投擲；扔
   - (C) ***choke***³ ﹝tʃok﹞ *v.* 使窒息；扼殺；使枯死
   - (D) camp¹ ﹝kæmp﹞ *v.* 露營
   - *weed³ ﹝wid﹞ *n.* 雜草　　plant¹ ﹝plænt﹞ *n.* 植物；草木

5. (**C**) She began exercising daily to improve her blood circulation.

She began exercising daily to improve her blood <u>circulation</u>.

她開始每天運動以增強血液<u>循環</u>。

(A) cafeteria [2] ﹝͵kæfə'tɪrɪə﹞ n. 自助餐廳

(B) calorie [4] ﹝'kælərɪ﹞ n. 卡路里

(C) ***circulation*** [4] ﹝͵sɝkjə'leʃən﹞ n. 循環

(D) citizen [2] ﹝'sɪtəzn̩﹞ n. 公民

＊exercise [2] ﹝'ɛksə͵saɪz﹞ v. 運動　　　daily [2] ﹝'delɪ﹞ adv. 每天

　improve [2] ﹝ɪm'pruv﹞ v. 增強　　　blood [1] ﹝blʌd﹞ n. 血

6. (**B**) Joe felt that none of the <u>candidates</u> for president was qualified, so he didn't vote.

喬覺得總統的<u>候選人</u>沒有一位是適任的，所以他沒有投票。

(A) canoe [3] ﹝kə'nu﹞ n. 獨木舟

(B) ***candidate*** [4] ﹝'kændə͵det﹞ n. 候選人

(C) campus [3] ﹝'kæmpəs﹞ n. 校園

(D) candle [2] ﹝'kændl̩﹞ n. 蠟燭

＊president [2] ﹝'prɛzədənt﹞ n. 總統

　qualified [5] ﹝'kwɑlə͵faɪd﹞ adj. 有資格的；適任的

　vote [2] ﹝vot﹞ v. 投票

7. (**C**) The theater has reached its full <u>capacity</u>; therefore, no more tickets will be sold.

那場戲已經<u>客滿</u>；因此，沒有票可以買了。

(A) calender [2] ﹝'kæləndə﹞ n. 日曆

(B) cable [2] ﹝'kebl̩﹞ n. 電纜

(C) ***capacity*** [4] ﹝kə'pæsətɪ﹞ n. 容量；客滿

(D) cap [1] ﹝kæp﹞ n. (無邊的) 帽子

＊theater [2] ﹝'θiətə﹞ n. 電影院；戲院

　therefore [2] ﹝'ðɛr͵for﹞ adv. 因此　　　ticket [1] ﹝'tɪkɪt﹞ n. 票

8. (**A**) The teacher attempted to <u>clarify</u> the essay question.

老師嘗試要<u>澄清</u>該作文題目。

(A) ***clarify*** [4] ﹝'klærə͵faɪ﹞ v. 清楚說明；澄清

(B) clash [4] ﹝klæʃ﹞ v. 起衝突

(C) cheat² 〔 tʃit 〕 *v.* 欺騙

(D) chase¹ 〔 tʃes 〕 *v.* 追趕;追求

*attempt³ 〔 əˋtɛmpt 〕 *v.* 嘗試　　essay⁴ 〔ˋɛse 〕 *n.* 論說文;作文

9. (**B**) She studied <u>classical</u> dance at an academy in Paris.

她在巴黎的一間專科學校研讀<u>古典</u>舞蹈。

(A) coarse⁴ 〔 kors 〕 *adj.* 粗糙的

(B) ***classical***³ 〔ˋklæsɪkl̩ 〕 *adj.* 古典的

(C) cloudy² 〔ˋklaʊdɪ 〕 *adj.* 多雲的

(D) calm² 〔 kɑm 〕 *adj.* 冷靜的

*academy⁵ 〔 əˋkædəmɪ 〕 *n.* 專科學校;學院

10. (**C**) The books in the library are <u>classified</u> by subject.

圖書館的書以學科<u>分類</u>。

(A) clip³ 〔 klɪp 〕 *v.* 修剪;夾住

(B) celebrate³ 〔ˋsɛlə‚bret 〕 *v.* 慶祝

(C) ***classify***⁴ 〔ˋklæsə‚faɪ 〕 *v.* 分類 (= *categorize*)

(D) clothe² 〔 kloð 〕 *v.* 穿衣 (= *dress*)

*subject² 〔ˋsʌbdʒɪkt 〕 *n.* 科目;學科

11. (**C**) Kevin has no coordination; he's too <u>clumsy</u> to play basketball.

凱文沒有肢體協調能力;他太<u>笨拙</u>無法打籃球。

(A) civil³ 〔ˋsɪvl̩ 〕 *adj.* 公民的

(B) chilly³ 〔ˋtʃɪlɪ 〕 *adj.* 寒冷的

(C) ***clumsy***⁴ 〔ˋklʌmzɪ 〕 *adj.* 笨拙的

(D) circular⁴ 〔ˋsɝkjələ 〕 *adj.* 圓的

*coordination⁶ 〔 ko‚ɔrdn̩ˋeʃən 〕 *n.* 協調

12. (**D**) Buenos Aires, Argentina, is considered the business <u>capital</u> of South America.

阿根廷的布宜諾斯艾利斯被認爲是南美洲的商業<u>中心</u>。

(A) capitalist⁴ 〔ˋkæpətl̩ɪst 〕 *n.* 資本家

(B) captain² 〔ˋkæptən 〕 *n.* 船長;機長

(C) charity⁴ 〔ˋtʃærətɪ 〕 *n.* 慈善機構

(D) **capital** [3,4] 〔'kæpətḷ 〕 *n.* 首都；中心

*Buenos Aires 〔'bonəs 'ɛriz 〕 *n.* 布宜諾斯艾利斯

Argentina 〔,ɑrdʒə'tinə 〕 *n.* 阿根廷

business [2] 〔'bɪznɪs 〕 *n.* 商業　　***South America*** 南美洲

13. (**A**) He struck up a <u>casual</u> conversation with the passenger sitting
to his right. 他和坐他右側的乘客開始<u>輕鬆</u>地交談。

(A) **casual** [3] 〔'kæʒuəl 〕 *adj.* 非正式的；輕鬆的

(B) capable [3] 〔'kepəbḷ 〕 *adj.* 能夠的 < *of* >

(C) ceramic [3] 〔 sə'ræmɪk 〕 *adj.* 陶器的

(D) central [2] 〔'sɛntrəl 〕 *adj.* 中心的

***strike up** 開始（交談）　　conversation [2] 〔,kɑnvɚ'seʃən 〕 *n.* 對話
passenger [2] 〔'pæsn̩dʒɚ 〕 *n.* 乘客

14. (**B**) The restaurant doesn't <u>charge</u> for delivery when the order is more
than $25. 那家餐廳訂餐超過 25 美元不<u>收運費</u>。

(A) chat [3] 〔 tʃæt 〕 *v.* 聊天

(B) **charge** [2] 〔 tʃɑrdʒ 〕 *v.* 收費

(C) cheer [3] 〔 tʃɪr 〕 *v.* 使振作；使高興

(D) chop [3] 〔 tʃɑp 〕 *v.* 砍；剁碎

*delivery [3] 〔 dɪ'lɪvərɪ 〕 *n.* 遞送　　order [1] 〔'ɔrdɚ 〕 *n.* 訂購

15. (**C**) The poor villagers are actually quite <u>cheerful</u> despite their awful
circumstances.
那些貧窮的村民們事實上很<u>快樂</u>，儘管他們的生活狀況很糟糕。

(A) childlike [2] 〔'tʃaɪld,laɪk 〕 *adj.* 純真的

(B) changeable [3] 〔'tʃendʒəbḷ 〕 *adj.* 可改變的；善變的

(C) **cheerful** [3] 〔'tʃɪrfəl 〕 *adj.* 愉快的；高興的

(D) chief [1] 〔 tʃif 〕 *adj.* 主要的 (= *main*)

*villager [2] 〔'vɪlɪdʒɚ 〕 *n.* 村民
actually [3] 〔'æktʃuəlɪ 〕 *adv.* 事實上
despite [4] 〔 dɪ'spaɪt 〕 *prep.* 儘管 (= *in spite of*)
awful [3] 〔'ɔful 〕 *adj.* 很糟的；極壞的
circumstances [4] 〔'sɝkəm,stænsɪz 〕 *n. pl.* 情況

TEST 5

【命題範圍：「高中生必背 4500 字」
p.41-50，coast～converse】

Directions: *Choose the one word that best completes the sentence.*

1. The building _____ during the earthquake.
   (A) collected
   (B) collapsed
   (C) combined
   (D) contained   (　)

2. Margaret writes a parenting _____ for a lifestyle magazine.
   (A) coast
   (B) cock
   (C) contest
   (D) column   (　)

3. She _____ me to leave the room immediately.
   (A) comforted
   (B) commanded
   (C) compared
   (D) complained   (　)

4. The real estate investor bought several _____ properties in London.
   (A) comic
   (B) continuous
   (C) cold
   (D) commercial   (　)

5. We should _____ our efforts to eliminate crime in our city.
   (A) concentrate
   (B) conclude
   (C) compose
   (D) confess   (　)

6. John broke up with Mary because he was not ready to _____ to a long-term relationship.
   (A) compete
   (B) commit
   (C) communicate
   (D) consider   (　)

7. Bob doesn't have enough confidence in his voice to enter the singing _____.
   (A) competition
   (B) company
   (C) companion
   (D) comparison   (　)

8. Unlike many artists, Nancy is open to _____ criticism of her work.
   (A) comfortable   (B) conscious
   (C) colorful   (D) constructive   (   )

9. The politician claimed his words were taken out of _____.
   (A) consumer   (B) context
   (C) container   (D) collar   (   )

10. A maze is a type of puzzle that consists of a _____ series of passages.
    (A) complex   (B) competitive
    (C) complete   (D) common   (   )

11. The police admitted they had no _____ evidence connecting Mr. Smith to the crime.
    (A) confident   (B) considerable
    (C) concrete   (D) consequent   (   )

12. The doctor's receptionist called this morning to _____ my appointment.
    (A) confirm   (B) confine
    (C) confuse   (D) connect   (   )

13. Her parents are very _____ and would not approve of her relationship with Tom.
    (A) consistent   (B) conservative
    (C) constant   (D) common   (   )

14. The relaxed pace of Terry's new job was a welcome _____ to his previous position.
    (A) contrast   (B) contract
    (C) convention   (D) controller   (   )

15. He received a letter of appreciation for his _____ to the fundraising drive.
    (A) contentment   (B) continent
    (C) contribution   (D) convenience   (   )

TEST 5　詳解

1. (**B**) The building <u>collapsed</u> during the earthquake.
   那棟建築物在地震中<u>倒塌</u>。
   (A) collect² 〔 kə'lɛkt 〕 *v.* 收集 (= *gather*)
   (B) ***collapse*** ⁴ 〔 kə'læps 〕 *v.* 倒塌；崩潰
   (C) combine³ 〔 kəm'baɪn 〕 *v.* 結合
   (D) contain² 〔 kən'ten 〕 *v.* 包含
   *earthquake² 〔'ɝθ,kwek 〕 *n.* 地震

2. (**D**) Margaret writes a parenting <u>column</u> for a lifestyle magazine.
   瑪格麗特替一本時尚生活雜誌寫育兒<u>專欄</u>。
   (A) coast¹ 〔 kost 〕 *n.* 海岸
   (B) cock² 〔 kɑk 〕 *n.* 公雞 (= *rooster*)
   (C) contest⁴ 〔'kɑntɛst 〕 *n.* 比賽
   (D) ***column*** ³ 〔'kɑləm 〕 *n.* 專欄
   *parenting¹ 〔'pɛrəntɪŋ 〕 *n.* 育兒
   　lifestyle 〔'laɪf,staɪl 〕 *adj.* 有關時尚生活的

3. (**B**) She <u>commanded</u> me to leave the room immediately.
   她<u>命令</u>我立即離開房間。
   (A) comfort³ 〔'kʌmfət 〕 *v.* 安慰
   (B) ***command*** ³ 〔 kə'mænd 〕 *v.* 命令 (= *order*)
   (C) compare² 〔 kəm'pɛr 〕 *v.* 比較
   (D) complain² 〔 kəm'plen 〕 *v.* 抱怨 (= *grumble*)
   *immediately³ 〔 ɪ'midɪɪtlɪ 〕 *v.* 立即；立刻

4. (**D**) The real estate investor bought several <u>commercial</u> properties in
   London.　那名房地產投資者在倫敦買了好幾筆<u>商業</u>地產。
   (A) comic⁴ 〔'kɑmɪk 〕 *adj.* 漫畫的；可笑的
   (B) continuous⁴ 〔 kən'tɪnjuəs 〕 *adj.* 連續的 (= *constant*)
   (C) cold¹ 〔 kold 〕 *adj.* 寒冷的 (= *chilly*)
   (D) ***commercial*** ³ 〔 kə'mɝʃəl 〕 *adj.* 商業的
   real estate 房地產　　investor⁴ 〔 ɪn'vɛstə 〕 *n.* 投資者
   　several¹ 〔'sɛvərəl 〕 *adj.* 幾個的　　property³ 〔'prɑpətɪ 〕 *n.* 地產

5. (**A**) We should <u>concentrate</u> our efforts to eliminate crime in our city.
我們應該<u>集中</u>努力消除我們市上的犯罪。

   (A) ***concentrate***[4] ﹝ˈkɑnsn̩ˌtret﹞ *v.* 集中 (= *focus*)
   (B) conclude[3] ﹝kənˈklud﹞ *v.* 下結論 (= *decide*)
   (C) compose[4] ﹝kəmˈpoz﹞ *v.* 組成 (= *constitute*)；作 (曲)
   (D) confess[4] ﹝kənˈfɛs﹞ *v.* 承認 (= *admit*)

   *effort[2] ﹝ˈɛfət﹞ *n.* 努力；費心　　eliminate[4] ﹝ɪˈlɪməˌnet﹞ *v.* 消除
   crime[2] ﹝kraɪm﹞ *n.* 犯罪

6. (**B**) John broke up with Mary because he was not ready to <u>commit</u> to a
long-term relationship.
約翰和瑪麗分手，因為他還沒準備好要<u>忠於</u>一段長期的關係。

   (A) compete[3] ﹝kəmˈpit﹞ *v.* 競爭 (= *contend*)
   (B) ***commit***[4] ﹝kəˈmɪt﹞ *v.* 致力於；承諾　　***commit to*** 承諾；忠於
   (C) communicate[3] ﹝kəˈmjunəˌket﹞ *v.* 溝通；聯繫 (= *contact*)
   (D) consider[2] ﹝kənˈsɪdə﹞ *v.* 認為；考慮 (= *think about*)

   break up 分手　　long-term ﹝ˌlɔŋˈtɜm﹞ *adj.* 長期的
   relationship[2] ﹝rɪˈleʃənˌʃɪp﹞ *n.* 關係

7. (**A**) Bob doesn't have enough confidence in his voice to enter the singing
<u>competition</u>. 鮑伯對自己的聲音不夠有自信去參加歌唱<u>比賽</u>。

   (A) ***competition***[4] ﹝ˌkɑmpəˈtɪʃən﹞ *n.* 競爭；比賽 (= *contest*)
   (B) company[2] ﹝ˈkʌmpənɪ﹞ *n.* 公司 (= *firm*)；同伴
   (C) companion[4] ﹝kəmˈpænjən﹞ *n.* 同伴；朋友 (= *partner*)
   (D) comparison[3] ﹝kəmˈpærəsn̩﹞ *n.* 比較

   *confidence[4] ﹝ˈkɑnfədəns﹞ *n.* 信心　　voice[1] ﹝vɔɪs﹞ *n.* (人) 聲音

8. (**D**) Unlike many artists, Nancy is open to <u>constructive</u> criticism of
her work. 不像很多的藝術家，南西接受對她作品<u>建設性的</u>批評。

   (A) comfortable[2] ﹝ˈkʌmfətəbl̩﹞ *adj.* 舒服的 (= *at ease*)
   (B) conscious[3] ﹝ˈkɑnʃəs﹞ *adj.* 知道的；察覺到的 (= *aware*)
   (C) colorful[2] ﹝ˈkʌləfəl﹞ *adj.* 多采多姿的
   (D) ***constructive***[4] ﹝kənˈstrʌktɪv﹞ *adj.* 建設性的 (= *positive*)

   *artist[2] ﹝ˈɑrtɪst﹞ *n.* 藝術家　　***be open to*** 接受；接納
   criticism[4] ﹝ˈkrɪtəˌsɪzəm﹞ *n.* 批評　　work[1] ﹝wɜk﹞ *n.* 作品

9. (**B**) The politician claimed his words were taken out of <u>context</u>.
那名政治家說他的話被<u>斷章</u>取義。

(A) consumer⁴〔kən'sumɚ〕*n.* 消費者

(B) ***context***⁴〔'kantɛkst〕*n.* 上下文（ = *framework* ）；背景

take sth. ***out of context*** 斷章取義

(C) container⁴〔kən'tenɚ〕*n.* 容器

(D) collar³〔'kalɚ〕*n.* 衣領（ = *neckband* ）

＊politician³〔,palə'tɪʃən〕*n.* 政治家　　claim²〔klem〕*v.* 聲明；陳述

words¹〔wɝds〕*n. pl.* 話

10. (**A**) A maze is a type of puzzle that consists of a <u>complex</u> series of passages. 迷宮是一種謎題，由一系列<u>複雜的</u>通道所組成。

(A) ***complex***³〔'kamplɛks〕*adj.* 複雜的（ = *complicated* ）

(B) competitive⁴〔kəm'pɛtətɪv〕*adj.* 競爭的；競爭激烈的

(C) complete²〔kəm'plit〕*adj.* 完整的

(D) common¹〔'kamən〕*adj.* 常見的

＊maze〔mez〕*n.* 迷宮　　type²〔taɪp〕*n.* 種類；類型

puzzle²〔'pʌzl̩〕*n.* 謎；難題　　***consist of*** 由…組成

series⁵〔'sɪrɪz〕*n.* 一系列　　passage³〔'pæsɪdʒ〕*n.* 通道

11. (**C**) The police admitted they had no <u>concrete</u> evidence connecting Mr. Smith to the crime.
警方承認，他們沒有史密斯先生和這項犯罪有關的<u>具體</u>證據。

(A) confident³〔'kanfədənt〕*adj.* 有信心的（ = *assured* ）

(B) considerable³〔kən'sɪdərəbl̩〕*adj.* 相當大的（ = *large* ）

(C) ***concrete***⁴〔kan'krit〕*adj.* 具體的（ = *substantial* ）

(D) consequent⁴〔'kansə,kwɛnt〕*adj.* 接著發生的（ = *subsequent* ）

＊***the police*** 警方　　admit³〔əd'mɪt〕*v.* 承認

evidence⁴〔'ɛvədəns〕*n.* 證據

connect³〔kə'nɛkt〕*v.* 連結；使有關係 < *to* >

12. (**A**) The doctor's receptionist called this morning to <u>confirm</u> my appointment. 醫生的櫃臺人員今早來電<u>確認</u>我的約診。

(A) ***confirm***²〔kən'fɝm〕*v.* 確認；證實

(B) confine⁴〔kən'faɪn〕*v.* 限制（ = *restrict* ）；關閉

(C) confuse³ ﹝kən'fjuz﹞v. 使困惑（= puzzle = baffle）

(D) connect³ ﹝kə'nɛkt﹞v. 連結（= link）

*receptionist⁴ ﹝rɪ'sɛpʃənɪst﹞n. 櫃臺人員

appointment⁴ ﹝ə'pɔɪntmənt﹞n. 約定；約診

13. (**B**) Her parents are very <u>conservative</u> and would not approve of her relationship with Tom. 她的父母很保守，不會同意她和湯姆的關係。

(A) consistent⁴ ﹝kən'sɪstənt﹞adj. 一致的

(B) ***conservative***⁴ ﹝kən'sɜvətɪv﹞adj. 保守的（= traditional）

(C) constant³ ﹝'kanstənt﹞adj. 不斷的；持續的

(D) common¹ ﹝'kamən﹞adj. 常見的

*approve³ ﹝ə'pruv﹞v. 贊同；同意 < of >

14. (**A**) The relaxed pace of Terry's new job was a welcome <u>contrast</u> to his previous position.
泰瑞新工作的步調很輕鬆，和上一份工作對比之下感到愉快。

(A) ***contrast***⁴ ﹝'kantræst﹞n. 對比（= opposition）；對照

(B) contract³ ﹝'kantrækt﹞n. 合約（= agreement）

(C) convention⁴ ﹝kən'vɛnʃən﹞n. 代表大會（= meeting）；習俗

(D) controller² ﹝kən'trolə﹞n. 管理者

*relaxed³ ﹝rɪ'lækst﹞adj. 輕鬆的；舒適的　　pace⁴ ﹝pes﹞n. 步調

welcome¹ ﹝'wɛlkəm﹞adj. 令人愉快的

previous³ ﹝'priviəs﹞adj. 以前的

position¹ ﹝pə'zɪʃən﹞n. 職位；工作

15. (**C**) He received a letter of appreciation for his <u>contribution</u> to the fundraising drive. 他收到一封感謝函，因為他對募款活動的貢獻。

(A) contentment⁴ ﹝kən'tɛntmənt﹞n. 滿足（= satisfaction）

(B) continent³ ﹝'kantənənt﹞n. 洲；大陸

(C) ***contribution***⁴ ﹝ˌkantrə'bjuʃən﹞n. 貢獻；捐贈

(D) convenience⁴ ﹝kən'vinjəns﹞n. 方便

*receive¹ ﹝rɪ'siv﹞v. 收到　　appreciation⁴ ﹝əˌpriʃɪ'eʃən﹞n. 感激

a letter of appreciation 感謝函

fundraising ﹝'fʌndˌrezɪŋ﹞n. 募款　　drive¹ ﹝draɪv﹞n. 活動

TEST 6

【命題範圍：「高中生必背 4500 字」
p.1-50，abandon～converse】

Directions: Choose the one word that best completes the sentence.

1. Tim's _____ in sales makes him a perfect candidate for the job.
   - (A) committee
   - (B) atmosphere
   - (C) basement
   - (D) background   (   )

2. He made a _____ decision to quit his job and enlist in the military.
   - (A) consequent
   - (B) bald
   - (C) bold
   - (D) classical   (   )

3. Police _____ with protestors outside the courthouse.
   - (A) acquainted
   - (B) clashed
   - (C) concentrated
   - (D) consulted   (   )

4. The company's new marketing campaign _____ to young consumers.
   - (A) bathes
   - (B) conquers
   - (C) appeals
   - (D) beats   (   )

5. Some mosquitoes _____ in shallow pools of water.
   - (A) breed
   - (B) construct
   - (C) await
   - (D) blame   (   )

6. It is often said that no two snowflakes can ever be _____.
   - (A) abstract
   - (B) alone
   - (C) alive
   - (D) alike   (   )

7. Charles attributes his success to a(n) _____ of hard work and good fortune.
   - (A) combination
   - (B) approval
   - (C) bandage
   - (D) conscience   (   )

8. Bob struck up a(n) _____ with his new neighbor.
   (A) conference   (B) acquaintance
   (C) characteristic   (D) civilization   (　)

9. With her father's help, Jessie was able to _____ a new bicycle.
   (A) acquire   (B) confirm
   (C) blend   (D) accompany   (　)

10. If all sides are _____, we can start the meeting now.
    (A) considerable   (B) concrete
    (C) clumsy   (D) agreeable   (　)

11. Make sure the _____ is open before starting a fire.
    (A) chimney   (B) bulletin
    (C) bubble   (D) balloon   (　)

12. During the speaking part of the test, you will read _____ a text on your screen.
    (A) aloud   (B) altogether
    (C) barely   (D) abroad   (　)

13. The sailors on merchant ships were often poorly paid and subject to _____ discipline.
    (A) bony   (B) capable
    (C) brutal   (D) childish   (　)

14. As you emerge from a dark room, it will take a minute for your eyes to _____ to the daylight.
    (A) contrast   (B) circulate
    (C) adjust   (D) accuse   (　)

15. The shoe company's new marketing _____ features several pro athletes.
    (A) authority   (B) campaign
    (C) attitude   (D) appetite   (　)

TEST 6 詳解

1. (**D**) Tim's <u>background</u> in sales makes him a perfect candidate for the job.
提姆在銷售部門的<u>經歷</u>讓他成為該工作最佳的候選人。
   - (A) committee [3] 〔 kə'mɪtɪ 〕 *n.* 委員會
   - (B) atmosphere [4] 〔'ætməs,fɪr 〕 *n.* 大氣；氣氛
   - (C) basement [2] 〔'besmənt 〕 *n.* 地下室
   - (D) ***background*** [3] 〔'bæk,graʊnd 〕 *n.* 背景；經歷 (= *experience*)

   * sales [1] 〔 selz 〕 *n. pl.* 銷售工作
   perfect [2] 〔'pɝfɪkt 〕 *adj.* 完美的；適合的
   candidate [4] 〔'kændə,det 〕 *n.* 候選人；可能成為⋯的人

2. (**C**) He made a <u>bold</u> decision to quit his job and enlist in the military.
他做了一個<u>大膽的</u>決定，辭職去從軍。
   - (A) consequent [4] 〔'kɑnsə,kwɛnt 〕 *adj.* 接著發生的 (= *subsequent*)
   - (B) bald [4] 〔 bɔld 〕 *adj.* 禿頭的
   - (C) ***bold*** [3] 〔 bold 〕 *adj.* 大膽的
   - (D) classical [3] 〔'klæsɪkḷ 〕 *adj.* 古典的

   * decision [2] 〔 dɪ'sɪʒən 〕 *n.* 決定　　***make a decision*** 下決定
   quit [2] 〔 kwɪt 〕 *v.* 停止；辭（職）　　enlist 〔 ɪn'lɪst 〕 *v.* 從軍；入伍
   military [2] 〔'mɪlə,tɛrɪ 〕 *n.* 軍隊；軍方

3. (**B**) Police <u>clashed</u> with protestors outside the courthouse.
警方和抗議民眾在法院外<u>起衝突</u>。
   - (A) acquaint [4] 〔 ə'kwent 〕 *v.* 使認識；使熟悉
   - (B) ***clash*** [4] 〔 klæʃ 〕 *v.* 起衝突 (= *order*)
   - (C) concentrate [4] 〔'kɑnsn̩,tret 〕 *v.* 集中；專心 (= *focus*)
   - (D) consult [4] 〔 kən'sʌlt 〕 *v.* 請教 (= *confer*)；查閱

   * police [1] 〔 pə'lis 〕 *n. pl.* 警察；警方
   protestor [4] 〔 prə'tɛstɚ 〕 *n.* 抗議者　　courthouse 〔'kort,haʊs 〕 *n.* 法院

4. (**C**) The company's new marketing campaign <u>appeals</u> to young
consumers. 那家公司新的行銷活動很<u>吸引</u>年輕的消費者。
   - (A) bathe [1] 〔 beð 〕 *v.* 洗澡

    (B) conquer[4]〔ˈkɑŋkɚ〕*v.* 征服

    (C) ***appeal***[3]〔əˈpil〕*v.* 吸引 < to >（= *attract*）

    (D) beat[1]〔bit〕*v.* 打；打敗

    *company[2]〔ˈkʌmpənɪ〕*n.* 公司   marketing[1]〔ˈmɑrkɪtɪŋ〕*n.* 行銷

    campaign[4]〔kæmˈpen〕*n.* 活動

    consumer[4]〔kənˈsumɚ〕*n.* 消費者

5. (**A**) Some mosquitoes <u>breed</u> in shallow pools of water.

    有些蚊子在淺水池裡繁殖。

    (A) ***breed***[4]〔brid〕*v.* 繁殖；養育

    (B) construct[4]〔kənˈstrʌkt〕*v.* 建造（= *build*）；建設

    (C) await[4]〔əˈwet〕*v.* 等待

    (D) blame[3]〔blem〕*v.* 責備

    *mosquito[2]〔məˈskito〕*n.* 蚊子   shallow[3]〔ˈʃælo〕*adj.* 淺的

    pool[1]〔pul〕*n.* 水塘；水池

6. (**D**) It is often said that no two snowflakes can ever be <u>alike</u>.

    人們常說，沒有兩片雪花是<u>一模一樣的</u>。

    (A) abstract[4]〔ˈækstrækt〕*adj.* 抽象的

    (B) alone[1]〔əˈlon〕*adj.* 單獨的

    (C) alive[2]〔əˈlaɪv〕*adj.* 活的（= *living*）；有活力的

    (D) ***alike***[2]〔əˈlaɪk〕*adj.* 相同的；相像的（= *similar*）

    *snowflake〔ˈsnoˌflek〕*n.* 雪花

7. (**A**) Charles attributes his success to a <u>combination</u> of hard work and good fortune. 查爾斯認為他成功的因素<u>綜合</u>了努力和好運。

    (A) ***combination***[4]〔ˌkɑmbəˈneʃən〕*n.* 結合（= *association*）；混合

    (B) approval[4]〔əˈpruvl̩〕*n.* 贊成

    (C) bandage[3]〔ˈbændɪdʒ〕*n.* 繃帶（= *dressing*）

    (D) conscience[4]〔ˈkɑnʃəns〕*n.* 良心（= *moral sense*）

    *attribute〔əˈtrɪbjut〕*v.* 歸因於 < to >   success[2]〔səkˈsɛs〕*n.* 成功

    hard work 努力   fortune[3]〔ˈfɔrtʃən〕*n.* 運氣

8. (**B**) Bob struck up an <u>acquaintance</u> with his new neighbor.

    鮑伯開始<u>認識</u>他的新鄰居。

(A) conference [4] ('kɑnfərəns) *n.* 會議 (= *meeting*)

(B) ***acquaintance*** [4] (ə'kwentəns) *n.* 認識的人；認識

(C) characteristic [4] (,kærɪktə'rɪstɪk) *n.* 特性 (= *feature*)

(D) civilzation [4] (,sɪvl̩'zeʃən) *n.* 文明 (= *culture*)

* ***strike up*** 開始　　neighbor [2] ('nebɚ) *n.* 鄰居

9. (**A**) With her father's help, Jessie was able to <u>acquire</u> a new bicycle.
有她父親的幫忙，潔西能夠<u>買到</u>一台新的腳踏車。

(A) ***acquire*** [4] (ə'kwaɪr) *v.* 獲得 (= *gain*)；購得；學會

(B) confirm [2] (kən'fɜm) *v.* 確認；證實

(C) blend [4] (blɛnd) *v.* 混合 (= *mix*)；調和

(D) accompany [4] (ə'kʌmpənɪ) *v.* 陪伴；伴隨 (= *go with*)

* ***be able to V.*** 能夠～　　bicycle [1] ('baɪ,sɪkl̩) *n.* 腳踏車

10. (**D**) If all sides are <u>agreeable</u>, we can start the meeting now.
如果各方都<u>同意</u>，我們現在開始開會。

(A) considerable [3] (kən'sɪdərəbl̩) *adj.* 相當大的 (= *large*)

(B) concrete [4] (kɑn'krit) *adj.* 具體的 (= *substantial*)

(C) clumsy [4] ('klʌmzɪ) *adj.* 笨拙的

(D) ***agreeable*** [4] (ə'griəbl̩) *adj.* 令人愉快的；同意的

* side [1] (saɪd) *n.* 一方　　meeting [2] ('mitɪŋ) *n.* 會議

11. (**A**) Make sure the <u>chimney</u> is open before starting a fire.
生火前要確認<u>煙囪</u>是開著的。

(A) ***chimney*** [3] ('tʃɪmnɪ) *n.* 煙囪

(B) bulletin [4] ('bʊlətɪn) *n.* 佈告 (= *report*)

(C) bubble [3] ('bʌbl̩) *n.* 泡泡

(D) balloon [1] (bə'lun) *n.* 氣球

* ***make sure*** 確認　　***start a fire*** 生火；點火

12. (**A**) During the speaking part of the test, you will read <u>aloud</u> a text on
your screen.
在進行考試口說部分的時候，你將會唸<u>出</u>一段你螢幕上的文字。

(A) ***aloud*** [2] (ə'laʊd) *adv.* 出聲地 (= *out loud*)

(B) altogether [2] (,ɔltə'gɛðɚ) *adv.* 總共 (= *all*)；完全地 (= *completely*)

(C) barely [3] (ˈbɛrlɪ) *adv.* 幾乎不 (= *hardly*)

(D) abroad [2] (əˈbrɔd) *adv.* 到國外 (= *overseas*)

*text [3] (tɛkst) *n.* 原文　　screen [2] (skrin) *n.* 螢幕

13. (**C**) The sailors on merchant ships were often poorly paid and subject to
brutal discipline.
商船上的水手常常是領低薪的，而且遭受殘酷的懲誡。

(A) bony [2] (ˈbonɪ) *adj.* 骨瘦如柴的

(B) capable [3] (ˈkepəbl̩) *adj.* 能夠的 < *of* >

(C) ***brutal*** [4] (ˈbrutl̩) *adj.* 殘忍的；無情的

(D) childish [2] (ˈtʃaɪldɪʃ) *adj.* 幼稚的 (= *immature*)

*sailor [2] (ˈselə) *n.* 水手　　merchant [3] (ˈmɜtʃənt) *adj.* 商人的；商船的
poorly-paid 低薪的；待遇差的
subject [2] (ˈsʌbdʒɪkt) *adj.* 易受…的 < *to* >
discipline [4] (ˈdɪsəplɪn) *n.* 紀律；懲戒

14. (**C**) As you emerge from a dark room, it will take a minute for your eyes
to adjust to the daylight.
當你從陰暗的房間走出來，你的眼睛需要幾分鐘來適應日光。

(A) contrast [4] (kənˈtræst) *v.* 對比；對照

(B) circulate [4] (ˈsɝkjəˌlet) *v.* 循環 (= *flow*)

(C) ***adjust*** [4] (əˈdʒʌst) *v.* 調整；適應 (= *adapt*) < *to* >

(D) accuse [4] (əˈkjuz) *v.* 控告 (= *charge*)

*emerge [4] (ɪˈmɝdʒ) *v.* 出現　　take [1] (tek) *v.* 花（時間）
daylight (ˈdeˌlaɪt) *n.* 日光

15. (**B**) The shoe company's new marketing campaign features several pro
athletes. 那家鞋業公司新的行銷活動以好幾個職業運動員為號召。

(A) authority [4] (ɔˈθɔrətɪ) *n.* 權威；權限

(B) ***campaign*** [4] (kæmˈpen) *n.* 活動

(C) attitude [3] (ˈætəˌtjud) *n.* 態度

(D) appetite [2] (ˈæpəˌtaɪt) *n.* 食慾；胃口

*feature [3] (ˈfitʃə) *v.* 以…為特色；以…為號召
pro (pro) *adj.* 職業選手的　　athlete [3] (ˈæθlit) *n.* 運動員

TEST 7

【命題範圍：「高中生必背 4500 字」
p.51-60，convey～depend】

Directions: Choose the one word that best completes the sentence.

1. Her eyes _____ great sadness.
   (A) cooperate　　　　　(B) convey
   (C) delay　　　　　　　(D) cope　　　　　　　　( )

2. He believed he was right and nothing would _____ him otherwise.
   (A) convince　　　　　(B) correspond
   (C) deny　　　　　　　(D) depart　　　　　　　( )

3. Teddy found painting to be a wonderful _____ outlet.
   (A) correct　　　　　　(B) crispy
   (C) creative　　　　　(D) delicious　　　　　( )

4. From the witness stand, the suspect _____ his innocence.
   (A) deepened　　　　　(B) declared
   (C) cracked　　　　　　(D) crawled　　　　　　( )

5. Wainwright received the Medal of Honor for his _____ leadership during the war.
   (A) costly　　　　　　(B) courageous
   (C) countable　　　　(D) defensible　　　　( )

6. People living there have a reputation for being very friendly and _____.
   (A) critical　　　　　(B) courteous
   (C) deaf　　　　　　　(D) crazy　　　　　　　( )

7. The teacher has a nice way of saying you're wrong without _____ your idea.
   (A) cramming　　　　　(B) crashing
   (C) covering　　　　　(D) criticizing　　　　( )

8. He bought a gun to _____ his family against potential intruders.
   (A) defend
   (B) demand
   (C) creep
   (D) deafen   ( )

9. Sasha said she _____ wouldn't attend the party.
   (A) definitely
   (B) dangerously
   (C) cunningly
   (D) delightfully   ( )

10. Although the paper kite is beautiful, it's too _____ to fly.
    (A) dense
    (B) democratic
    (C) defensive
    (D) delicate   ( )

11. As he passed the new restaurant, he stopped and looked in the window out of _____.
    (A) courtesy
    (B) craft
    (C) curiosity
    (D) department   ( )

12. This research team is composed of experts from different _____ backgrounds.
    (A) curious
    (B) crunchy
    (C) cruel
    (D) cultural   ( )

13. All essays submitted after the _____ will be marked down a full letter grade.
    (A) cushion
    (B) crisis
    (C) dealer
    (D) deadline   ( )

14. The two old men enjoyed _____ who the greatest boxer of all time was.
    (A) delivering
    (B) cursing
    (C) debating
    (D) daring   ( )

15. The famous chef's cooking _____ was broadcast live on national television.
    (A) decoration
    (B) cottage
    (C) corner
    (D) demonstration   ( )

TEST 7 詳解

1. (**B**) Her eyes <u>convey</u> great sadness. 她的雙眼<u>表達出</u>極大的悲傷。
   - (A) cooperate [4] (ko'ɑpə‚ret) v. 合作
   - (B) ***convey*** [4] (kən've) v. 傳達；表達
   - (C) delay [2] (dɪ'le) v., n. 延遲；耽誤
   - (D) cope [4] (kop) v. 處理；應付
   - *sadness [1] ('sædnɪs) n. 悲傷

2. (**A**) He believed he was right and nothing would <u>convince</u> him otherwise.
   他相信自己是對的，沒有事情能<u>使他相信</u>自己是錯的。
   - (A) ***convince*** [4] (kən'vɪns) v. 使相信；說服
   - (B) correspond [4] (‚kɔrə'spɑnd) v. 通信；符合
   - (C) deny [2] (dɪ'naɪ) v. 否認；拒絕給予
   - (D) depart [4] (dɪ'pɑrt) v. 離開
   - *otherwise [4] ('ʌðə‚waɪz) adv. 否則；在其他方面

3. (**C**) Teddy found painting to be a wonderful <u>creative</u> outlet.
   泰迪發現繪畫是很好的<u>創作</u>管道。
   - (A) correct [1] (kə'rɛkt) adj. 正確的
   - (B) crispy [3] ('krɪspɪ) adj. 酥脆的
   - (C) ***creative*** [3] (krɪ'etɪv) adj. 有創造力的
   - (D) delicious [2] (dɪ'lɪʃəs) adj. 美味的
   - *painting [2] ('pentɪŋ) n. 繪畫　　outlet [6] ('aʊt‚lɛt) n. 出口；發洩管道

4. (**B**) From the witness stand, the suspect <u>declared</u> his innocence.
   在證人席上，嫌犯<u>宣布</u>自己是清白的。
   - (A) deepen [3] ('dipən) v. 加深
   - (B) ***declare*** [4] (dɪ'klɛr) v. 宣布
   - (C) crack [4] (kræk) v. 使破裂
   - (D) crawl [3] (krɔl) v. 爬行
   - *witness [4] ('wɪtnɪs) n. 目擊者；證人
     stand [1] (stænd) n. 攤子；看台　　***witness stand*** 證人席
     suspect [3] ('sʌspɛkt) n. 嫌疑犯　　innocence [4] ('ɪnəsn̩s) n. 清白

5. (**B**) Wainwright received the Medal of Honor for his <u>courageous</u>
leadership during the war.
溫萊特因為戰爭時<u>英勇的</u>領導，獲得榮譽勳章。

    (A) costly² 〔'kɔstlɪ 〕*adj.* 昂貴的

    (B) ***courageous***⁴ 〔kə'redʒəs 〕*adj.* 勇敢的

    (C) countable³ 〔'kaʊntəbḷ 〕*adj.* 可數的

    (D) defensible⁴ 〔dɪ'fɛnsəbḷ 〕*adj.* 可防禦的

    ＊receive¹ 〔rɪ'siv 〕*v.* 收到；得到

      medal³ 〔'mɛdḷ 〕*n.* 獎牌；勳章   honor³ 〔'ɑnɚ 〕*n.* 光榮

      leadership² 〔'lidɚˏʃɪp 〕*n.* 領導能力

6. (**B**) People living there have a reputation for being very friendly and
<u>courteous</u>. 住在那裡的人以非常友善、<u>有禮貌</u>著稱。

    (A) critical⁴ 〔'krɪtɪkḷ 〕*adj.* 批評的；危急的

    (B) ***courteous***⁴ 〔'kɜtɪəs 〕*adj.* 有禮貌的

    (C) deaf² 〔dɛf 〕*adj.* 聾的

    (D) crazy² 〔'krezɪ 〕*adj.* 瘋狂的

    ＊reputation⁴ 〔ˏrɛpjə'teʃən 〕*n.* 名聲

7. (**D**) The teacher has a nice way of saying you're wrong without
<u>criticizing</u> your idea.
那位老師很會說話，他可以說你是錯的，卻不會<u>批評</u>你的想法。

    (A) cram⁴ 〔kræm 〕*v.* 填塞；K 書

    (B) crash³ 〔kræʃ 〕*v., n.* 墜毀；撞毀

    (C) cover¹ 〔'kʌvɚ 〕*v.* 覆蓋；涵蓋

    (D) ***criticize***⁴ 〔'krɪtəˏsaɪz 〕*v.* 批評

8. (**A**) He bought a gun to <u>defend</u> his family against potential intruders.
他買了一枝槍，來<u>保護</u>家人抵抗可能的入侵者。

    (A) ***defend***⁴ 〔dɪ'fɛnd 〕*v.* 保衛

    (B) demand⁴ 〔dɪ'mænd 〕*v., n.* 要求

    (C) creep³ 〔krip 〕*v.* 爬行；悄悄地前進

    (D) deafen³ 〔'dɛfən 〕*v.* 使耳聾

*gun¹〔gʌn〕n. 槍　　against¹〔ə'gɛnst〕prep. 反對
potential⁵〔pə'tɛnʃəl〕adj. 可能的
intruder⁶〔ɪn'trudɚ〕n. 入侵者

9. (**A**) Sasha said she <u>definitely</u> wouldn't attend the party.
莎夏說，她<u>一定</u>不會去參加派對。

(A) ***definitely***⁴〔'dɛfənɪtlɪ〕adv. 明確地；一定
(B) dangerously²〔'dendʒərəslɪ〕adv. 危險地
(C) cunningly⁴〔'kʌnɪŋlɪ〕adv. 狡猾地
(D) delightfully⁴〔dɪ'laɪtfəlɪ〕adv. 令人高興地

*attend²〔ə'tɛnd〕v. 參加

10. (**D**) Although the paper kite is beautiful, it's too <u>delicate</u> to fly.
雖然這個紙風箏很漂亮，但是它太<u>細緻</u>了飛不起來。

(A) dense⁴〔dɛns〕adj. 濃密的；密集的
(B) democratic³〔,dɛmə'krætɪk〕adj. 民主的
(C) defensive⁴〔dɪ'fɛnsɪv〕adj. 防禦的
(D) ***delicate***⁴〔'dɛləkɪt〕adj. 細緻的

*kite¹〔kaɪt〕n. 風箏

11. (**C**) As he passed the new restaurant, he stopped and looked in the
window out of <u>curiosity</u>.
當他經過那家新餐廳時，出於<u>好奇心</u>，他停下來看窗戶裡面。

(A) courtesy⁴〔'kɜtəsɪ〕n. 禮貌
(B) craft⁴〔kræft〕n. 技藝；技術
(C) ***curiosity***⁴〔,kjʊrɪ'ɑsətɪ〕n. 好奇心　　***out of curiosity*** 出於好奇心
(D) department²〔dɪ'pɑrtmənt〕n. 部門；系

12. (**D**) This research team is composed of experts from different <u>cultural</u>
backgrounds.　這個研究小隊由來自不同<u>文化</u>背景的專家所組成。

(A) curious²〔'kjʊrɪəs〕adj. 好奇的
(B) crunchy³〔'krʌntʃɪ〕adj. 鬆脆的
(C) cruel²〔'kruəl〕adj. 殘忍的
(D) ***cultural***³〔'kʌltʃərəl〕adj. 文化的

*research [4] ('risɜtʃ, rɪ'sɜtʃ) *n.* 研究　　team [2] (tim) *n.* 隊伍
compose [4] (kəm'poz) *v.* 組成　　***be composed of*** 由～組成
expert [2] ('ɛkspɜt) *n.* 專家
background [3] ('bæk,graʊnd) *n.* 背景

13. (**D**) All essays submitted after the <u>deadline</u> will be marked down
a full letter grade.
所有過了<u>期限</u>才交的文章，都會被扣一整個字母等級的分數。
(A) cushion [4] ('kuʃən) *n.* 墊子
(B) crisis [2] ('kraɪsɪs) *n.* 危機
(C) dealer [3] ('dilə) *n.* 商人
(D) ***deadline*** [4] ('dɛd,laɪn) *n.* 最後期限
*essay [4] ('ɛse) *n.* 論文；文章　　submit [5] (səb'mɪt) *v.* 提交
mark down 給低分；扣分　　***letter grade*** 字母等級

14. (**C**) The two old men enjoyed <u>debating</u> who the greatest boxer of all
time was.　這二位老先生喜歡<u>爭辯</u>誰是史上最偉大的拳擊手。
(A) deliver [2] (dɪ'lɪvə) *v.* 遞送
(B) curse [4] (kɜs) *v., n.* 詛咒
(C) ***debate*** [2] (dɪ'bet) *v., n.* 辯論；爭辯
(D) dare [3] (dɛr) *v.* 敢
*boxer [5] ('bɑksə) *n.* 拳擊手　　***of all time*** 史上；有史以來

15. (**D**) The famous chef's cooking <u>demonstration</u> was broadcast live
on national television.
這位名主廚的烹飪<u>示範</u>在全國的電視上現場轉播。
(A) decoration [4] (,dɛkə'reʃən) *n.* 裝飾
(B) cottage [4] ('kɑtɪdʒ) *n.* 農舍
(C) corner [2] ('kɔrnə) *n.* 角落；轉角
(D) ***demonstration*** [4] (,dɛmən'streʃən) *n.* 示範；示威
*chef [5] (ʃɛf) *n.* 主廚　　broadcast [2] ('brɔd,kæst) *v.* 廣播；播送
live [1] (laɪv) *adv.* 現場地　　national [2] ('næʃənl) *adj.* 全國的

TEST 8

【命題範圍：「高中生必背 4500 字」
p.61-70，dependable～dragonfly】

Directions: Choose the one word that best completes the sentence.

1. Eric has been working hard and doing a good job. He _____ a raise.
   - (A) depresses
   - (B) disagrees
   - (C) deserves
   - (D) dominates　　　( )

2. Most photographers are now using _____ cameras.
   - (A) desperate
   - (B) different
   - (C) difficult
   - (D) digital　　　( )

3. With _____ practice, he taught himself to play piano.
   - (A) distinguished
   - (B) direct
   - (C) distant
   - (D) diligent　　　( )

4. Taking a taxi to the airport is expensive and our least _____ option.
   - (A) dependent
   - (B) doubtful
   - (C) double
   - (D) desirable　　　( )

5. Showing great _____, Kiki finally got her driver's license after six attempts.
   - (A) determination
   - (B) description
   - (C) depression
   - (D) discussion　　　( )

6. Mothers are _____ to their children and fathers are dedicated to the family.
   - (A) described
   - (B) devoted
   - (C) destroyed
   - (D) disputed　　　( )

7. Homeowner's insurance policies generally don't cover natural _____ like earthquakes.
   - (A) deposits
   - (B) designers
   - (C) disasters
   - (D) dragonflies　　　( )

8. He never let failure _____ him from achieving his dream.
   - (A) discuss
   - (B) discourage
   - (C) disappear
   - (D) download
   ( )

9. She tried to _____ her anger with a bright smile.
   - (A) desert
   - (B) discover
   - (C) disguise
   - (D) disconnect
   ( )

10. The singer has a _____ voice that seems to cut through the music.
    - (A) dishonest
    - (B) disappointed
    - (C) distinct
    - (D) dim
    ( )

11. Larry keeps a _____ of his daily activities.
    - (A) devil
    - (B) diary
    - (C) depth
    - (D) disco
    ( )

12. Children are able to _____ right from wrong as early as two years old.
    - (A) distinguish
    - (B) disturb
    - (C) doubt
    - (D) drag
    ( )

13. They hired two temporary workers to _____ promotional materials on the street.
    - (A) determine
    - (B) distribute
    - (C) dial
    - (D) devise
    ( )

14. He likes to drink _____ beer, but enjoys an occasional imported brew.
    - (A) domestic
    - (B) dominant
    - (C) dependable
    - (D) divine
    ( )

15. Gina lived in an on-campus _____ during her freshman and sophomore years of college.
    - (A) discount
    - (B) development
    - (C) dormitory
    - (D) distance
    ( )

TEST 8 詳解

1. (**C**) Eric has been working hard and doing a good job. He <u>deserves</u> a raise. 愛瑞克一直都很努力工作，表現得也很好。他<u>值得</u>加薪。
   - (A) depress[4] 〔 dɪˈprɛs 〕 v. 使沮喪
   - (B) disagree[2] 〔ˌdɪsəˈgri 〕 v. 不同意
   - (C) ***deserve***[4] 〔 dɪˈzɜv 〕 v. 應得；值得
   - (D) dominate[4] 〔ˈdɑməˌnet 〕 v. 支配；控制
   * ***do a good job*** 表現得很好　　raise[1] 〔 rez 〕 n. 提高；加薪

2. (**D**) Most photographers are now using <u>digital</u> cameras.
   大部分攝影師現在都使用<u>數位</u>相機。
   - (A) desperate[4] 〔ˈdɛspərɪt 〕 adj. 絕望的
   - (B) different[1] 〔ˈdɪfərənt 〕 adj. 不同的
   - (C) difficult[1] 〔ˈdɪfəˌkʌlt 〕 adj. 困難的
   - (D) ***digital***[4] 〔ˈdɪdʒətḷ 〕 adj. 數位的
     digital camera 數位相機
   * photographer[2] 〔 fəˈtɑgrəfɚ 〕 n. 攝影師

3. (**D**) With <u>diligent</u> practice, he taught himself to play piano.
   他<u>勤奮</u>練習，自學彈鋼琴。
   - (A) distinguished[4] 〔 dɪˈstɪŋgwɪʃt 〕 adj. 卓越的；著名的
   - (B) direct[1] 〔 dəˈrɛkt 〕 adj. 直接的
   - (C) distant[2] 〔ˈdɪstənt 〕 adj. 遙遠的
   - (D) ***diligent***[3] 〔ˈdɪlədʒənt 〕 adj. 勤勉的；勤奮的
   * practice[1] 〔ˈpræktɪs 〕 n. 練習

4. (**D**) Taking a taxi to the airport is expensive and our least <u>desirable</u> option. 搭計程車去機場很貴，是我們最不<u>想要的</u>選擇。
   - (A) dependent[4] 〔 dɪˈpɛndənt 〕 adj. 依賴的
   - (B) doubtful[3] 〔ˈdautfəl 〕 adj. 懷疑的；不確定的
   - (C) double[4] 〔ˈdʌbḷ 〕 adj. 兩倍的
   - (D) ***desirable***[3] 〔 dɪˈzaɪrəbḷ 〕 adj. 合意的
   * least[1] 〔 list 〕 adv. 最不　　option[6] 〔ˈɑpʃən 〕 n. 選擇

5. (**A**) Showing great <u>determination</u>, Kiki finally got her driver's license after six attempts.

琪琪展現出很大的<u>決心</u>，在嘗試六次之後終於拿到駕照。

   (A) **determination** [4] ﹝ dɪˌtɝmə'neʃən ﹞ *n.* 決心

   (B) description [3] ﹝ dɪ'skrɪpʃən ﹞ *n.* 描述

   (C) depression [4] ﹝ dɪ'prɛʃən ﹞ *n.* 沮喪

   (D) discussion [2] ﹝ dɪ'skʌʃən ﹞ *n.* 討論

   * license [4] ﹝'laɪsn̩s ﹞ *n.* 執照　***driver's license*** 駕照

   attempt [3] ﹝ ə'tɛmpt ﹞ *n.* 嘗試

6. (**B**) Mothers are <u>devoted</u> to their children and fathers are dedicated to the family. 母親們<u>致力於</u>孩子，而父親們致力於整個家庭。

   (A) describe [2] ﹝ dɪ'skraɪb ﹞ *v.* 描述

   (B) **devote** [4] ﹝ dɪ'vot ﹞ *v.* 使致力於　***be devoted to*** 致力於

   (C) destroy [3] ﹝ dɪ'strɔɪ ﹞ *v.* 破壞

   (D) dispute [1] ﹝ dɪ'spjut ﹞ *v., n.* 爭論

   * dedicate [6] ﹝'dɛdəˌket ﹞ *v.* 使致力於（ = *devote* ）

   be dedicated to 致力於（ = *be devoted to* ）

7. (**C**) Homeowner's insurance policies generally don't cover natural <u>disasters</u> like earthquakes.

房屋保險（房主的保單）通常不包含像地震等的<u>天災</u>。

   (A) deposit [3] ﹝ dɪ'pɑzɪt ﹞ *n.* 存款

   (B) designer [3] ﹝ dɪ'zaɪnɚ ﹞ *n.* 設計師

   (C) **disaster** [3] ﹝ dɪz'æstɚ ﹞ *n.* 災難

   natural disaster 天然災難；天災

   (D) dragonfly [2] ﹝'drægənˌflaɪ ﹞ *n.* 蜻蜓

   * homeowner ﹝'homˌonɚ ﹞ *n.* 屋主；房主

   insurance [4] ﹝ ɪn'ʃʊrəns ﹞ *n.* 保險

   policy [2] ﹝'pɑləsɪ ﹞ *n.* 政策；保單（ = *insurance policy* ）

   generally [1,2] ﹝'dʒɛnərəlɪ ﹞ *adv.* 一般地；通常

   cover [1] ﹝'kʌvɚ ﹞ *v.* 涵蓋；包含

   natural [2] ﹝'nætʃərəl ﹞ *adj.* 自然的；天然的

   earthquake [2] ﹝'ɝθˌkwek ﹞ *n.* 地震

8. (**B**) He never let failure <u>discourage</u> him from achieving his dream.
他從來不會<u>因失敗而氣餒</u>，因而未能達成他的夢想。

(A) discuss [2] 〔 dɪ'skʌs 〕 *v.* 討論

(B) ***discourage*** [4] 〔 dɪs'kɝɪdʒ 〕 *v.* 使氣餒

(C) disappear [2] 〔 ,dɪsə'pɪr 〕 *v.* 消失

(D) download [4] 〔 'daʊn,lod 〕 *v.* 下載

* failure [2] 〔 'feljɚ 〕 *n.* 失敗　　　achieve [3] 〔 ə'tʃiv 〕 *v.* 達到

9. (**C**) She tried to <u>disguise</u> her anger with a bright smile.
她試著用燦爛的微笑來<u>偽裝</u>她的憤怒。

(A) desert [2] 〔 dɪ'zɝt 〕 *v.* 拋棄　〔'dɛzɚt 〕 *n.* 沙漠

(B) discover [1] 〔 dɪ'skʌvɚ 〕 *v.* 發現

(C) ***disguise*** [4] 〔 dɪs'gaɪz 〕 *v.* 偽裝

(D) disconnect [4] 〔 ,dɪskə'nɛkt 〕 *v.* 切斷

* anger [1] 〔 'æŋgɚ 〕 *n.* 憤怒　　　bright [1] 〔 braɪt 〕 *adj.* 明亮的；燦爛的

10. (**C**) The singer has a <u>distinct</u> voice that seems to cut through the music.
這位歌手的嗓音非常<u>獨特</u>，似乎能穿透音樂。

(A) dishonest [2] 〔 dɪs'ɑnɪst 〕 *adj.* 不誠實的

(B) disappointed [4] 〔 ,dɪsə'pɔɪntɪd 〕 *adj.* 感到失望的

(C) ***distinct*** [4] 〔 dɪ'stɪŋkt 〕 *adj.* 獨特的；不同的

(D) dim [3] 〔 dɪm 〕 *adj.* 昏暗的

* voice [1] 〔 vɔɪs 〕 *n.* 聲音　　　***cut through*** 穿過；穿透

11. (**B**) Larry keeps a <u>diary</u> of his daily activities.
賴瑞把他每天的活動都寫成<u>日記</u>。

(A) devil [3] 〔 'dɛvḷ 〕 *n.* 魔鬼

(B) ***diary*** [2] 〔 'daɪərɪ 〕 *n.* 日記

(C) depth [2] 〔 dɛpθ 〕 *n.* 深度

(D) disco [3] 〔 'dɪsko 〕 *n.* 迪斯可舞廳

* daily [2] 〔 'delɪ 〕 *adj.* 每天的　　　activity [3] 〔 æk'tɪvətɪ 〕 *n.* 活動

12. (**A**) Children are able to <u>distinguish</u> right from wrong as early as two
years old.　小孩早在兩歲時就可以<u>分辨</u>對與錯。

(A) *distinguish* [4] 〔 dɪ'stɪŋgwɪʃ 〕 *v.* 分辨;區分

    distinguish A from B 區分 A 和 B

(B) disturb [4] 〔 dɪ'stɜb 〕 *v.* 打擾

(C) doubt [2] 〔 daʊt 〕 *v., n.* 懷疑;不相信

(D) drag [2] 〔 dræg 〕 *v.* 拖

* *be able* [1] *to V* 能夠

13. (**B**) They hired two temporary workers to <u>distribute</u> promotional materials on the street. 他們雇用了兩名臨時工,在街上<u>發</u>促銷品。

    (A) determine [3] 〔 dɪ'tɜmɪn 〕 *v.* 決定

    (B) *distribute* [4] 〔 dɪ'strɪbjut 〕 *v.* 分配;分發

    (C) dial [2] 〔 'daɪəl 〕 *v.* 撥(號)

    (D) devise [4] 〔 dɪ'vaɪz 〕 *v.* 設計;發明

  * hire [2] 〔 haɪr 〕 *v.* 雇用   temporary [3] 〔 'tɛmpə,rɛrɪ 〕 *adj.* 臨時的

    promotional 〔 prə'moʃənḷ 〕 *adj.* 促銷的

    material [2,6] 〔 mə'tɪrɪəl 〕 *n.* 物質;材料;物品

14. (**A**) He likes to drink <u>domestic</u> beer, but enjoys an occasional imported brew. 他喜歡喝<u>國產的</u>啤酒,但是偶爾也會享受一下進口啤酒。

    (A) *domestic* [3] 〔 də'mɛstɪk 〕 *adj.* 國內的

    (B) dominant [4] 〔 'dɑmənənt 〕 *adj.* 支配的;佔優勢的

    (C) dependable [4] 〔 dɪ'pɛndəbḷ 〕 *adj.* 可靠的

    (D) divine [4] 〔 də'vaɪn 〕 *adj.* 神聖的

  * occasional [4] 〔 ə'keʒənḷ 〕 *adj.* 偶爾的

    imported [3] 〔 ɪm'portɪd 〕 *adj.* 進口的   brew [6] 〔 bru 〕 *n.* 釀造;啤酒

15. (**C**) Gina lived in an on-campus <u>dormitory</u> during her freshman and sophomore years of college.

    吉娜在大學大一和大二兩年,住在校內的<u>宿舍</u>裡。

    (A) discount [3] 〔 'dɪskaʊnt 〕 *n.* 折扣

    (B) development [2] 〔 dɪ'vɛləpmənt 〕 *n.* 發展

    (C) *dormitory* [4,5] 〔 'dɔrmə,torɪ 〕 *n.* 宿舍

    (D) distance [2] 〔 'dɪstəns 〕 *n.* 距離

  * campus [3] 〔 'kæmpəs 〕 *n.* 校園   freshman [4] 〔 'frɛʃmən 〕 *adj.* 大一的

    sophomore [4] 〔 'sɑfm̩,or 〕 *adj.* 大二的

TEST 9

【命題範圍：「高中生必背 4500 字」
p.71-80，drain～evident】

Directions: *Choose the one word that best completes the sentence.*

1. Charles will _____ if he goes in the water; he can't swim.

    (A) drain　　　　　　　(B) drip

    (C) drown　　　　　　　(D) dread　　　　　　　　( )

2. The author has an _____ writing style and rarely uses big words.

    (A) economic　　　　　　(B) economics

    (C) economical　　　　　(D) economy　　　　　　( )

3. The recycling program aims to _____ waste in the school system.

    (A) employ　　　　　　　(B) educate

    (C) escape　　　　　　　(D) eliminate　　　　　　( )

4. He waited for her to _____ from the building.

    (A) emerge　　　　　　　(B) edit

    (C) emphasize　　　　　　(D) dump　　　　　　　( )

5. Ms. Brown is a _____ teacher whose classes are extremely popular with students.

    (A) dynamic　　　　　　　(B) equal

    (C) dusty　　　　　　　　(D) drowsy　　　　　　( )

6. The article about our company will appear in today's _____ of the newspaper.

    (A) dynasty　　　　　　　(B) edition

    (C) effect　　　　　　　　(D) electricity　　　　　( )

7. Instant messaging has become the most _____ form of communication.

    (A) earnest　　　　　　　(B) eager

    (C) efficient　　　　　　　(D) durable　　　　　　( )

8. If you _____ a bear in the forest, try not to make eye contact with it.
   (A) enforce
   (B) endanger
   (C) encounter
   (D) enclose
   ( )

9. The girl was _____ of her much more attractive younger sister.
   (A) enormous
   (B) emotional
   (C) envious
   (D) elegant
   ( )

10. The apartment is _____ with all new modern appliances.
    (A) erased
    (B) estimated
    (C) equipped
    (D) entertained
    ( )

11. The new lighting system will be installed by a licensed _____.
    (A) employer
    (B) electrician
    (C) emperor
    (D) economist
    ( )

12. The broken window was _____ that a burglary had taken place.
    (A) eventual
    (B) dramatic
    (C) evidence
    (D) empty
    ( )

13. The money in your savings account must only be used in case of _____.
    (A) engagement
    (B) element
    (C) emergency
    (D) embassy
    ( )

14. The singer's _____ performances impressed both audiences and critics alike.
    (A) energetic
    (B) elastic
    (C) effective
    (D) elementary
    ( )

15. Jack is not the best student, but his _____ for knowledge is inspiring.
    (A) evaluation
    (B) enthusiasm
    (C) enlargement
    (D) equality
    ( )

TEST 9 詳解

1. (**C**) Charles will <u>drown</u> if he goes in the water; he can't swim.
查爾斯如果掉到水裡會<u>淹死</u>的；他不會游泳。

(A) drain³ 〔 dren 〕 *v.* 排水　　*n.* 排水溝
(B) drip³ 〔 drɪp 〕 *v.* 滴下
(C) ***drown***³ 〔 draʊn 〕 *v.* 淹死
(D) dread⁴ 〔 drɛd 〕 *v.* 害怕

2. (**C**) The author has an <u>economical</u> writing style and rarely uses big
words. 這位作者的寫作風格<u>簡約</u>，他很少使用艱深的字彙。

(A) economic⁴ 〔͵ikə'namɪk 〕 *adj.* 經濟的
(B) economics⁴ 〔͵ikə'namɪks 〕 *n.* 經濟學
(C) ***economical***⁴ 〔͵ikə'namɪkḷ 〕 *adj.* 節省的
(D) economy⁴ 〔 ɪ'kanəmɪ 〕 *n.* 經濟

* author³ 〔'ɔθɚ 〕 *n.* 作者　　style³ 〔 staɪl 〕 *n.* 風格；方式
rarely² 〔'rɛrlɪ 〕 *adv.* 罕見地　　***big word*** 艱深的字

3. (**D**) The recycling program aims to <u>eliminate</u> waste in the school system.
這個回收計劃目標在於<u>除去學校系統中的廢物</u>。

(A) employ³ 〔 ɪm'plɔɪ 〕 *v.* 雇用
(B) educate³ 〔'ɛdʒə͵ket 〕 *v.* 教育
(C) escape³ 〔 ə'skep 〕 *v.* 逃走；逃脫
(D) ***eliminate***⁴ 〔 ɪ'lɪmə͵net 〕 *v.* 除去；排除

* recycle⁴ 〔 ri'saɪkḷ 〕 *v.* 回收再利用　　program³ 〔'progræm 〕 *n.* 計劃
aim² 〔 em 〕 *v.* 目標在於　　waste¹ 〔 west 〕 *n.* 浪費；廢物
system³ 〔'sɪstəm 〕 *n.* 系統

4. (**A**) He waited for her to <u>emerge</u> from the building.
他等她從大樓裡<u>出來</u>。

(A) ***emerge***⁴ 〔 ɪ'mɝdʒ 〕 *v.* 出現
(B) edit³ 〔'ɛdɪt 〕 *v.* 編輯
(C) emphasize³ 〔'ɛmfə͵saɪz 〕 *v.* 強調
(D) dump³ 〔 dʌmp 〕 *v.* 傾倒

5. (**A**) Ms. Brown is a <u>dynamic</u> teacher whose classes are extremely popular with students.
布朗女士是一位很<u>有活力的</u>老師，她的課非常受到學生的歡迎。

(A) ***dynamic*** [4] ﹝daɪ'næmɪk﹞ *adj.* 有活力的

(B) equal [1] ﹝'ikwəl﹞ *adj.* 平等的

(C) dusty [4] ﹝'dʌstɪ﹞ *adj.* 滿是灰塵的

(D) drowsy [3] ﹝'draʊzɪ﹞ *adj.* 想睡的

***be popular with** 受～的歡迎

6. (**B**) The article about our company will appear in today's <u>edition</u> of the newspaper. 那篇有關我們公司的報導會出現在今天報紙的<u>版面</u>上。

(A) dynasty [4] ﹝'daɪnəstɪ﹞ *n.* 朝代

(B) ***edition*** [3] ﹝ɪ'dɪʃən﹞ *n.* (發行物的) 版

(C) effect [2] ﹝ɪ'fɛkt﹞ *n.* 影響

(D) electricity [3] ﹝ɪ,lɛk'trɪsətɪ﹞ *n.* 電

*article [2,4] ﹝'ɑrtɪkl̩﹞ *n.* 文章；報導　　appear [1] ﹝ə'pɪr﹞ *v.* 出現

7. (**C**) Instant messaging has become the most <u>efficient</u> form of communication. 即時通訊已經成為最<u>有效率的</u>溝通方式。

(A) earnest [4] ﹝'ɝnɪst﹞ *adj.* 認真的

(B) eager [3] ﹝'igɚ﹞ *adj.* 渴望的

(C) ***efficient*** [3] ﹝ɪ'fɪʃənt﹞ *adj.* 有效率的

(D) durable [4] ﹝'djʊrəbl̩﹞ *adj.* 耐用的；持久的

*instant [2] ﹝'ɪnstənt﹞ *adj.* 立即的　　***instant messaging*** 即時通訊
form [2] ﹝fɔrm﹞ *n.* 形式；方式
communication [4] ﹝kə,mjunə'keʃən﹞ *n.* 溝通

8. (**C**) If you <u>encounter</u> a bear in the forest, try not to make eye contact with it. 如果你在森林裡<u>遇到</u>一隻熊，試著不要和牠有目光接觸。

(A) enforce [4] ﹝ɪn'fors﹞ *v.* 實施；執行

(B) endanger [4] ﹝ɪn'dendʒɚ﹞ *v.* 危害

(C) ***encounter*** [4] ﹝ɪn'kaʊntɚ﹞ *v.* 遭遇

(D) enclose [4] ﹝ɪn'kloz﹞ *v.* (隨函) 附寄

*forest [1] ﹝'fɑrɪst﹞ *n.* 森林　　contact [2] ﹝'kɑntækt﹞ *n.* 接觸；聯絡
eye contact 目光接觸

9. (**C**) The girl was <u>envious</u> of her much more attractive younger sister.
這個女孩很<u>羨慕</u>比她更加吸引人的妹妹。

    (A) enormous⁴ 〔 ɪ'nɔrməs 〕 *adj.* 巨大的

    (B) emotional⁴ 〔 ɪ'moʃənḷ 〕 *adj.* 感情的

    (C) *envious*⁴ 〔'ɛnvɪəs 〕 *adj.* 嫉妒的;羨慕的

        be envious of 嫉妒;羨慕

    (D) elegant⁴ 〔'ɛləgənt 〕 *adj.* 優雅的

    ＊attractive³ 〔 ə'træktɪv 〕 *adj.* 吸引人的

10. (**C**) The apartment is <u>equipped</u> with all new modern appliances.
這間公寓<u>配備</u>有所有全新的現代化家電用品。

    (A) erase³ 〔 ɪ'res 〕 *v.* 擦掉

    (B) estimate⁴ 〔'ɛstə,met 〕 *v.* 估計

    (C) *equip*⁴ 〔 ɪ'kwɪp 〕 *v.* 裝備;使配備　*be equipped with* 有～配備

    (D) entertain⁴ 〔,ɛntə'ten 〕 *v.* 娛樂

    ＊apartment² 〔 ə'partmənt 〕 *n.* 公寓　modern² 〔'madən 〕 *adj.* 現代的

      appliance⁴ 〔 ə'plaɪəns 〕 *n.* 家電用品

11. (**B**) The new lighting system will be installed by a licensed <u>electrician</u>.
這組新的照明系統將請一位有執照的<u>電工</u>來安裝。

    (A) employer³ 〔 ɪm'plɔɪə 〕 *n.* 雇主

    (B) *electrician*⁴ 〔 ɪ,lɛk'trɪʃən 〕 *n.* 電工

    (C) emperor³ 〔'ɛmpərə 〕 *n.* 皇帝

    (D) economist⁴ 〔 ɪ'kɑnəmɪst 〕 *n.* 經濟學家

    ＊lighting¹ 〔'laɪtɪŋ 〕 *n.* 照明　*lighting system* 照明系統

      install⁴ 〔 ɪn'stɔl 〕 *v.* 安裝　licensed⁴ 〔'laɪsṇst 〕 *adj.* 有執照的

12. (**C**) The broken window was <u>evidence</u> that a burglary had taken place.
破掉的窗戶就是<u>證據</u>,證明有竊案發生。

    (A) eventual³ 〔 ɪ'vɛntʃuəl 〕 *adj.* 最後的

    (B) dramatic² 〔 drə'mætɪk 〕 *adj.* 戲劇性的

    (C) *evidence*⁴ 〔'ɛvədəns 〕 *n.* 證據

    (D) empty³ 〔'ɛmptɪ 〕 *adj.* 空的

    ＊burglary 〔'bɝglərɪ 〕 *n.* 竊案　*take place* 發生

13. (**C**) The money in your savings account must only be used in case
of <u>emergency</u>.

在你的儲蓄存款帳戶裡的錢，只有在<u>緊急情況</u>時才能使用。

(A) engagement [3] 〔 ɪn'gedʒmənt 〕 *n.* 訂婚

(B) element [2] 〔'ɛləmənt 〕 *n.* 要素

(C) *emergency* [3] 〔 ɪ'mɝdʒənsɪ 〕 *n.* 緊急情況

(D) embassy [4] 〔'ɛmbəsɪ 〕 *n.* 大使館

＊saving [3] 〔'sevɪŋ 〕 *n.* 節省；*(pl.)* 儲蓄　　account [3] 〔 ə'kaʊnt 〕 *n.* 帳戶

savings account 儲蓄存款帳戶　　*in case of* 萬一發生～

14. (**A**) The singer's <u>energetic</u> performances impressed both audiences
and critics alike.

這位歌手<u>充滿活力的</u>表演，讓觀眾和評論者印象都非常深刻。

(A) *energetic* [3] 〔,ɛnɚ'dʒɛtɪk 〕 *adj.* 充滿活力的

(B) elastic [4] 〔 ɪ'læstɪk 〕 *adj.* 有彈性的；可變通的

(C) effective [2] 〔 ə'fɛktɪv 〕 *adj.* 有效的

(D) elementary [4] 〔,ɛlə'mɛntərɪ 〕 *adj.* 基本的

＊performance [3] 〔 pɚ'fɔrməns 〕 *n.* 表演

impress [3] 〔 ɪm'prɛs 〕 *v.* 使印象深刻　　audience [3] 〔'ɔdɪəns 〕 *n.* 觀眾

critic [4] 〔'krɪtɪk 〕 *n.* 評論家　　alike [2] 〔 ə'laɪk 〕 *adv.* 同樣地

15. (**B**) Jack is not the best student, but his <u>enthusiasm</u> for knowledge
is inspiring.

傑克不是最優秀的學生，但是他對知識的<u>熱忱</u>非常激勵人心。

(A) evaluation [4] 〔 ɪ,væljʊ'eʃən 〕 *n.* 評價；評估

(B) *enthusiasm* [4] 〔 ɪn'θjuzɪ,æzəm 〕 *n.* 熱忱

(C) enlargement [4] 〔 ɪn'lɑrdʒmənt 〕 *n.* 擴大；放大

(D) equality [4] 〔 ɪ'kwɑlətɪ 〕 *n.* 相等；平等

＊knowledge [2] 〔'nɑlɪdʒ 〕 *n.* 知識

inspiring [4] 〔 ɪn'spaɪrɪŋ 〕 *adj.* 激勵人心的；令人振奮的

TEST 10

【命題範圍：「高中生必背 4500 字」
p.81-90，evil～flea】

Directions: *Choose the one word that best completes the sentence.*

1. John is a big talker who tends to _____ his accomplishments.

 (A) examine (B) exchange

 (C) expand (D) exaggerate ( )

2. Crops like corn and tobacco _____ the soil of nutrients.

 (A) exhibit (B) exist

 (C) explain (D) exhaust ( )

3. He saw a flash of light, followed by a loud _____.

 (A) explosion (B) experiment

 (C) exception (D) expression ( )

4. The pianist was _____ to classical music from a very young age.

 (A) exported (B) explored

 (C) exposed (D) expected ( )

5. Lauren has a(n) _____ talent for learning new languages.

 (A) expressive (B) extraordinary

 (C) faithful (D) familiar ( )

6. The basketball team's new training _____ will open next month.

 (A) feature (B) festival

 (C) facility (D) fence ( )

7. Some say climate change will cause more _____ weather conditions.

 (A) extreme (B) explosive

 (C) farther (D) fatal ( )

8. His _____ is to be rich and famous.
   (A) fable   (B) farewell
   (C) factor   (D) fantasy   (   )

9. The taxi driver told us to _____ our seatbelts.
   (A) fade   (B) extend
   (C) fasten   (D) excite   (   )

10. Paul's version of the event is pure _____. It's just not true.
   (A) ferry   (B) fiction
   (C) flame   (D) feast   (   )

11. The baby put up a _____ battle, but she eventually fell asleep.
   (A) fertile   (B) firm
   (C) fierce   (D) fashionable   (   )

12. You should keep a _____ on hand in case of power outages.
   (A) flashlight   (B) faucet
   (C) figure   (D) feather   (   )

13. He's such a good liar that we never know if what he's saying is true or _____.
   (A) exact   (B) extra
   (C) fake   (D) false   (   )

14. The architecture of Venice was _____, but not nearly as exciting as the ride on a gondola.
   (A) famous   (B) fantastic
   (C) fearful   (D) financial   (   )

15. He went down to the market on the corner to _____ the morning newspapers.
   (A) flatter   (B) fetch
   (C) explode   (D) faint   (   )

TEST 10 詳解

1. (**D**) John is a big talker who tends to <u>exaggerate</u> his accomplishments.
約翰很會吹牛，他通常會<u>誇大</u>自己的成就。
   (A) examine [1] 〔 ɪgˈzæmɪn 〕 v. 檢查；測驗
   (B) exchange [3] 〔 ɪksˈtʃendʒ 〕 v. 交換
   (C) expand [4] 〔 ɪkˈspænd 〕 v. 擴大
   (D) *exaggerate* [4] 〔 ɪgˈzædʒəˌret 〕 v. 誇大
   * *big talker* 吹牛的人　　 tend [3] 〔 tɛnd 〕 v. 傾向於；通常 < to V >
   accomplishment [4] 〔 əˈkɑmplɪʃmənt 〕 n. 成就

2. (**D**) Crops like corn and tobacco <u>exhaust</u> the soil of nutrients.
像玉米和煙草等農作物會將土壤中的養分<u>用光</u>。
   (A) exhibit [4] 〔 ɪgˈzɪbɪt 〕 v. 展示；展現
   (B) exist [2] 〔 ɪgˈzɪst 〕 v. 存在
   (C) explain [2] 〔 ɪkˈsplen 〕 v. 解釋
   (D) *exhaust* [4] 〔 ɪgˈzɔst 〕 v. 使筋疲力盡；使用光
   exhaust A of B 將 A 中的 B 用光
   * crop [2] 〔 krɑp 〕 n. 農作物　　 corn [1] 〔 kɔrn 〕 n. 玉米
   tobacco [3] 〔 təˈbæko 〕 n. 煙草　　 soil [1] 〔 sɔɪl 〕 n. 土壤
   nutrient [6] 〔ˈnjutrɪənt 〕 n. 營養素；養分

3. (**A**) He saw a flash of light, followed by a loud <u>explosion</u>.
他看到了一道閃光，隨後就聽到了很大的<u>爆炸聲</u>。
   (A) *explosion* [4] 〔 ɪkˈsploʒən 〕 n. 爆炸 (聲)
   (B) experiment [3] 〔 ɪkˈspɛrəmənt 〕 n. 實驗
   (C) exception [4] 〔 ɪkˈsɛpʃən 〕 n. 例外
   (D) expression [3] 〔 ɪkˈsprɛʃən 〕 n. 表達；表情；說法
   * flash [2] 〔 flæʃ 〕 n. 閃光；閃爍　　 light [1] 〔 laɪt 〕 n. 燈；光；光線
   follow [1] 〔ˈfɑlo 〕 v. 跟隨　　 loud [1] 〔 laʊd 〕 adj. 大聲的

4. (**C**) The pianist was <u>exposed</u> to classical music from a very young age.
這位鋼琴家從很小的時候就<u>接觸</u>了古典音樂。

(A) export⁴ 〔 ɪk'sport 〕 v. 出口

(B) explore⁴ 〔 ɪk'splor 〕 v. 探險;探索

(C) **expose**⁴ 〔 ɪk'spoz 〕 v. 暴露;使接觸

　　　be exposed to 暴露;接觸

(D) expect² 〔 ɪk'spɛkt 〕 v. 期待

*pianist⁴ 〔 pɪ'ænɪst 〕 n. 鋼琴家　　classical³ 〔'klæsɪkl̩ 〕 adj. 古典的

5. (**B**) Lauren has an <u>extraordinary</u> talent for learning new languages.
羅倫對於學習新語言有著<u>不尋常的</u>天分。

(A) expressive³ 〔 ɪk'sprɛsɪv 〕 adj. 表達的

(B) **extraordinary**⁴ 〔 ɪk'strɔrdn̩ˌɛrɪ 〕 adj. 不尋常的;特別的

(C) faithful⁴ 〔'feθfəl 〕 adj. 忠實的

(D) familiar¹ 〔 fə'mɪljə 〕 adj. 熟悉的

*talent² 〔'tælənt 〕 n. 天分;才能

6. (**C**) The basketball team's new training <u>facility</u> will open next month.
那個籃球隊新的訓練<u>設備</u>下個月即將開放。

(A) feature³ 〔'fitʃə 〕 n. 特色

(B) festival² 〔'fɛstəvl̩ 〕 n. 節日

(C) **facility**⁴ 〔 fə'sɪlətɪ 〕 n. 設備;設施

(D) fence² 〔 fɛns 〕 n. 籬笆;圍牆

*training¹ 〔'trenɪŋ 〕 n. 訓練

7. (**A**) Some say climate change will cause more <u>extreme</u> weather conditions.
有些人說,氣候變遷會造成更多<u>極端的</u>天氣狀態。

(A) **extreme**³ 〔 ɪk'strim 〕 adj. 極端的

(B) explosive⁴ 〔 ɪk'splosɪv 〕 adj. 爆炸性的　　n. 炸藥

(C) farther³ 〔'fɑrðə 〕 adj. 更遠的

(D) fatal⁴ 〔'fetl̩ 〕 adj. 致命的

*climate² 〔'klaɪmɪt 〕 n. 氣候　　condition³ 〔 kən'dɪʃən 〕 n. 情況

8. (**D**) His <u>fantasy</u> is to be rich and famous.
他的<u>幻想</u>是想要發財和出名。

(A) fable³ (ˈfebḷ) *n.* 寓言；故事

(B) farewell⁴ (ˌfɛrˈwɛl) *n.* 告別

(C) factor³ (ˈfæktɚ) *n.* 因素

(D) ***fantasy***⁴ (ˈfæntəsɪ) *n.* 幻想

9. (**C**) The taxi driver told us to <u>fasten</u> our seatbelts.
計程車司機要我們把安全帶<u>繫上</u>。

(A) fade³ (fed) *v.* 褪色；逐漸消失

(B) extend⁴ (ɪkˈstɛnd) *v.* 延伸；延長

(C) ***fasten***³ (ˈfæsn̩) *v.* 繫上

(D) excite² (ɪkˈsaɪt) *v.* 使興奮

*seatbelt (ˈsitˌbɛlt) *n.* 安全帶

10. (**B**) Paul's version of the event is pure <u>fiction</u>. It's just not true.
保羅對於這個事件的說法完全就是<u>虛構的事</u>。那不是真的。

(A) ferry⁴ (ˈfɛrɪ) *n.* 渡輪

(B) ***fiction***⁴ (ˈfɪkʃən) *n.* 小說；虛構的事

(C) flame³ (flem) *n.* 火焰

(D) feast⁴ (fist) *n.* 盛宴

*version⁶ (ˈvɝʒən) *n.* 版本；說法　　event² (ɪˈvɛnt) *n.* 活動；事件
pure³ (pjur) *adj.* 純粹的；完全的

11. (**C**) The baby put up a <u>fierce</u> battle, but she eventually fell asleep.
小寶寶進行了<u>激烈的戰鬥</u>，不過最後終於睡著了。

(A) fertile⁴ (ˈfɝtḷ) *adj.* 肥沃的

(B) firm² (fɝm) *adj.* 堅定的　*n.* 公司

(C) ***fierce***⁴ (fɪrs) *adj.* 凶猛的；激烈的

(D) fashionable³ (ˈfæʃənəbḷ) *adj.* 流行的

****put up*** 進行　　battle² (ˈbætḷ) *n.* 戰役；戰鬥
eventually⁴ (ɪˈvɛntʃuəlɪ) *adv.* 最後；終於　　***fall asleep*** 睡著

12. (**A**) You should keep a <u>flashlight</u> on hand in case of power outages.
你手邊應該準備<u>手電筒</u>，以防發生停電。

(A) ***flashlight***² (ˈflæʃˌlaɪt) *n.* 手電筒

(B) faucet³ 〔'fɔsɪt 〕 *n.* 水龍頭

(C) figure² 〔'fɪgɚ 〕 *n.* 數字；人物

(D) feather³ 〔'fɛðɚ 〕 *n.* 羽毛

*on hand 在手邊　　***in case of** 萬一發生～；以防～

power¹ 〔'pauɚ 〕 *n.* 力量；電力　　outage 〔'autɪdʒ 〕 *n.* 停止供應

13. (**D**) He's such a good liar that we never know if what he's saying is true or <u>false</u>. 他實在太會說謊了，我們永遠不知道他說的是真是<u>假</u>。

(A) exact² 〔 ɪg'zækt 〕 *adj.* 精確的

(B) extra² 〔'ɛkstrə 〕 *adj.* 額外的

(C) fake³ 〔 fek 〕 *adj.* 假的；仿冒的

(D) ***false**¹ 〔 fɔls 〕 *adj.* 錯誤的；假的；不實的【和 true 相對】

*liar³ 〔'laɪɚ 〕 *n.* 說謊者

14. (**B**) The architecture of Venice was <u>fantastic</u>, but not nearly as exciting as the ride on a gondola.
威尼斯的建築<u>非常棒</u>，但遠不及乘坐平底遊覽船來的令人興奮。

(A) famous² 〔'feməs 〕 *adj.* 有名的

(B) ***fantastic**⁴ 〔 fæn'tæstɪk 〕 *adj.* 極好的

(C) fearful² 〔'fɪrfəl 〕 *adj.* 害怕的；可怕的

(D) financial⁴ 〔 faɪ'nænʃəl , fə- 〕 *adj.* 財務的

*architecture⁶ 〔'ɑrkə,tɛktʃɚ 〕 *n.* 建築

Venice 〔'vɛnɪs 〕 *n.* 威尼斯【義大利東北部港市】

nearly² 〔'nɪrlɪ 〕 *adv.* 幾乎　　***not nearly** 遠不及

ride¹ 〔 raɪd 〕 *n.* 搭乘；乘坐

gondola 〔'gɑndələ 〕 *n.* (威尼斯的) 平底遊覽船

15. (**B**) He went down to the market on the corner to <u>fetch</u> the morning newspapers. 他下去到轉角的市場<u>拿來</u>今天的報紙。

(A) flatter⁴ 〔'flætɚ 〕 *v.* 奉承；諂媚

(B) ***fetch**⁴ 〔 fɛtʃ 〕 *v.* 去拿來

(C) explode³ 〔 ɪk'splod 〕 *v.* 爆炸；爆發

(D) faint³ 〔 fent 〕 *v.* 昏倒

*corner² 〔'kɔrnɚ 〕 *n.* 角落；轉角

TEST 11

【命題範圍：「高中生必背 4500 字」
p.91-100，flee～graceful】

Directions: *Choose the one word that best completes the sentence.*

1. Tom is looking for a part-time job with ＿＿＿＿ hours.
   (A) flexible　　　　　　(B) foggy
   (C) foreign　　　　　　(D) fortunate　　　　( )

2. The weather ＿＿＿＿ calls for rain throughout the week.
   (A) formation　　　　　(B) forehead
   (C) forecast　　　　　　(D) giant　　　　　　( )

3. This traditional medicine is based on an ancient ＿＿＿＿.
   (A) fossil　　　　　　　(B) foam
   (C) former　　　　　　(D) formula　　　　　( )

4. Many different types of birds use this ＿＿＿＿ to bathe and drink.
   (A) furniture　　　　　(B) fountain
   (C) fright　　　　　　　(D) garden　　　　　( )

5. Vivian is ＿＿＿＿ in four languages: German, French, Italian, and English.
   (A) frank　　　　　　　(B) fluent
   (C) frequent　　　　　(D) gentle　　　　　　( )

6. The math teacher may ＿＿＿＿ the students from using calculators on the exam.
   (A) float　　　　　　　(B) flock
   (C) forbid　　　　　　(D) flunk　　　　　　( )

7. Despite not having any ＿＿＿＿ training in music, Susan composed an opera.
   (A) formal　　　　　　(B) fragrant
   (C) functional　　　　(D) global　　　　　　( )

8. Bad luck always seemed to ＿＿＿＿＿ his ambitions.

(A) frustrate　　　　　　(B) gamble

(C) flee　　　　　　　　(D) flush　　　　　　　　　（　）

9. She ＿＿＿＿＿ her promise to return in the summer.

(A) focused　　　　　　(B) froze

(C) fulfilled　　　　　　(D) frowned　　　　　　　（　）

10. They spent the afternoon at an art ＿＿＿＿＿.

(A) gallon　　　　　　　(B) gallery

(C) gate　　　　　　　　(D) garage　　　　　　　（　）

11. Mr. Smith accepted the gift, touched by her ＿＿＿＿＿.

(A) glance　　　　　　　(B) glory

(C) generosity　　　　　(D) generation　　　　　（　）

12. Tests proved that the document was ＿＿＿＿＿, not a forgery.

(A) gifted　　　　　　　(B) graceful

(C) general　　　　　　(D) genuine　　　　　　　（　）

13. He caught a ＿＿＿＿＿ of the newspaper headline and started to panic.

(A) genius　　　　　　　(B) glimpse

(C) gesture　　　　　　(D) ginger　　　　　　　（　）

14. Rick isn't one to ＿＿＿＿＿, so I believe what he says is true.

(A) giggle　　　　　　　(B) govern

(C) gaze　　　　　　　　(D) gossip　　　　　　　（　）

15. The parents were ＿＿＿＿＿ to learn their son had dropped out of school.

(A) furious　　　　　　　(B) fundamental

(C) further　　　　　　　(D) funny　　　　　　　（　）

TEST 11 詳解

1. (**A**) Tom is looking for a part-time job with <u>flexible</u> hours.
   湯姆正在尋找一個有<u>彈性</u>工時的兼職工作。
   - (A) *flexible* [4]〔ˋflɛksəbḷ〕 *adj.* 有彈性的
   - (B) foggy [2]〔ˋfɑgɪ〕 *adj.* 多霧的
   - (C) foreign [1]〔ˋfɔrɪn〕 *adj.* 外國的；外來的
   - (D) fortunate [4]〔ˋfɔrtʃənɪt〕 *adj.* 幸運的
   - * *look for* 尋找　　part-time〔ˋpɑrtˏtaɪm〕 *adj.* 兼職的
     hour [1]〔aʊr〕 *n.* 小時；(*pl.*) 時間

2. (**C**) The weather <u>forecast</u> calls for rain throughout the week.
   氣象<u>預報</u>預測一整週都會下雨。
   - (A) formation [4]〔fɔrˋmeʃən〕 *n.* 形成
   - (B) forehead [3]〔ˋfɔrˏhɛd〕 *n.* 額頭
   - (C) *forecast* [4]〔ˋforˏkæst〕 *n., v.* 預測
   - (D) giant [2]〔ˋdʒaɪənt〕 *n.* 巨人
   - * *call for* 預測　　throughout [2]〔θruˋaʊt〕 *prep.* 遍及；自始至終

3. (**D**) This traditional medicine is based on an ancient <u>formula</u>.
   這個傳統的藥是以一個古老的<u>配方</u>爲根據。
   - (A) fossil [4]〔ˋfɑsḷ〕 *n.* 化石
   - (B) foam [4]〔fom〕 *n.* 泡沫
   - (C) former [2]〔ˋfɔrmɚ〕 *n.* 前者　*adj.* 前任的；前者的
   - (D) *formula* [4]〔ˋfɔrmjələ〕 *n.* 公式；式；配方
   - * traditional [2]〔trəˋdɪʃənḷ〕 *adj.* 傳統的　　*be based on* 以～爲根據
     ancient [2]〔ˋenʃənt〕 *adj.* 古老的

4. (**B**) Many different types of birds use this <u>fountain</u> to bathe and drink.
   許多種類的鳥都使用這座<u>噴泉</u>來洗澡和喝水。
   - (A) furniture [3]〔ˋfɝnɪtʃɚ〕 *n.* 家具
   - (B) *fountain* [3]〔ˋfaʊntṇ〕 *n.* 噴泉
   - (C) fright [2]〔fraɪt〕 *n.* 驚嚇；害怕

(D) garden¹〔'gɑrdn〕 *n.* 花園

*type²〔taɪp〕 *n.* 種類　　bathe¹〔beð〕 *v.* 洗澡

5. (**B**) Vivian is <u>fluent</u> in four languages: German, French, Italian, and English.　薇薇安四種語言很<u>流利</u>：德語、法語、義大利語和英語。

(A) frank²〔fræŋk〕 *adj.* 坦白的

(B) ***fluent*** ⁴〔'fluənt〕 *adj.* 流利的

(C) frequent³〔'frikwənt〕 *adj.* 經常的；頻繁的

(D) gentle²〔'dʒɛntl̩〕 *adj.* 溫和的

*German〔'dʒɝmən〕 *n.* 德語　　French〔frɛntʃ〕 *n.* 法語
　Italian〔ɪ'tæljən〕 *n.* 義大利語

6. (**C**) The math teacher may <u>forbid</u> the students from using calculators on the exam.　數學老師可能會<u>禁止</u>學生考試中使用計算機。

(A) float³〔flot〕 *v.* 飄浮；漂浮

(B) flock³〔flɑk〕 *v.* 聚集　　*n.* (鳥、羊) 群

(C) ***forbid*** ⁴〔fɚ'bɪd〕 *v.* 禁止

(D) flunk⁴〔flʌŋk〕 *v.* 使不及格；當掉

*calculator⁴〔'kælkjə,letɚ〕 *n.* 計算機

7. (**A**) Despite not having any <u>formal</u> training in music, Susan composed an opera.
儘管沒有音樂方面<u>正式的</u>訓練，蘇珊還是作了一齣歌劇。

(A) ***formal*** ²〔'fɔrml̩〕 *adj.* 正式的

(B) fragrant⁴〔'fregrənt〕 *adj.* 芳香的

(C) functional⁴〔'fʌŋkʃənl̩〕 *adj.* 功能的

(D) global³〔'globl̩〕 *adj.* 全球的

*despite⁴〔dɪ'spaɪt〕 *prep.* 儘管　　training¹〔'trenɪŋ〕 *n.* 訓練
　compose⁴〔kəm'poz〕 *v.* 組成；作 (曲)
　opera⁴〔'ɑpərə〕 *n.* 歌劇

8. (**A**) Bad luck always seemed to <u>frustrate</u> his ambitions.
他似乎運氣不好，抱負總是受到<u>挫敗</u>。

(A) **frustrate**[3] ('frʌstret) *v.* 使受挫折

(B) gamble[3] ('gæmbl̩) *v.* 賭博

(C) flee[4] (fli) *v.* 逃走；逃離

(D) flush[4] (flʌʃ) *v.* 臉紅

*ambition[3] (æm'bɪʃən) *n.* 抱負；志向

9. (**C**) She <u>fulfilled</u> her promise to return in the summer.

她<u>履行</u>了她的承諾，在夏天時歸來。

(A) focus[1] ('fokəs) *v.* 對焦；集中

(B) freeze[3] (friz) *v.* 結冰

(C) **fulfill**[4] (fʊl'fɪl) *v.* 履行；實現

(D) frown[4] (fraʊn) *v.* 皺眉頭

*promise[2] ('prɑmɪs) *n., v.* 承諾

10. (**B**) They spent the afternoon at an art <u>gallery</u>.

他們下午的時間都待在<u>藝廊</u>裡。

(A) gallon[3] ('gælən) *n.* 加侖【容量單位】

(B) **gallery**[4] ('gælərɪ) *n.* 畫廊；藝廊

(C) gate[2] (get) *n.* 大門

(D) garage[2] (gə'rɑʒ) *n.* 車庫

11. (**C**) Mr. Smith accepted the gift, touched by her <u>generosity</u>.

史密斯先生被她的<u>慷慨</u>所感動，接受了這份禮物。

(A) glance[3] (glæns) *n., v.* 看一眼

(B) glory[3] ('glorɪ) *n.* 光榮；榮譽

(C) **generosity**[4] (ˌdʒɛnə'rɑsətɪ) *n.* 慷慨；大方

(D) generation[4] (ˌdʒɛnə'reʃən) *n.* 世代

*accept[2] (ək'sɛpt) *v.* 接受　　touch[1] (tʌtʃ) *v.* 觸摸；使感動

12. (**D**) Tests proved that the document was <u>genuine</u>, not a forgery.

檢驗鑑定證明這份文件是<u>真的</u>，不是偽造的。

(A) gifted[4] ('gɪftɪd) *adj.* 有天分的

(B) graceful[4] ('gresfəl) *adj.* 優雅的

(C) general [1,2] ('dʒɛnərəl) *adj.* 一般的　　*n.* 將軍

(D) *genuine* [4] ('dʒɛnjuɪn) *adj.* 眞正的

*test [2] (tɛst) *n.* 測驗；檢驗；鑑定　　prove [1] (pruv) *v.* 證明

document [5] ('dɑkjəmənt) *n.* 文件

forgery ('fɔrdʒərɪ) *n.* 僞造物

13. (**B**) He caught a <u>glimpse</u> of the newspaper headline and started to panic.
他瞄了一眼報紙標題，開始感到驚慌。

(A) genius [4] ('dʒiniəs) *n.* 天才；天賦

(B) *glimpse* [1] (glɪmps) *n., v.* 看一眼；瞥見
catch a glimpse of 瞥見

(C) gesture [3] ('dʒɛstʃɚ) *n.* 姿勢；手勢

(D) ginger [4] ('dʒɪndʒɚ) *n.* 薑

*headline [3] ('hɛd,laɪn) *n.* 標題　　panic [3] ('pænɪk) *v., n.* 驚慌；恐慌

14. (**D**) Rick isn't one to <u>gossip</u>, so I believe what he says is true.
瑞克不是愛八卦的人，所以我相信他說的是眞的。

(A) giggle [4] ('gɪgl) *v.* 咯咯地笑

(B) govern [2] ('gʌvən) *v.* 統治

(C) gaze [4] (gez) *v., n.* 凝視；注視

(D) *gossip* [3] ('gɑsəp) *v.* 說閒話；八卦

15. (**A**) The parents were <u>furious</u> to learn their son had dropped out of
school. 這對父母得知他們的兒子輟學十分震怒。

(A) *furious* [4] ('fjurɪəs) *adj.* 狂怒的

(B) fundamental [4] (,fʌndə'mɛntl) *adj.* 基本的

(C) further [2] ('fɝðɚ) *adj.* 更進一步的

(D) funny [1] ('fʌnɪ) *adj.* 好笑的

drop out of school 輟學

TEST 12

【命題範圍：「高中生必背 4500 字」
p.51-100，convey～graceful】

Directions: Choose the one word that best completes the sentence.

1. He refused to _____ with the investigation.
   (A) convey
   (B) correspond
   (C) cooperate
   (D) convince
   (　)

2. We need to go shopping. There's no food in the _____.
   (A) curtain
   (B) council
   (C) cupboard
   (D) cucumber
   (　)

3. Many people _____ whether it's right to clone an individual.
   (A) declare
   (B) debate
   (C) defend
   (D) decrease
   (　)

4. He does not have a _____ idea about what to do for a career.
   (A) democratic
   (B) desirable
   (C) definite
   (D) desperate
   (　)

5. The task requires strong attention to _____.
   (A) device
   (B) dessert
   (C) detective
   (D) detail
   (　)

6. She was a(n) _____ woman who dared to break the stereotypes of gender.
   (A) courageous
   (B) dependent
   (C) dizzy
   (D) economic
   (　)

7. He didn't have time to _____ all the information before making a decision.
   (A) digest
   (B) disconnect
   (C) disguise
   (D) dispute
   (　)

8. He noticed the _____ aroma of burning plastic.
   (A) distant
   (B) dominant
   (C) distinct
   (D) domestic   (   )

9. The _____'s long neck allows it to reach fruit at the top of a tree.
   (A) dragonfly
   (B) duckling
   (C) giraffe
   (D) dinosaur   (   )

10. Our speaker this evening is a(n) _____ member of the Royal Society.
    (A) endangered
    (B) distinguished
    (C) embarrassed
    (D) depressed   (   )

11. She has a _____ imagination and a love of telling stories.
    (A) fertile
    (B) dense
    (C) genuine
    (D) drowsy   (   )

12. Terry has been very _____ of my work lately.
    (A) critical
    (B) fantastic
    (C) essential
    (D) fierce   (   )

13. The garden is _____ by a white picket fence.
    (A) encountered
    (B) endured
    (C) enclosed
    (D) exaggerated   (   )

14. The computer will automatically _____ software updates as needed.
    (A) download
    (B) drain
    (C) determine
    (D) disappoint   (   )

15. Nobody in the accounting department noticed the _____ until it was too late.
    (A) errand
    (B) eraser
    (C) error
    (D) essay   (   )

TEST 12 詳解

1. (**C**) He refused to <u>cooperate</u> with the investigation.
　　他拒絕與這次調查合作。

　　(A) convey⁴ 〔kən'νe〕 ν. 傳達
　　(B) correspond⁴ 〔,kɔrɪ'spɑnd〕 ν. 通信
　　(C) ***cooperate***⁴ 〔ko'ɑpə,ret〕 ν. 合作
　　(D) convince⁴ 〔kən'νɪns〕 ν. 使相信

　　*refuse² 〔rɪ'fjuz〕 ν. 拒絕　　investigation⁴ 〔ɪn,νɛstə'geʃən〕 n. 調查

2. (**C**) We need to go shopping. There's no food in the <u>cupboard</u>.
　　我們需要去購物了。碗櫥裡沒有食物了。

　　(A) curtain² 〔'kɝtn̩〕 n. 窗簾
　　(B) council⁴ 〔'kaʊnsl̩〕 n. 議會
　　(C) ***cupboard***³ 〔'kʌbəd〕 n. 碗櫥
　　(D) cucumber⁴ 〔'kjukʌmbə〕 n. 黃瓜

　　****go shopping*** 去購物

3. (**B**) Many people <u>debate</u> whether it's right to clone an individual.
　　許多人在辯論複製人是否是正確的。

　　(A) declare⁴ 〔dɪ'klɛr〕 ν. 宣布
　　(B) ***debate***² 〔dɪ'bet〕 ν., n. 辯論；爭論
　　(C) defend⁴ 〔dɪ'fɛnd〕 ν. 保衛
　　(D) decrease⁴ 〔dɪ'kris〕 ν., n. 減少

　　*clone⁶ 〔klon〕 ν. 複製　　individual³ 〔,ɪndə'νɪdʒʊəl〕 n. 個人

4. (**C**) He does not have a <u>definite</u> idea about what to do for a career.
　　對於一份職業要做什麼，他沒有明確的想法。

　　(A) democratic³ 〔,dɛmə'krætɪk〕 adj. 民主的
　　(B) desirable³ 〔dɪ'zaɪrəbl̩〕 adj. 合意的
　　(C) ***definite***⁴ 〔'dɛfənɪt〕 adj. 明確的
　　(D) desperate⁴ 〔'dɛspərɪt〕 adj. 絕望的；不顧一切的

　　*career⁴ 〔kə'rɪr〕 n. 職業；生涯

5. (**D**) The task requires strong attention to <u>detail</u>.
　　　這份工作需要非常注意<u>細節</u>。

　　(A) device [4] 〔 dɪ'vaɪs 〕 n. 裝置
　　(B) dessert [2] 〔 dɪ'zɜt 〕 n. 甜點
　　(C) detective [4] 〔 dɪ'tɛktɪv 〕 n. 偵探　adj. 偵探的
　　(D) **detail** [3] 〔'ditel 〕 n. 細節

　　*task [2] 〔 tæsk 〕 n. 工作　　require [2] 〔 rɪ'kwaɪr 〕 v. 需要
　　attention [2] 〔 ə'tɛnʃən 〕 n. 專注；注意 < to >

6. (**A**) She was a <u>courageous</u> woman who dared to break the stereotypes
　　of gender. 她是個很<u>勇敢的</u>女性，敢於破除關於性別的刻板印象。

　　(A) **courageous** [4] 〔 kə'redʒəs 〕 adj. 勇敢的
　　(B) dependent [4] 〔 dɪ'pɛndənt 〕 adj. 依賴的
　　(C) dizzy [2] 〔'dɪzɪ 〕 adj. 頭暈的
　　(D) economic [4] 〔,ikə'namɪk 〕 adj. 經濟的

　　*dare [3] 〔 dɛr 〕 v. 敢　　stereotype [5] 〔'stɛrɪə,taɪp 〕 n. 刻板印象
　　gender [5] 〔'dʒɛndɚ 〕 n. 性別

7. (**A**) He didn't have time to <u>digest</u> all the information before making
　　a decision. 在做決定之前，他沒有時間<u>消化</u>所有的資訊。

　　(A) **digest** [4] 〔 daɪ'dʒɛst 〕 v. 消化
　　(B) disconnect [4] 〔,dɪskə'nɛkt 〕 v. 切斷
　　(C) disguise [4] 〔 dɪs'gaɪz 〕 v., n. 偽裝
　　(D) dispute [4] 〔 dɪ'spjut 〕 v., n. 爭論

　　*information [4] 〔,ɪnfɚ'meʃən 〕 n. 資訊　　decision [2] 〔 dɪ'sɪʒən 〕 n. 決定

8. (**C**) He noticed the <u>distinct</u> aroma of burning plastic.
　　他注意到燃燒塑膠的<u>獨特</u>味道。

　　(A) distant [2] 〔'dɪstənt 〕 adj. 遙遠的
　　(B) dominant [4] 〔'damənənt 〕 adj. 支配的；佔優勢的
　　(C) **distinct** [4] 〔 dɪ'stɪŋkt 〕 adj. 獨特的；不同的
　　(D) domestic [3] 〔 də'mɛstɪk 〕 adj. 國內的；家庭的

　　*notice [1] 〔'notɪs 〕 v. 注意到　　aroma 〔 ə'romə 〕 n. 味道
　　plastic [3] 〔'plæstɪk 〕 n. 塑膠

9. (**C**) The <u>giraffe</u>'s long neck allows it to reach fruit at the top of a tree.
長頸鹿長長的脖子讓牠能搆到樹頂的果實。

    (A) dragonfly² ('drægən,flaɪ) *n.* 蜻蜓

    (B) duckling¹ ('dʌklɪŋ) *n.* 小鴨子

    (C) *giraffe*² (dʒə'ræf) *n.* 長頸鹿

    (D) dinosaur² ('daɪnə,sɔr) *n.* 恐龍

    *allow¹ (ə'laʊ) *v.* 允許；使能夠   reach¹ (ritʃ) *v.* 到達

10. (**B**) Our speaker this evening is a <u>distinguished</u> member of the Royal Society. 今晚我們的演講者是皇家學會一位<u>卓越的</u>會員。

    (A) endangered⁴ (ɪn'dendʒəd) *adj.* 瀕臨絕種的

    (B) *distinguished*⁴ (dɪ'stɪŋgwɪʃt) *adj.* 卓越的；傑出的

    (C) embarrassed⁴ (ɪm'bærəst) *adj.* 尷尬的

    (D) depressed⁴ (dɪ'prɛst) *adj.* 沮喪的

    *member² ('mɛmbə) *n.* 成員；會員   royal² ('rɔɪəl) *adj.* 皇家的
    society² (sə'saɪətɪ) *n.* 社會；學會   *the Royal Society* 皇家學會

11. (**A**) She has a <u>fertile</u> imagination and a love of telling stories.
她有<u>豐富的</u>想像力，而且熱愛說故事。

    (A) *fertile*⁴ ('fɜtḷ) *adj.* 肥沃的；豐富的

    (B) dense⁴ (dɛns) *adj.* 濃密的；密集的

    (C) genuine⁴ ('dʒɛnjuɪn) *adj.* 真正的

    (D) drowsy³ ('draʊzɪ) *adj.* 想睡的

    *imagination³ (ɪ,mædʒə'neʃən) *n.* 想像力

12. (**A**) Terry has been very <u>critical</u> of my work lately.
泰瑞最近一直在<u>挑</u>我工作的<u>毛病</u>。

    (A) *critical*⁴ ('krɪtɪkḷ) *adj.* 批評的；挑毛病的

    (B) fantastic⁴ (fæn'tæstɪk) *adj.* 極好的

    (C) essential⁴ (ə'sɛnʃəl) *adj.* 必要的

    (D) fierce⁴ (fɪrs) *adj.* 兇猛的；激烈的

    *lately⁴ ('letlɪ) *adv.* 最近

13. (**C**) The garden is <u>enclosed</u> by a white picket fence.
　　　　這座花園被白色的柵欄<u>圍起來</u>。

　　　(A) encounter [4] 〔 ɪn'kaʊntɚ 〕 v. 遭遇

　　　(B) endure [4] 〔 ɪn'djʊr 〕 v. 忍受

　　　(C) **enclose** [4] 〔 ɪn'kloz 〕 v. (隨函) 附寄；圍住

　　　(D) exaggerate [4] 〔 ɪg'zædʒə,ret 〕 v. 誇大

　　　* picket 〔'pɪkɪt 〕 n. 木樁　　fence [2] 〔 fɛns 〕 n. 籬笆；圍牆
　　　　picket fence 柵欄

14. (**A**) The computer will automatically <u>download</u> software updates as
　　　　needed. 這台電腦會自動<u>下載</u>所需的軟體最新資訊。

　　　(A) **download** [4] 〔'daʊn,lod 〕 v. 下載

　　　(B) drain [3] 〔 dren 〕 v. 排出～的水　　n. 排水溝

　　　(C) determine [3] 〔 dɪ'tɝmɪn 〕 v. 決定

　　　(D) disappoint [3] 〔,dɪsə'pɔɪnt 〕 v. 使失望

　　　* automatically [3] 〔,ɔtə'mætɪkl̩ɪ 〕 adv. 自動地
　　　　software [4] 〔'sɔft,wɛr 〕 n. 軟體
　　　　update [5] 〔'ʌp,det 〕 n. 更新；最新資訊

15. (**C**) Nobody in the accounting department noticed the <u>error</u> until it was
　　　　too late.
　　　　會計部門沒有人注意到這個<u>錯誤</u>，最後太遲了。

　　　(A) errand [4] 〔'ɛrənd 〕 n. 差事

　　　(B) eraser [2] 〔 ɪ'resɚ 〕 n. 橡皮擦

　　　(C) **error** [2] 〔'ɛrɚ 〕 n. 錯誤

　　　(D) essay [4] 〔'ɛse 〕 n. 論說文；文章

　　　* accounting [6] 〔 ə'kaʊntɪŋ 〕 n. 會計
　　　　department [2] 〔 dɪ'pɑrtmənt 〕 n. 部門

TEST 13

【命題範圍：「高中生必背 4500 字」
p.101-110，gracious～humble】

Directions: *Choose the one word that best completes the sentence.*

1. Learning to write well is a _____ process.

    (A) gracious   (B) grand
    (C) gradual   (D) grassy   (　)

2. The drowning boy _____ at the lifeguard's hand.

    (A) grasped   (B) graduated
    (C) greeted   (D) grieved   (　)

3. The widow expressed her _____ for the community's support.

    (A) grade   (B) grammar
    (C) gratitude   (D) grave   (　)

4. He's a _____ boy, only looking out for himself.

    (A) gray   (B) greedy
    (C) greasy   (D) grateful   (　)

5. There's no _____ that it won't rain again tomorrow.

    (A) guide   (B) guard
    (C) guarantee   (D) guidance   (　)

6. He has enough experience to _____ such a difficult situation.

    (A) hang   (B) harden
    (C) hasten   (D) handle   (　)

7. The villagers lived in _____ until the arrival of the white men.

    (A) harmony   (B) harmonica
    (C) harbor   (D) hesitation   (　)

8. The company's _____ are located in Los Angeles.

   (A) headlines   (B) headphones

   (C) headquarters   (D) handkerchiefs   ( )

9. The president arrived at the ceremony in a _____.

   (A) helicopter   (B) heater

   (C) helmet   (D) hammer   ( )

10. His _____ apology was not accepted by the family of the victim.

   (A) healthful   (B) holy

   (C) hollow   (D) historical   ( )

11. Changes are coming and good things are on the _____.

   (A) homeland   (B) grass

   (C) horizon   (D) hallway   ( )

12. A _____ sleeping underwater rises and breathes without waking up.

   (A) hawk   (B) hippopotamus

   (C) hen   (D) herd   ( )

13. She is too _____ to brag about her achievements.

   (A) horrible   (B) healthy

   (C) humble   (D) honorable   ( )

14. Some of them thought Mike's punishment was too _____, and he should have been allowed to stay in school.

   (A) harmful   (B) hasty

   (C) harsh   (D) hateful   ( )

15. He _____ to pick up the phone, knowing Jenny was on the other end.

   (A) hatched   (B) hesitated

   (C) healed   (D) harvested   ( )

TEST 13 詳解

1. (**C**) Learning to write well is a <u>gradual</u> process.
   學習好好地寫作是個漸進的過程。
   (A) gracious [4] (ˈgreʃəs) *adj.* 親切的
   (B) grand [1] (grænd) *adj.* 宏偉的
   (C) ***gradual*** [3] (ˈgrædʒʊəl) *adj.* 逐漸的;漸進的
   (D) grassy [2] (ˈgræsɪ) *adj.* 多草的
   * process [3] (ˈprɑsɛs) *n.* 過程

2. (**A**) The drowning boy <u>grasped</u> at the lifeguard's hand.
   那個快淹死的男孩想抓住救生員的手。
   (A) ***grasp*** [3] (græsp) *v.* 抓住　　**grasp at** 試圖抓住
   (B) graduate [3] (ˈgrædʒʊ‚et) *v.* 畢業
   (C) greet [2] (grit) *v.* 問候;迎接
   (D) grieve [4] (griv) *v.* 悲傷
   * drown [3] (draʊn) *v.* 淹死　　lifeguard [3] (ˈlaɪf‚gɑrd) *n.* 救生員

3. (**C**) The widow expressed her <u>gratitude</u> for the community's support.
   那位寡婦對於社會的援助表示感激。
   (A) grade [2] (gred) *n.* 成績
   (B) grammar [4] (ˈgræmə) *n.* 文法
   (C) ***gratitude*** [4] (ˈgrætə‚tjud) *n.* 感激
   (D) grave [4] (grev) *n.* 墳墓
   * widow [5] (ˈwɪdo) *n.* 寡婦　　express [2] (ɪkˈsprɛs) *v.* 表達;表示
   community [4] (kəˈmjunətɪ) *n.* 社區;社會
   support [2] (səˈport) *n.* 支持;援助

4. (**B**) He's a <u>greedy</u> boy, only looking out for himself.
   他是個貪心的男孩,一心只顧自己。
   (A) gray [1] (gre) *adj.* 灰色的
   (B) ***greedy*** [2] (ˈgridɪ) *adj.* 貪心的

(C) greasy [4] 〔'grisɪ 〕 *adj.* 油膩的

(D) grateful [4] 〔'gretfəl 〕 *adj.* 感激的

* ***look out for*** *oneself* 一心只顧自己（不顧他人）

5. (**C**) There's no guarantee that it won't rain again tomorrow.
   無法保證明天不會再下雨。

    (A) guide [1] 〔 gaɪd 〕 *n.* 導遊　*v.* 引導

    (B) guard [2] 〔 gɑrd 〕 *n.* 警衛　*v.* 看守

    (C) ***guarantee*** 〔ˌgærən'ti 〕 *n. v.* 保證

    (D) guidance [4] 〔'gaɪdəns 〕 *n.* 指導

6. (**D**) He has enough experience to handle such a difficult situation.
   他有足夠的經驗，能應付這樣困難的情況。

    (A) hang [2] 〔 hæŋ 〕 *v.* 懸掛

    (B) harden [4] 〔'hɑrdn̩ 〕 *v.* 變硬

    (C) hasten [4] 〔'hesn̩ 〕 *v.* 趕快

    (D) ***handle*** [2] 〔'hændl̩ 〕 *v.* 應付；處理

7. (**A**) The villagers lived in harmony until the arrival of the white men.
   直到那些白人到達之前，村民們一直過著和諧的生活。

    (A) ***harmony*** [4] 〔'hɑrmənɪ 〕 *n.* 和諧

    (B) harmonica [4] 〔 hɑr'mɑnɪkə 〕 *n.* 口琴

    (C) harbor [3] 〔'hɑrbɚ 〕 *n.* 港口

    (D) hesitation [4] 〔ˌhɛzə'teʃən 〕 *n.* 猶豫

    * villager [2] 〔'vɪlɪdʒɚ 〕 *n.* 村民　　arrival [3] 〔 ə'raɪvl̩ 〕 *n.* 到達

8. (**C**) The company's headquarters are located in Los Angeles.
   那家公司的總部位於洛杉磯。

    (A) headline [3] 〔'hɛd,laɪn 〕 *n.* 頭條新聞

    (B) headphones [4] 〔'hɛd,fonz 〕 *n. pl.* 耳機

    (C) ***headquarters*** [3] 〔'hɛd,kwɔrtɚz 〕 *n. pl.* 總部

    (D) handkerchief [2] 〔'hæŋkɚtʃɪf 〕 *n.* 手帕

* be located in 位於

Los Angeles〔ləs'ændʒələs〕*n.* 洛杉磯

9. (**A**) The president arrived at the ceremony in a <u>helicopter</u>.

總統搭乘<u>直升機</u>抵達典禮現場。

(A) *helicopter* [4]〔'hɛlɪ,kɑptɚ〕*n.* 直升機

(B) heater [2]〔'hitɚ〕*n.* 暖氣機

(C) helmet [3]〔'hɛlmɪt〕*n.* 安全帽

(D) hammer [2]〔'hæmɚ〕*n.* 鐵鎚

* president [2]〔'prɛzədənt〕*n.* 總統

ceremony [5]〔'sɛrə,monɪ〕*n.* 典禮

10. (**C**) His <u>hollow</u> apology was not accepted by the family of the victim.

他<u>無誠意的</u>道歉不被受害者的家人接受。

(A) healthful [4]〔'hɛlθfəl〕*adj.* 有益健康的

(B) holy [3]〔'holɪ〕*adj.* 神聖的

(C) *hollow* [3]〔'hɑlo〕*adj.* 中空的；虛假的；無誠意的

(D) historical [3]〔hɪs'tɔrɪkl̩〕*adj.* 歷史的

* apology [4]〔ə'pɑlədʒɪ〕*n.* 道歉　　accept [2]〔ək'sɛpt〕*v.* 接受

victim〔'vɪktɪm〕*n.* 受害者

11. (**C**) Changes are coming and good things are on the <u>horizon</u>.

改變就要來臨，而且好事<u>即將發生</u>。

(A) homeland [4]〔'hom,lænd〕*n.* 祖國

(B) grass [1]〔græs〕*n.* 草

(C) *horizon* [4]〔hə'raɪzn̩〕*n.* 地平線　　*on the horizon* 即將發生

(D) hallway [3]〔'hɔl,we〕*n.* 走廊

12. (**B**) A <u>hippopotamus</u> sleeping underwater rises and breathes without waking up.

有隻在水中睡覺的<u>河馬</u>浮到水面呼吸，但並未醒來。

(A) hawk [3]〔hɔk〕*n.* 老鷹

(B) *hippopotamus* [2]〔,hɪpə'pɑtəməs〕*n.* 河馬（= *hippo* [2]）

(C) hen² 〔 hɛn 〕 n. 母雞

(D) herd⁴ 〔 hɝd 〕 n.（牛）群

＊underwater 〔͵ʌndɚˈwɔtɚ 〕 adv. 在水中

rise¹ 〔 raɪz 〕 v. 浮（到水面）

breathe³ 〔 brið 〕 v. 呼吸　**wake up** 醒來

13. (**C**) She is too <u>humble</u> to brag about her achievements.
她太謙虛，不會吹噓自己的成就。

(A) horrible³ 〔ˈhɔrəb!͵ˈhɑrəb! 〕 adj. 可怕的

(B) healthy² 〔ˈhɛlθɪ 〕 adj. 健康的

(C) **humble²** 〔ˈhʌmb! 〕 adj. 謙虛的

(D) honorable⁴ 〔ˈɑnərəb! 〕 adj. 值得尊敬的

＊**too⋯to V**. 太⋯以致於不～

brag 〔 bræg 〕 v. 自誇；吹噓＜about＞

achievements³ 〔 əˈtʃivmənts 〕 n. pl. 成就

14. (**C**) Some of them thought Mike's punishment was too <u>harsh</u>, and he should have been allowed to stay in school. 他們當中有些人認為，對麥可的處罰太嚴厲了，他當時應該被准許留在學校。

(A) harmful³ 〔ˈhɑrmfəl 〕 adj. 有害的

(B) hasty³ 〔ˈhestɪ 〕 adj. 匆忙的

(C) **harsh⁴** 〔 hɑrʃ 〕 adj. 嚴厲的

(D) hateful² 〔ˈhetfəl 〕 adj. 可恨的

＊punishment² 〔ˈpʌnɪʃmənt 〕 n. 處罰　　allow¹ 〔 əˈlaʊ 〕 v. 允許

15. (**B**) He <u>hesitated</u> to pick up the phone, knowing Jenny was on the other end. 他很猶豫要不要接電話，因為他知道電話的另一頭是珍妮。

(A) hatch³ 〔 hætʃ 〕 v. 孵化

(B) **hesitate³** 〔ˈhɛzə͵tet 〕 v. 猶豫

(C) heal³ 〔 hil 〕 v. 痊癒；（使）復原

(D) harvest³ 〔ˈhɑrvɪst 〕 v. 收穫

＊**pick up** 接起（電話）　　end¹ 〔 ɛnd 〕 n. 一頭；一端

TEST 14

【命題範圍：「高中生必背 4500 字」
p.111-120，humid～interview】

Directions: Choose the one word that best completes the sentence.

1. Being _____ of the law is not an excuse for breaking it.
   (A) industrial
   (B) influential
   (C) ignorant
   (D) informative
   (　　)

2. Dave preferred to be alone with his _____ friends.
   (A) imaginable
   (B) imagine
   (C) imagination
   (D) imaginary
   (　　)

3. His speech didn't _____ us.
   (A) impress
   (B) insist
   (C) imply
   (D) immigrate
   (　　)

4. He pointed to _____ a spot on the map.
   (A) include
   (B) indicate
   (C) increase
   (D) ignore
   (　　)

5. The boat sank after striking a(n) _____ 30 miles off the coast of Norway.
   (A) iceberg
   (B) hydrogen
   (C) hurricane
   (D) humidity
   (　　)

6. The fingerprints found at the crime scene are _____ to those of the suspect.
   (A) ideal
   (B) identical
   (C) idle
   (D) independent
   (　　)

7. The latest epidemic _____ the need for stricter enforcement of health regulations.
   (A) hushes
   (B) identifies
   (C) illustrates
   (D) inspects
   (　　)

8. A virus must have _____ your computer.

   (A) infected   (B) informed

   (C) influenced   (D) injured   (   )

9. In our judicial system, everyone is _____ until proven guilty.

   (A) innocent   (B) intensive

   (C) intelligent   (D) instant   (   )

10. The artist was _____ by the beautiful landscapes of the region.

   (A) installed   (B) inspired

   (C) instructed   (D) insulted   (   )

11. He based most of his decisions on _____. He trusted his feelings.

   (A) instance   (B) inspection

   (C) instinct   (D) inspiration   (   )

12. His _____ response to the proposal was negative, but he eventually agreed to it.

   (A) inner   (B) internal

   (C) initial   (D) intermediate   (   )

13. All citizens are required to pay into the national health care _____ system.

   (A) instrument   (B) intensity

   (C) interview   (D) insurance   (   )

14. During the heat of an _____ argument, she broke down and started sobbing.

   (A) inferior   (B) intense

   (C) intellectual   (D) imaginative   (   )

15. He was _____ several times during the meeting before finally turning off his mobile phone.

   (A) interested   (B) interpreted

   (C) interfered   (D) interrupted   (   )

TEST 14 詳解

1. (**C**) Being <u>ignorant</u> of the law is not an excuse for breaking it.
<u>不知道</u>法律不是違反法律的藉口。
- (A) industrial[3] 〔 ɪnˈdʌstrɪəl 〕 *adj.* 工業的
- (B) influential[4] 〔ˌɪnfluˈɛnʃəl 〕 *adj.* 有影響力的
- (C) ***ignorant***[4] 〔ˈɪgnərənt 〕 *adj.* 無知的；不知道的
  be ignorant of 不知道
- (D) informative[4] 〔 ɪnˈfɔrmətɪv 〕 *adj.* 知識性的
- *excuse[2] 〔 ɪkˈskjus 〕 *n.* 藉口　　break[1] 〔 brek 〕 *v.* 違反

2. (**D**) Dave preferred to be alone with his <u>imaginary</u> friends.
戴夫比較喜歡跟他<u>假想的</u>朋友單獨在一起。
- (A) imaginable[4] 〔 ɪˈmædʒənəbḷ 〕 *adj.* 想像得到的
- (B) imagine[2] 〔 ɪˈmædʒɪn 〕 *v.* 想像
- (C) imagination[3] 〔 ɪˌmædʒəˈneʃən 〕 *n.* 想像力
- (D) ***imaginary***[4] 〔 ɪˈmædʒəˌnɛrɪ 〕 *adj.* 虛構的；想像的；假想的
- *prefer[2] 〔 prɪˈfɝ 〕 *v.* 比較喜歡　　alone[1] 〔 əˈlon 〕 *adj.* 單獨的
  be alone with 和⋯單獨在一起

3. (**A**) His speech didn't <u>impress</u> us.
他的演講並未<u>使我們印象深刻</u>。
- (A) ***impress***[3] 〔 ɪmˈprɛs 〕 *v.* 使印象深刻
- (B) insist[2] 〔 ɪnˈsɪst 〕 *v.* 堅持
- (C) imply[4] 〔 ɪmˈplaɪ 〕 *v.* 暗示
- (D) immigrate[4] 〔ˈɪməˌgret 〕 *v.* 移入
- *speech[1] 〔 spitʃ 〕 *n.* 演講

4. (**B**) He pointed to <u>indicate</u> a spot on the map.
他用手指<u>指出</u>地圖上的一個地點。
- (A) include[2] 〔 ɪnˈklud 〕 *v.* 包括　　(B) ***indicate***[2] 〔ˈɪndəˌket 〕 *v.* 指出
- (C) increase[2] 〔 ɪnˈkris 〕 *v.* 增加　　(D) ignore[2] 〔 ɪgˈnor 〕 *v.* 忽視
- *point[1] 〔 pɔɪnt 〕 *v.* 指著；指出
  spot[2] 〔 spat 〕 *n.* 點；地點　　map[2] 〔 mæp 〕 *n.* 地圖

5. (**A**) The boat sank after striking an <u>iceberg</u> 30 miles off the coast of Norway. 那艘船在離挪威海岸 30 哩外，撞上一座<u>冰山</u>之後沈沒。

(A) *iceberg* [4]〔'aɪs,bɝg〕 *n.* 冰山

(B) hydrogen [4]〔'haɪdrədʒən〕 *n.* 氫

(C) hurricane [4]〔'hɝɪ,ken〕 *n.* 颶風

(D) humidity [4]〔hju'mɪdətɪ〕 *n.* 濕氣；濕度

*sink [2]〔sɪŋk〕 *v.* 下沉　　strike [2]〔straɪk〕 *v.* 撞擊
off [1]〔ɔf〕 *prep.* 在…之外　　coast [1]〔kost〕 *n.* 海岸
Norway〔'nɔrwe〕 *n.* 挪威

6. (**B**) The fingerprints found at the crime scene are <u>identical</u> to those of the suspect. 在犯罪現場發現的指紋，和嫌犯的<u>完全相同</u>。

(A) ideal [3]〔aɪ'diəl〕 *adj.* 理想的

(B) *identical* [4]〔aɪ'dɛntɪkḷ〕 *adj.* 完全相同的 < *to* / *with* >

(C) idle [4]〔'aɪdḷ〕 *adj.* 遊手好閒的

(D) independent [2]〔,ɪndɪ'pɛndənt〕 *adj.* 獨立的

*fingerprint〔'fɪŋgɚ,prɪnt〕 *n.* 指紋　　crime [2]〔kraɪm〕 *n.* 犯罪
scene [1]〔sin〕 *n.* 現場　　suspect [3]〔'sʌspɛkt〕 *n.* 嫌疑犯

7. (**C**) The latest epidemic <u>illustrates</u> the need for stricter enforcement of health regulations. 最新的流行病<u>說明</u>了必須更嚴格執行衛生規定。

(A) hush [3]〔hʌʃ〕 *v.* 使安靜

(B) identify [4]〔aɪ'dɛntə,faɪ〕 *v.* 辨識

(C) *illustrate* [4]〔'ɪləstret〕 *v.* 圖解說明；說明

(D) inspect [3]〔ɪn'spɛkt〕 *v.* 檢查

*latest [2]〔'letɪst〕 *adj.* 最新的　　epidemic [6]〔,ɛpə'dɛmɪk〕 *n.* 流行病
strict [2]〔strɪkt〕 *adj.* 嚴格的　　enforcement [4]〔ɪn'forsmənt〕 *n.* 執行
health [1]〔hɛlθ〕 *n.* 保健；衛生　　regulation [4]〔,rɛgjə'leʃən〕 *n.* 規定

8. (**A**) A virus must have <u>infected</u> your computer.
一定有某種病毒<u>感染</u>了你的電腦。

(A) *infect* [4]〔ɪn'fɛkt〕 *v.* 感染　　(B) inform [3]〔ɪn'fɔrm〕 *v.* 通知
(C) influence [2]〔'ɪnfluəns〕 *v.* 影響　　(D) injure [3]〔'ɪndʒɚ〕 *v.* 傷害

*virus [4]〔'vaɪrəs〕 *n.* 病毒

9. (**A**) In our judicial system, everyone is <u>innocent</u> until proven guilty.
在我們的司法制度中，任何人在被證明有罪之前，都是<u>無罪的</u>。

(A) ***innocent*** [3] ('ɪnəsṇt) *adj.* 清白的；無罪的；天眞的

(B) intensive [4] (ɪn'tɛnsɪv) *adj.* 密集的

(C) intelligent [4] (ɪn'tɛlədʒənt) *adj.* 聰明的

(D) instant [2] ('ɪnstənt) *adj.* 立即的

*judicial (dʒu'dɪʃəl) *adj.* 司法的　　system [3] ('sɪstəm) *n.* 制度
prove [1] (pruv) *v.* 證明　　guilty [4] ('gɪltɪ) *adj.* 有罪的

10. (**B**) The artist was <u>inspired</u> by the beautiful landscapes of the region.
那位藝術家因爲這個地區漂亮的風景而<u>有了靈感</u>。

(A) install [4] (ɪn'stɔl) *v.* 安裝

(B) ***inspire*** [4] (ɪn'spaɪr) *v.* 激勵；給予靈感

(C) instruct [4] (ɪn'strʌkt) *v.* 教導

(D) insult [4] (ɪn'sʌlt) *v.* 侮辱

*artist [4] ('ɑrtɪst) *n.* 藝術家；畫家　　landscape [4] ('lænskep) *n.* 風景
region [2] ('ridʒən) *n.* 地區

11. (**C**) He based most of his decisions on <u>instinct</u>. He trusted his feelings.
他大部分的決定都是根據<u>直覺</u>。他信任自己的感覺。

(A) instance [2] ('ɪnstəns) *n.* 實例　　for instance 例如

(B) inspection [4] (ɪn'spɛkʃən) *n.* 檢查

(C) ***instinct*** [4] ('ɪnstɪŋkt) *n.* 本能；直覺

(D) inspiration [4] (,ɪnspə'reʃən) *n.* 激勵；靈感

*base [1] (bes) *v.* 使以⋯爲基礎 < *on* >　　trust [2] (trʌst) *v.* 信任

12. (**C**) His <u>initial</u> response to the proposal was negative, but he eventually
agreed to it. 他對這項提議<u>最初的</u>反應是否定的，但最後就同意了。

(A) inner [3] ('ɪnɚ) *adj.* 內部的

(B) internal [3] (ɪn'tɝnḷ) *adj.* 內部的

(C) ***initial*** [4] (ɪ'nɪʃəl) *adj.* 最初的

(D) intermediate [4] (,ɪntɚ'midɪɪt) *adj.* 中級的

*response [3] (rɪ'spɑns) *n.* 反應　　proposal [3] (prə'pozḷ) *n.* 提議
negative [2] ('nɛgətɪv) *adj.* 否定的
eventually [4] (ɪ'vɛntʃʊəlɪ) *adv.* 最後　　***agree to*** *sth.* 同意某事

13. (**D**) All citizens are required to pay into the national health care <u>insurance</u> system. 所有的人民都被要求將錢存入全民健保系統中。

(A) instrument [2] 〔ˋɪnstrəmənt 〕 *n.* 儀器；樂器

(B) intensity [4] 〔 ɪnˋtɛnsətɪ 〕 *n.* 強度

(C) interview [2] 〔ˋɪntɚ͵vju 〕 *n.* 面試

(D) *insurance* [4] 〔 ɪnˋʃʊrəns 〕 *n.* 保險

*citizen [2] 〔ˋsɪtəzn̩ 〕 *n.* 公民；國民；人民

require [2] 〔 rɪˋkwaɪr 〕 *v.* 要求　　*pay into* 把錢存到（帳戶）

national [2] 〔ˋnæʃən̩l 〕 *adj.* 全國的

health care 醫療保健（服務）

14. (**B**) During the heat of an <u>intense</u> argument, she broke down and started sobbing. 在<u>激烈</u>的爭論最白熱化的時候，她突然崩潰，開始啜泣。

(A) inferior [3] 〔 ɪnˋfɪrɪɚ 〕 *adj.* 較差的（↔ *superior* ）

(B) *intense* [4] 〔 ɪnˋtɛns 〕 *adj.* 激烈的

(C) intellectual [4] 〔͵ɪntl̩ˋɛktʃʊəl 〕 *adj.* 智力的

(D) imaginative [3] 〔 ɪˋmædʒə͵netɪv 〕 *adj.* 有想像力的

*heat [1] 〔 hit 〕 *n.* 熱；激烈；猛烈

during the heat of sth. 在…最激烈的階段

argument [2] 〔ˋɑrgjəmənt 〕 *n.* 爭論

break down 崩潰　　sob [4] 〔 sɑb 〕 *v.* 啜泣

15. (**D**) He was <u>interrupted</u> several times during the meeting before finally turning off his mobile phone.

他在開會時被<u>打斷</u>好幾次，最後終於關掉他的手機。

(A) interest [1] 〔ˋɪntrɪst 〕 *v.* 使感興趣　 *n.* 興趣

(B) interpret [4] 〔 ɪnˋtɝprɪt 〕 *v.* 口譯；詮釋

(C) interfere [4] 〔͵ɪntɚˋfɪr 〕 *v.* 干涉

(D) *interrupt* [3] 〔͵ɪntəˋrʌpt 〕 *v.* 打斷

*time [1] 〔 taɪm 〕 *n.* 次　　meeting [2] 〔ˋmitɪŋ 〕 *n.* 會議

turn off 關掉（電源）　　mobile [3] 〔ˋmobl̩ 〕 *adj.* 可移動的

mobile phone 行動電話；手機（ = *cell phone* ）

TEST 15

【命題範圍：「高中生必背 4500 字」
p.121-130，intimate～lifetime】

Directions: Choose the one word that best completes the sentence.

1. The unchanging _____ of his speech made it boring to listen to him.
   (A) introduction　　　　　(B) invasion
   (C) intonation　　　　　　(D) invention　　　　　　(　　)

2. She heard a noise in the kitchen and went downstairs to _____.
   (A) isolate　　　　　　　(B) judge
   (C) investigate　　　　　(D) kneel　　　　　　　(　　)

3. He wants to join a school club that doesn't _____ sports.
   (A) kick　　　　　　　　(B) involve
   (C) knock　　　　　　　(D) lack　　　　　　　(　　)

4. Mr. Thomas kept a _____ during his time in prison.
   (A) justice　　　　　　　(B) journey
   (C) jewelry　　　　　　　(D) journal　　　　　　(　　)

5. Once cockroaches have _____ a building, they're almost impossible to get rid of.
   (A) invaded　　　　　　(B) invested
   (C) invented　　　　　　(D) invited　　　　　　(　　)

6. He's a _____ man who doesn't like his wife to socialize with other men.
   (A) joyful　　　　　　　(B) juicy
   (C) jealous　　　　　　(D) junior　　　　　　(　　)

7. A gorilla emerged from the edge of the _____ and stared at the tourists.
   (A) jungle　　　　　　　(B) keyboard
   (C) kingdom　　　　　　(D) jail　　　　　　　(　　)

8. He bent down on one _____ and proposed to his girlfriend.

(A) joint

(B) knuckle

(C) knee

(D) kidney

(　　)

9. The statue is probably the most famous _____ in town.

(A) landmark

(B) landscape

(C) lantern

(D) landslide

(　　)

10. If you have _____ problems, see a lawyer.

(A) intimate

(B) learned

(C) legal

(D) liberal

(　　)

11. _____ has it that a dragon used to live in this cave.

(A) Leisure

(B) Lecture

(C) Legend

(D) Laundry

(　　)

12. Citizens of this country are very protective of their civil _____.

(A) leadership

(B) isolation

(C) liberties

(D) jealousy

(　　)

13. The _____ was placed under quarantine after an experiment with bacteria went wrong.

(A) kindergarten

(B) island

(C) laboratory

(D) library

(　　)

14. The _____ is native to Australia and feeds chiefly on eucalyptus leaves.

(A) ladybug

(B) koala

(C) kitten

(D) leopard

(　　)

15. The airport's main runway had to be _____ to accommodate larger aircraft.

(A) knitted

(B) lengthened

(C) ironed

(D) itched

(　　)

TEST 15 詳解

1. (**C**) The unchanging <u>intonation</u> of his speech made it boring to listen
to him. 他說話的<u>語調</u>一成不變,所以聽他說話很無聊。
 (A) introduction³ ﹝͵ɪntrə'dʌkʃən﹞ *n.* 介紹
 (B) invasion⁴ ﹝ɪn'veʒən﹞ *n.* 入侵
 (C) ***intonation***⁴ ﹝͵ɪntə'neʃən﹞ *n.* 語調
 (D) invention⁴ ﹝ɪn'vɛnʃən﹞ *n.* 發明
 * unchanging² ﹝ʌn'tʃendʒɪŋ﹞ *adj.* 不變的
  speech¹ ﹝spitʃ﹞ *n.* 說話;演講　　boring³ ﹝'borɪŋ﹞ *adj.* 無聊的

2. (**C**) She heard a noise in the kitchen and went downstairs to <u>investigate</u>.
她聽到廚房有聲音,所以就下樓去<u>查看</u>。
 (A) isolate⁴ ﹝'aɪsḷ͵et﹞ *v.* 隔離
 (B) judge² ﹝dʒʌdʒ﹞ *v.* 判斷
 (C) ***investigate***³ ﹝ɪn'vɛstə͵get﹞ *v.* 調查
 (D) kneel³ ﹝nil﹞ *v.* 跪下
 * downstairs¹ ﹝'daʊn'stɛrz﹞ *adv.* 到樓下

3. (**B**) He wants to join a school club that doesn't <u>involve</u> sports.
他想要加入<u>跟</u>運動無<u>關</u>的學校社團。
 (A) kick¹ ﹝kɪk﹞ *v.* 踢
 (B) ***involve***⁴ ﹝ɪn'vɑlv﹞ *v.* 牽涉;和⋯有關
 (C) knock² ﹝nɑk﹞ *v.* 敲
 (D) lack¹ ﹝læk﹞ *v.* 缺乏
 * join¹ ﹝dʒɔɪn﹞ *v.* 加入　　club² ﹝klʌb﹞ *n.* 社團

4. (**D**) Mr. Thomas kept a <u>journal</u> during his time in prison.
湯瑪斯先生在監獄服刑期間都有寫<u>日記</u>。
 (A) justice³ ﹝'dʒʌstɪs﹞ *n.* 正義;公正;公平
 (B) journey³ ﹝'dʒɝnɪ﹞ *n.* 旅程
 (C) jewelry³ ﹝'dʒuəlrɪ﹞ *n.* 珠寶【集合名詞】
 (D) ***journal***³ ﹝'dʒɝnḷ﹞ *n.* 日誌;日記;期刊
  keep a journal 寫日記 (= *keep a diary*)
 * time¹ ﹝taɪm﹞ *n.* 刑期　　prison² ﹝'prɪzn̩﹞ *n.* 監獄

5. (**A**) Once cockroaches have <u>invaded</u> a building, they're almost impossible to get rid of. 一旦蟑螂入侵一棟建築物，幾乎不可能擺脫它們。

(A) ***invade*** [4] [ɪn'ved] *v.* 入侵   (B) invest [4] [ɪn'vɛst] *v.* 投資
(C) invent [2] [ɪn'vɛnt] *v.* 發明   (D) invite [2] [ɪn'vaɪt] *v.* 邀請

* cockroach [2] ['kɑk,rotʃ] *n.* 蟑螂   ***get rid of*** 除去；擺脫

6. (**C**) He's a <u>jealous</u> man who doesn't like his wife to socialize with other men. 他是個嫉妒心重的男人，不喜歡他的太太和其他男人交往。

(A) joyful [3] ['dʒɔɪfəl] *adj.* 愉快的
(B) juicy [2] ['dʒusɪ] *adj.* 多汁的
(C) ***jealous*** [3] ['dʒɛləs] *adj.* 嫉妒心重的；善嫉妒的
(D) junior [4] ['dʒunjɚ] *adj.* 年少的；資淺的

* socialize [6] ['soʃəl,aɪz] *v.* 交際

7. (**A**) A gorilla emerged from the edge of the <u>jungle</u> and stared at the tourists. 有隻黑猩猩從叢林的邊緣出現，然後盯著觀光客看。

(A) ***jungle*** [3] ['dʒʌŋgḷ] *n.* 叢林
(B) keyboard [3] ['ki,bord] *n.* 鍵盤
(C) kingdom [2] ['kɪŋdəm] *n.* 王國
(D) jail [3] [dʒel] *n.* 監獄 (= *prison* [2])

* gorilla [2] [gə'rɪlə] *n.* 黑猩猩   emerge [4] [ɪ'mɝdʒ] *v.* 出現
edge [1] [ɛdʒ] *n.* 邊緣   stare [3] [stɛr] *v.* 凝視；瞪眼看 < *at* >
tourist [3] ['tʊrɪst] *n.* 觀光客

8. (**C**) He bent down on one <u>knee</u> and proposed to his girlfriend.
他單膝跪地，向他的女朋友求婚。

(A) joint [2] [dʒɔɪnt] *n.* 關節
(B) knuckle [4] ['nʌkḷ] *n.* 指關節
(C) ***knee*** [1] [ni] *n.* 膝蓋
(D) kidney [3] ['kɪdnɪ] *n.* 腎臟

* ***bend down*** 彎下身子   propose [2] [prə'poz] *v.* 求婚

9. (**A**) The statue is probably the most famous <u>landmark</u> in town.
那座雕像可能是城裡最著名的地標。

(A) *landmark*[4]〔'lænd,mɑrk〕*n.* 地標

(B) landscape[4]〔'lænskep〕*n.* 風景

(C) lantern[2]〔'læntən〕*n.* 燈籠

(D) landslide[4]〔'lænd,slaɪd〕*n.* 山崩

*statue[3]〔'stætʃʊ〕*n.* 雕像　　famous[2]〔'feməs〕*adj.* 有名的

10. (**C**) If you have <u>legal</u> problems, see a lawyer.

如果你有<u>法律</u>問題，去找律師。

(A) intimate[4]〔'ɪntəmɪt〕*adj.* 親密的

(B) learned[4]〔'lɜnɪd〕*adj.* 有學問的【注意發音】

(C) *legal*[2]〔'ligl〕*adj.* 法律的；合法的

(D) liberal[3]〔'lɪbərəl〕*adj.* 開明的

*lawyer[2]〔'lɔjə〕*n.* 律師

11. (**C**) <u>Legend</u> has it that a dragon used to live in this cave.

<u>傳說</u>指出，以前有一隻龍住在這個洞穴裡。

(A) leisure[3]〔'liʒə〕*n.* 空閒；悠閒　*adj.* 空閒的

leisure time　空閒時間

(B) lecture[4]〔'lɛktʃə〕*n. v.* 講課；演講

(C) *legend*[4]〔'lɛdʒənd〕*n.* 傳說　　***Legend has it that*** 傳說指出

(D) laundry[3]〔'lɔndrɪ〕*n.* 待洗的衣物　　do the laundry 洗衣服

*dragon[2]〔'drægən〕*n.* 龍　　***used to V.*** 以前…

cave[2]〔kev〕*n.* 洞穴

12. (**C**) Citizens of this country are very protective of their civil <u>liberties</u>.

這個國家的人民非常保護自己的公民<u>自由</u>。

(A) leadership[2]〔'lidə,ʃɪp〕*n.* 領導能力

(B) isolation[4]〔,aɪsl̩'eʃən〕*n.* 隔離

(C) *liberty*[3]〔'lɪbətɪ〕*n.* 自由　　*civil liberties* 公民的自由【受法律保障的思想上、言論上、行動上的自由】

(D) jealousy[4]〔'dʒɛləsɪ〕*n.* 嫉妒

*citizen[2]〔'sɪtɪzn̩〕*n.* 公民；國民；人民

protective[3]〔prə'tɛktɪv〕*adj.* 保護的；捍衛的

civil[3]〔'sɪvl̩〕*adj.* 公民的；國民的

13. (**C**) The <u>laboratory</u> was placed under quarantine after an experiment
with bacteria went wrong.
這間<u>實驗室</u>在用細菌做實驗失敗後，就被隔離檢疫。

   (A) kindergarten² (ˈkɪndəˌgɑrtn̩) *n.* 幼稚園

   (B) island² (ˈaɪlənd) *n.* 島

   (C) *laboratory*⁴ (ˈlæbrəˌtorɪ) *n.* 實驗室（= *lab*⁴ ）

   (D) library² (ˈlaɪˌbrɛrɪ) *n.* 圖書館

   *place¹ (ples) *v.* 使處於（某種狀態）
under¹ (ˈʌndə) *prep.* 在…之中；接受
quarantine (ˈkwɔrənˌtin) *n.* 隔離；檢疫
experiment³ (ɪkˈspɛrəmənt) *n.* 實驗
bacteria³ (bækˈtɪrɪə) *n. pl.* 細菌　　***go wrong*** 出錯

14. (**B**) The <u>koala</u> is native to Australia and feeds chiefly on eucalyptus
leaves. 無尾熊原產於澳洲，主要是以尤加利樹的葉子爲食。

   (A) ladybug² (ˈledɪˌbʌg) *n.* 瓢蟲

   (B) *koala*² (koˈalə) *n.* 無尾熊

   (C) kitten¹ (ˈkɪtn̩) *n.* 小貓

   (D) leopard² (ˈlɛpəd) *n.* 豹【注意發音】

   *native³ (ˈnetɪv) *adj.* 原產的　　***be native to*** 原產於
Australia (ɔˈstreljə) *n.* 澳洲　　***feed on*** 以…爲食
chiefly¹ (ˈtʃiflɪ) *adv.* 主要地
eucalyptus (ˌjukəˈlɪptəs) *n.* 尤加利樹
leaves¹ (livz) *n. pl.* 葉子【單數是 leaf】

15. (**B**) The airport's main runway had to be <u>lengthened</u> to accommodate
larger aircraft. 機場的主要跑道必須<u>加長</u>，以容納較大型的飛機。

   (A) knit³ (nɪt) *v.* 編織

   (B) *lengthen*³ (ˈlɛŋθən) *v.* 加長

   (C) iron¹ (ˈaɪən) *v.* 熨燙　　*n.* 鐵；熨斗

   (D) itch⁴ (ɪtʃ) *v. n.* 癢

   *main² (men) *adj.* 主要的　　runway (ˈrʌnˌwe) *n.* 跑道
accommodate⁶ (əˈkɑməˌdet) *v.* 容納
aircraft² (ˈɛrˌkræft) *n.* 飛機【集合名詞】

TEST 16

【命題範圍：「高中生必背 4500 字」
p.131-140，lift～microphone】

Directions: *Choose the one word that best completes the sentence.*

1. To stay healthy, drink plenty of _____ and get ample rest.
   (A) limbs　　　　　　　(B) liquors
   (C) linens　　　　　　　(D) liquids　　　　　　　　(　)

2. He studied 18th century _____ before joining the Navy.
   (A) location　　　　　　(B) limitation
   (C) lightning　　　　　　(D) literature　　　　　　(　)

3. Dave's plan seems the most _____, so let's agree to follow it.
   (A) logical　　　　　　　(B) mechanical
   (C) medical　　　　　　　(D) lonely　　　　　　　　(　)

4. That was a _____ thing for him to do. He should apologize.
   (A) likely　　　　　　　(B) magical
   (C) lousy　　　　　　　　(D) lovely　　　　　　　　(　)

5. The mother sang a _____ to her infant son.
   (A) luggage　　　　　　(B) lullaby
   (C) luncheon　　　　　　(D) luxury　　　　　　　　(　)

6. The newlywed couple rented a _____ villa in the south of France.
   (A) luxurious　　　　　　(B) literary
   (C) lunar　　　　　　　　(D) loose　　　　　　　　(　)

7. That boy is a _____ for trouble. Bad things happen wherever he goes.
   (A) melody　　　　　　　(B) madam
   (C) magnet　　　　　　　(D) melon　　　　　　　　(　)

8. The larger the home, the more expensive it is to _____.

    (A) match   (B) march

    (C) melt   (D) maintain   ( )

9. They won the game by a large _____.

    (A) majority   (B) marble

    (C) manual   (D) margin   ( )

10. The library has a _____ collection of rare and antique books.

    (A) mathematical   (B) manageable

    (C) marvelous   (D) mature   ( )

11. The _____ height for new buildings in the city is 50 meters.

    (A) measurable   (B) maximum

    (C) meaningful   (D) magnificent   ( )

12. He _____ the distance between the floor and ceiling.

    (A) lightened   (B) measured

    (C) mastered   (D) managed   ( )

13. The students must _____ these vocabulary words.

    (A) limit   (B) mend

    (C) memorize   (D) manufacture   ( )

14. She cut her foot on a piece of _____.

    (A) metal   (B) medal

    (C) merit   (D) mercy   ( )

15. Each student will be assigned a _____ at the beginning of the school year.

    (A) lollipop   (B) locker

    (C) makeup   (D) lobster   ( )

TEST 16 詳解

1. (**D**) To stay healthy, drink plenty of <u>liquids</u> and get ample rest.
要保持健康，就要喝許多<u>液體</u>，並獲得充分的休息。
   (A) limbs [3] ﹝lɪmbs﹞ *n. pl.* 四肢
   (B) liquor [4] ﹝'lɪkɚ﹞ *n.* 烈酒
   (C) linen [3] ﹝'lɪnɪn﹞ *n.* 亞麻布；(*pl.*) 亞麻布製品
   (D) *liquid* [2] ﹝'lɪkwɪd﹞ *n.* 液體
   * stay [1] ﹝ste﹞ *v.* 保持　　healthy [2] ﹝'hɛlθɪ﹞ *adj.* 健康的
   plenty of 許多的　　ample [5] ﹝'æmpḷ﹞ *adj.* 豐富的；充裕的
   rest [1] ﹝rɛst﹞ *n.* 休息

2. (**D**) He studied 18th century <u>literature</u> before joining the Navy.
他在加入海軍之前，研讀了十八世紀的<u>文學作品</u>。
   (A) location [4] ﹝lo'keʃən﹞ *n.* 位置
   (B) limitation [4] ﹝͵lɪmə'teʃən﹞ *n.* 限制
   (C) lightning [2] ﹝'laɪtnɪŋ﹞ *n.* 閃電　【比較】thunder [2] ﹝'θʌndɚ﹞ *n.* 雷
   (D) *literature* [4] ﹝'lɪtərətʃɚ﹞ *n.* 文學；文學作品
   * century [2] ﹝'sɛntʃərɪ﹞ *n.* 世紀　　join [1] ﹝dʒɔɪn﹞ *v.* 加入
   navy [3] ﹝'nevɪ﹞ *n.* 海軍

3. (**A**) Dave's plan seems the most <u>logical</u>, so let's agree to follow it.
戴夫的計劃似乎是最<u>合邏輯的</u>，所以我們就同意遵循它吧。
   (A) *logical* [4] ﹝'lɑdʒɪkḷ﹞ *adj.* 合邏輯的
   (B) mechanical [4] ﹝mə'kænɪkḷ﹞ *adj.* 機械的
   (C) medical [3] ﹝'mɛdɪkḷ﹞ *adj.* 醫學的；醫療的
   (D) lonely [2] ﹝'lonlɪ﹞ *adj.* 寂寞的
   * seem [1] ﹝sim﹞ *v.* 似乎　　follow [1] ﹝'falo﹞ *v.* 遵循；奉行

4. (**C**) That was a <u>lousy</u> thing for him to do. He should apologize.
他做這件事很<u>差勁</u>。他應該道歉。
   (A) likely [1] ﹝'laɪklɪ﹞ *adj.* 可能的

(B) magical [3] (ˈmædʒɪkḷ) *adj.* 神奇的

(C) ***lousy*** [4] (ˈlaʊzɪ) *adj.* 差勁的

(D) lovely [2] (ˈlʌvlɪ) *adj.* 可愛的

＊apologize [4] (əˈpɑləˌdʒaɪz) *v.* 道歉

5. (**B**) The mother sang a <u>lullaby</u> to her infant son.
那位母親對她年幼的兒子唱了一首<u>搖籃曲</u>。

   (A) luggage [3] (ˈlʌgɪdʒ) *n.* 行李

   (B) ***lullaby*** [3] (ˈlʌləˌbaɪ) *n.* 搖籃曲

   (C) luncheon [1] (ˈlʌntʃən) *n.* 午餐

   (D) luxury [4] (ˈlʌkʃərɪ) *n.* 豪華

   ＊infant [4] (ˈɪnfənt) *adj.* 幼兒的；嬰兒的

6. (**A**) The newlywed couple rented a <u>luxurious</u> villa in the south of France.
這對新婚夫妻在法國南部租了一間<u>豪華</u>別墅。

   (A) ***luxurious*** [4] (lʌgˈʒʊrɪəs , lʌkˈʃʊrɪəs) *adj.* 豪華的

   (B) literary [4] (ˈlɪtəˌrɛrɪ) *adj.* 文學的

   (C) lunar [4] (ˈlunɚ) *adj.* 月亮的   lunar calendar 農曆

   (D) loose [3] (lus) *adj.* 鬆的 (↔ *tight*)

   ＊newlywed [6] (ˈnjulɪˌwɛd) *n.* 新婚者

    couple [2] (ˈkʌpḷ) *n.* 夫妻   rent [3] (rɛnt) *v.* 租

    villa [6] (ˈvɪlə) *n.* 別墅   south [1] (saʊθ) *n.* 南部

7. (**C**) That boy is a <u>magnet</u> for trouble. Bad things happen wherever he goes. 那個男孩會<u>吸引</u>麻煩。無論他到哪裡，總會有壞事發生。

   (A) melody [2] (ˈmɛlədɪ) *n.* 旋律

   (B) madam [4] (ˈmædəm) *n.* 女士

   (C) ***magnet*** [3] (ˈmægnɪt) *n.* 磁鐵；有吸引力的人或物

   (D) melon [2] (ˈmɛlən) *n.* 甜瓜

8. (**D**) The larger the home, the more expensive it is to <u>maintain</u>.
房子越大，<u>維護</u>的費用就越貴。

(A) match³〔mætʃ〕*v.* 搭配；與…匹敵

(B) march³〔martʃ〕*v.* 行軍；行進

(C) melt³〔mɛlt〕*v.* 融化

(D) ***maintain*** ²〔men'ten〕*v.* 維持；養護；維修

* 「the + 比較級…the + 比較級」表「越…就越～」。

9. (**D**) They won the game by a large <u>margin</u>.

他們以極大的<u>差距</u>贏得比賽。

(A) majority³〔mə'dʒɔrətɪ〕*n.* 大多數

(B) marble³〔'marbl̩〕*n.* 大理石；彈珠

(C) manual⁴〔'mænjʊəl〕*n.* 手冊

(D) ***margin*** ⁴〔'mardʒɪn〕*n.* 差距；邊緣；頁邊的空白

10. (**C**) The library has a <u>marvelous</u> collection of rare and antique books.

那間圖書館<u>很棒</u>，有收藏稀有而且古老的珍貴書籍。

(A) mathematical³〔‚mæθə'mætɪkl̩〕*adj.* 數學的

(B) manageable³〔'mænɪdʒəbl̩〕*adj.* 可管理的

(C) ***marvelous*** ³〔'marvl̩əs〕*adj.* 很棒的

(D) mature³〔mə'tʃʊr〕*adj.* 成熟的

* library²〔'laɪ‚brɛrɪ〕*n.* 圖書館

collection³〔kə'lɛkʃən〕*n.* 收集；收藏

rare²〔rɛr〕*adj.* 稀有的；罕見的

antique⁵〔æn'tik〕*adj.* 古董的；古舊而有價值的

11. (**B**) The <u>maximum</u> height for new buildings in the city is 50 meters.

在這個城市，新建築物的高度<u>極限</u>是五十公尺。

(A) measurable²〔'mɛʒərəbl̩〕*adj.* 可測量的

(B) ***maximum*** ⁴〔'mæksəməm〕*adj.* 最大的；最高的；極限的

n. 最大量（↔ *minimum*）

(C) meaningful³〔'minɪŋfəl〕*adj.* 有意義的

(D) magnificent⁴〔mæg'nɪfəsn̩t〕*adj.* 壯麗的

* height²〔haɪt〕*n.* 高度　building¹〔'bɪldɪŋ〕*n.* 建築物

meter²〔'mitɚ〕*n.* 公尺

12. (**B**) He <u>measured</u> the distance between the floor and ceiling.
他<u>測量</u>地板和天花板之間的距離。

    (A) lighten[4]〔'laɪtn̩〕v. 照亮;變亮;減輕

    (B) ***measure***[2,4]〔'mɛʒɚ〕v. 測量　　n. 措施

    (C) master[1]〔'mæstɚ〕v. 精通　　n. 主人;大師;碩士

    (D) manage[3]〔'mænɪdʒ〕v. 管理;設法

    *distance[2]〔'dɪstəns〕n. 距離　　ceiling[2]〔'silɪŋ〕n. 天花板

13. (**C**) The students must <u>memorize</u> these vocabulary words.
學生必須<u>背</u>這些字彙。

    (A) limit[2]〔'lɪmɪt〕v. n. 限制

    (B) mend[3]〔mɛnd〕v. 修補;改正

    (C) ***memorize***[3]〔'mɛmə,raɪz〕v. 背誦;記憶

    (D) manufacture[4]〔,mænjə'fæktʃɚ〕v. 製造

    *vocabulary[2]〔və'kæbjə,lɛrɪ〕n. 字彙

14. (**A**) She cut her foot on a piece of <u>metal</u>.
她被一片<u>金屬</u>割傷了腳。

    (A) ***metal***[1]〔'mɛtl̩〕n. 金屬

    (B) medal[2]〔'mɛdl̩〕n. 獎牌　　gold medal 金牌

    (C) merit[2]〔'mɛrɪt〕n. 優點

    (D) mercy[3]〔'mɝsɪ〕n. 慈悲

    *cut[1]〔kʌt〕v. 割傷;切傷

15. (**B**) Each student will be assigned a <u>locker</u> at the beginning of the school
year. 學年的一開始,每個學生都會被分配一個<u>置物櫃</u>。

    (A) lollipop[3]〔'lalɪ,pap〕n. 棒棒糖

    (B) ***locker***[4]〔'lakɚ〕n. 置物櫃

    (C) makeup[4]〔'mek,ʌp〕n. 化粧品

    (D) lobster[3]〔'labstɚ〕n. 龍蝦

    *assign[4]〔ə'saɪn〕v. 分配;分派

    school year 學年【英、美通常指九月至六月】

TEST 17

【命題範圍：「高中生必背 4500 字」
p.141-150，microscope～noise】

Directions: Choose the one word that best completes the sentence.

1. The refugees are housed at a temporary shelter in _____ conditions.
   (A) miserable   (B) mighty
   (C) mild   (D) military   (　)

2. A _____ amount of stress can be beneficial for ambitious students.
   (A) missing   (B) moderate
   (C) mobile   (D) modern   (　)

3. The security cameras _____ activity in the hotel lobby.
   (A) mow   (B) multiply
   (C) monitor   (D) murder   (　)

4. When viewed under a _____, some bacteria look like scary monsters.
   (A) missile   (B) microwave
   (C) mommy   (D) microscope   (　)

5. Hank is only 165 centimeters tall, which is just below the _____ for a police officer.
   (A) millionaire   (B) mineral
   (C) monument   (D) minimum   (　)

6. Don't let her pleasant attitude _____ you into thinking she can be trusted.
   (A) misunderstand   (B) mix
   (C) mislead   (D) mop   (　)

7. The most important characteristic of farmland is the soil's ability to retain _____.
   (A) moisture   (B) mixture
   (C) ministry   (D) miracle   (　)

8. The student _____ something to the teacher and left the classroom.

(A) moved   (B) negotiated

(C) neglected   (D) murmured   ( )

9. The couple met through _____ friends at college.

(A) musical   (B) nearsighted

(C) mutual   (D) naughty   ( )

10. She wiped her mouth with a _____.

(A) network   (B) napkin

(C) nickname   (D) needle   ( )

11. Tom could be from the U.S., but it's hard to guess his _____.

(A) modesty   (B) nationality

(C) minority   (D) necessity   ( )

12. I was very _____ about driving again after the accident.

(A) negative   (B) needy

(C) naked   (D) nervous   ( )

13. Teaching is one of the most _____ professions.

(A) noble   (B) narrow

(C) mysterious   (D) natural   ( )

14. A group of her friends attended the performance, offering _____ support.

(A) muddy   (B) moveable

(C) moist   (D) moral   ( )

15. My _____ got in a fight with a boy at school and broke the other kid's nose.

(A) minister   (B) nephew

(C) model   (D) merchant   ( )

TEST　17　詳解

1. (**A**) The refugees are housed at a temporary shelter in <u>miserable</u> conditions. 那些難民被收容在一個暫時的避難所，情況很<u>悲慘</u>。

　　(A) ***miserable***[4] 〔ˈmɪzərəbḷ 〕 *adj.* 悲慘的
　　(B) mighty[3] 〔ˈmaɪtɪ 〕 *adj.* 強有力的
　　(C) mild[4] 〔 maɪld 〕 *adj.* 溫和的
　　(D) military[2] 〔ˈmɪləˌtɛrɪ 〕 *adj.* 軍事的

　　*refugee[4] 〔ˌrɛfjʊˈdʒi 〕 *n.* 難民
　　house[1] 〔 haʊz 〕 *v.* 收容；提供…住所
　　temporary[3] 〔ˈtɛmpəˌrɛrɪ 〕 *adj.* 暫時的
　　shelter[4] 〔ˈʃɛltɚ 〕 *n.* 避難所　　condition[3] 〔 kənˈdɪʃən 〕 *n.* 情況

2. (**B**) A <u>moderate</u> amount of stress can be beneficial for ambitious students. <u>適量</u>的壓力對有抱負的學生而言，可能是有益的。

　　(A) missing[3] 〔ˈmɪsɪŋ 〕 *adj.* 失蹤的
　　(B) ***moderate***[4] 〔ˈmɑdərɪt 〕 *adj.* 適度的
　　(C) mobile[3] 〔ˈmobḷ 〕 *adj.* 可移動的
　　(D) modern[2] 〔ˈmɑdɚn 〕 *adj.* 現代的

　　*amount[2] 〔 əˈmaʊnt 〕 *n.* 數量　　stress[2] 〔 strɛs 〕 *n.* 壓力
　　beneficial[5] 〔ˌbɛnəˈfɪʃəl 〕 *adj.* 有益的
　　ambitious[4] 〔 æmˈbɪʃəs 〕 *adj.* 有抱負的；有野心的

3. (**C**) The security cameras <u>monitor</u> activity in the hotel lobby.
保全攝影機<u>監視</u>著飯店大廳裡的活動。

　　(A) mow[4] 〔 mo 〕 *v.* 割（草）
　　(B) multiply[2] 〔ˈmʌltəˌplaɪ 〕 *v.* 繁殖；乘
　　(C) ***monitor***[4] 〔ˈmɑnətɚ 〕 *v.* 監視
　　(D) murder[3] 〔ˈmɝdɚ 〕 *v.* 謀殺

　　*security[3] 〔 sɪˈkjʊrətɪ 〕 *adj.* 安全的；保安的
　　camera[1] 〔ˈkæmərə 〕 *n.* 攝影機　　lobby[3] 〔ˈlabɪ 〕 *n.* 大廳

4. (**D**) When viewed under a <u>microscope</u>, some bacteria look like scary monsters. 在<u>顯微鏡</u>底下，有些細菌看起來像是可怕的怪物。

(A) missile [3] ('mɪsḷ) *n.* 飛彈

(B) microwave [3] ('maɪkrə,wev) *n.* 微波爐

(C) mommy [1] ('mamɪ) *n.* 木乃伊

(D) ***microscope*** [4] ('maɪkrə,skop) *n.* 顯微鏡

*view [1] (vju) *v.* 看　　bacteria [3] (bæk'tɪrɪə) *n. pl.* 細菌

scary [3] ('skɛrɪ) *adj.* 可怕的　　monster [2] ('manstə) *n.* 怪物

5. (**D**) Hank is only 165 centimeters tall, which is just below the <u>minimum</u> for a police officer.

漢克只有 165 公分高，剛好低於警員的<u>最低標準</u>。

(A) millionaire [3] (,mɪljən'ɛr) *n.* 百萬富翁

(B) mineral [4] ('mɪnərəl) *n.* 礦物；礦物質　　mineral water　礦泉水

(C) monument [4] ('manjəmənt) *n.* 紀念碑

(D) ***minimum*** [4] ('mɪnəməm) *n.* 最小量；最低限度 (↔ *maximum*)

*centimeter [3] ('sɛntə,mitə) *n.* 公分

below [1] (bə'lo) *prep.* 在…之下　　***police officer***　警官；警員

6. (**C**) Don't let her pleasant attitude <u>mislead</u> you into thinking she can be trusted.　不要讓她友善的態度<u>誤導</u>你，認爲她是可以信任的。

(A) misunderstand [4] (,mɪsʌndə'stænd) *v.* 誤會

(B) mix [2] (mɪks) *v.* 混合

(C) ***mislead*** [4] (mɪs'lid) *v.* 誤導

(D) mop [3] (map) *v.* 用拖把拖 (地板)

*pleasant [2] ('plɛzṇt) *adj.* 令人愉快的；友善的

attitude [3] ('ætə,tjud) *n.* 態度　　trust [2] (trʌst) *v.* 信任

7. (**A**) The most important characteristic of farmland is the soil's ability to retain <u>moisture</u>.

農地最重要的特性，就是土壤有能力能留住<u>水分</u>。

(A) ***moisture*** [3] ('mɔɪstʃə) *n.* 濕氣；水分

(B) mixture [3] ('mɪkstʃə) *n.* 混合物

(C) ministry [4] ('mɪnɪstrɪ) *n.* 部

(D) miracle [3] ('mɪrəkḷ) *n.* 奇蹟

*characteristic [4] (,kærɪktə'rɪstɪk) *n.* 特性

farmland〔'farm,lænd〕*n.* 農地

soil[1]〔sɔɪl〕*n.* 土壤　　ability[2]〔ə'bɪlətɪ〕*n.* 能力

retain[4]〔rɪ'ten〕*v.* 保留；保持

8. (**D**) The student <u>murmured</u> something to the teacher and left the
classroom. 那位學生向老師<u>低聲說</u>了某些話，然後離開教室。

　　(A) move[1]〔muv〕*v.* 移動；搬家；使感動

　　(B) negotiate[4]〔nɪ'goʃɪ,et〕*v.* 談判；協商

　　(C) neglect[4]〔nɪ'glɛkt〕*v.* 忽略

　　(D) *murmur*[4]〔'mɝmɚ〕*v.* 喃喃地說；低聲說

9. (**C**) The couple met through <u>mutual</u> friends at college.
那對夫妻是透過大學時期<u>共同</u>的朋友認識的。

　　(A) musical[3]〔'mjuzɪk!〕*adj.* 音樂的　*n.* 音樂劇

　　(B) nearsighted[4]〔'nɪr'saɪtɪd〕*adj.* 近視的

　　(C) *mutual*[4]〔'mjutʃʊəl〕*adj.* 互相的；共同的

　　(D) naughty[2]〔'nɔtɪ〕*adj.* 頑皮的

　　*couple[2]〔'kʌp!〕*n.* 夫妻；一對男女　　meet[1]〔mit〕*v.* 認識

10. (**B**) She wiped her mouth with a <u>napkin</u>.
她用<u>餐巾</u>來擦嘴。

　　(A) network[3]〔'nɛt,wɝk〕*n.* (電腦) 網路；網路系統；網狀組織

　　(B) *napkin*[2]〔'næpkɪn〕*n.* 餐巾

　　(C) nickname[3]〔'nɪk,nem〕*n.* 綽號

　　(D) needle[2]〔'nid!〕*n.* 針　【比較】noodle[2]〔'nud!〕*n.* 麵

　　*wipe[3]〔waɪp〕*v.* 擦　　mouth[1]〔maʊθ〕*n.* 嘴巴

11. (**B**) Tom could be from the U.S., but it's hard to guess his <u>nationality</u>.
湯姆可能來自美國，但是很難猜他的<u>國籍</u>。

　　(A) modesty[4]〔'madəstɪ〕*n.* 謙虛

　　(B) *nationality*[4]〔,næʃən'ælətɪ〕*n.* 國籍

　　(C) minority[3]〔maɪ'nɔrətɪ〕*n.* 少數（↔ *majority*）

　　(D) necessity[3]〔nə'sɛsətɪ〕*n.* 必要；需要

　　*hard[1]〔hard〕*adj.* 困難的　　guess[1]〔gɛs〕*v.* 猜

12. (**D**) I was very <u>nervous</u> about driving again after the accident.
發生意外之後，對於再次開車我非常緊張。

    (A) negative² 〔'nɛgətɪv 〕 *adj.* 負面的 (↔ *positive*)

    (B) needy⁴ 〔'nidɪ 〕 *adj.* 窮困的

    (C) naked² 〔'nekɪd 〕 *adj.* 赤裸的

    (D) ***nervous***³ 〔'nɜvəs 〕 *adj.* 緊張的

13. (**A**) Teaching is one of the most <u>noble</u> professions.
教書是最高尚的職業之一。

    (A) ***noble***³ 〔'nobḷ 〕 *adj.* 高貴的；高尚的

    (B) narrow² 〔'næro 〕 *adj.* 窄的；勉強的

        have a narrow escape 千鈞一髮；好險

    (C) mysterious⁴ 〔 mɪs'tɪrɪəs 〕 *adj.* 神祕的

    (D) natural² 〔'nætʃərəl 〕 *adj.* 自然的；天生的

    *profession⁴ 〔 prə'fɛʃən 〕 *n.* 職業

14. (**D**) A group of her friends attended the performance, offering <u>moral</u> support. 她的一群朋友出席那場表演，提供精神上的支持。

    (A) muddy⁴ 〔'mʌdɪ 〕 *adj.* 泥濘的   mud¹ *n.* 泥巴

    (B) moveable² 〔'muvəbḷ 〕 *adj.* 可移動的

    (C) moist³ 〔 mɔɪst 〕 *adj.* 潮濕的 (= *damp*⁴ = *humid*² = *wet*²)

    (D) ***moral***³ 〔'mɔrəl 〕 *adj.* 道德的；道義上的；精神上的

    *attend² 〔 ə'tɛnd 〕 *v.* 參加；出席

    performance³ 〔 pə'fɔrməns 〕 *n.* 表演

    offer² 〔'ɔfə 〕 *v.* 提供   support² 〔 sə'port 〕 *n.* 支持

15. (**B**) My <u>nephew</u> got in a fight with a boy at school and broke the other kid's nose. 我的姪子在學校和一個男孩打架，打斷了那個孩子的鼻子。

    (A) minister⁴ 〔'mɪnɪstə 〕 *n.* 部長

    (B) ***nephew***² 〔'nɛfju 〕 *n.* 姪子；外甥

        【比較】niece² 〔 nis 〕 *n.* 姪女；外甥女

    (C) model² 〔'madḷ 〕 *n.* 模特兒；模型；模範

    (D) merchant³ 〔'mɜtʃənt 〕 *n.* 商人

    *fight¹ 〔 faɪt 〕 *n.* 打架   ***get in a fight with*** *sb.* 和某人打架

    break¹ 〔 brek 〕 *v.* 折斷；使碎裂

TEST 18

【命題範圍：「高中生必背 4500 字」
p.101-150，gracious～noise】

Directions: Choose the one word that best completes the sentence.

1. The train pulled out of the station, _____ building up speed.
   - (A) gradually
   - (B) gratefully
   - (C) greedily
   - (D) grammatically
   ( )

2. He snatched the ticket from my hand without a moment's _____.
   - (A) imagination
   - (B) hesitation
   - (C) indication
   - (D) identification
   ( )

3. The child's disappearance remains a _____.
   - (A) memory
   - (B) marathon
   - (C) luxury
   - (D) mystery
   ( )

4. He took off his jacket and _____ his necktie.
   - (A) loosened
   - (B) located
   - (C) nodded
   - (D) memorized
   ( )

5. Due to _____, the price of milk has more than tripled over the last year.
   - (A) impression
   - (B) illustration
   - (C) instruction
   - (D) inflation
   ( )

6. The seminar was very _____. It told us everything we need to know about starting a small business.
   - (A) mental
   - (B) negative
   - (C) informative
   - (D) intense
   ( )

7. _____ the cloth over the table and I'll get the dishes and silverware.
   - (A) Lie
   - (B) Lay
   - (C) Lick
   - (D) Link
   ( )

8. The man fell from the seventh floor and died on _____.
    (A) miracle   (B) impact
    (C) harmony   (D) liberty   ( )

9. If Oscar is busy, why don't you ask George _____?
    (A) however   (B) moreover
    (C) instead   (D) namely   ( )

10. The country has obtained the technology to _____ a nuclear missile.
    (A) lean   (B) launch
    (C) kneel   (D) motivate   ( )

11. When Freddie gets depressed, he tends to _____ himself from his friends and family.
    (A) murmur   (B) measure
    (C) investigate   (D) isolate   ( )

12. The wife of an Italian nobleman was Da Vinci's _____ for the *Mona Lisa*.
    (A) interaction   (B) intention
    (C) inspiration   (D) interruption   ( )

13. Only _____ friends were invited to their wedding.
    (A) intimate   (B) magical
    (C) mature   (D) luxurious   ( )

14. It became clear that Mr. Irving needed _____ treatment for his injuries.
    (A) immediate   (B) nervous
    (C) identical   (D) humble   ( )

15. Dad was on his way home and Mom was in the kitchen. _____, my sister was chatting on her phone.
    (A) Hardly   (B) Lately
    (C) Mostly   (D) Meanwhile   ( )

TEST 18 詳解

1. (**A**) The train pulled out of the station, <u>gradually</u> building up speed.
　　火車開出車站，<u>逐漸</u>加快速度。
　　(A) **gradually** [3] ('grædʒʊəlɪ) *adv.* 逐漸地
　　(B) gratefully [4] ('gretfəlɪ) *adv.* 感激地
　　(C) greedily [2] ('gridɪlɪ) *adv.* 貪心地
　　(D) grammatically [4] (grə'mætɪklɪ) *adv.* 在文法上
　　***pull out** （列車）出站　　　**build up** 增加
　　speed [2] (spid) *n.* 速度

2. (**B**) He snatched the ticket from my hand without a moment's <u>hesitation</u>.
　　他沒有片刻的<u>猶豫</u>，就從我的手中把票搶走。
　　(A) imagination [3] (ɪ,mædʒə'neʃən) *n.* 想像力
　　(B) **hesitation** [4] (,hɛzə'teʃən) *n.* 猶豫
　　(C) indication [4] (,ɪndə'keʃən) *n.* 跡象；指標
　　(D) identification [4] (aɪ,dɛntəfə'keʃən) *n.* 確認身份；身份證明（文件）
　　*snatch [5] (snætʃ) *v.* 搶奪　　　moment [1] ('momənt) *n.* 片刻

3. (**D**) The child's disappearance remains a <u>mystery</u>.
　　那個小孩的失蹤，仍然是個<u>謎</u>。
　　(A) memory [2] ('mɛmərɪ) *n.* 記憶
　　(B) marathon [4] ('mærə,θɑn) *n.* 馬拉松
　　(C) luxury [4] ('lʌkʃərɪ) *n.* 豪華
　　(D) **mystery** [3] ('mɪstrɪ) *n.* 謎；奧祕
　　*disappearance [2] (,dɪsə'pɪrəns) *n.* 消失；失蹤
　　remain [3] (rɪ'men) *v.* 仍然是

4. (**A**) He took off his jacket and <u>loosened</u> his necktie.
　　他脫掉他的夾克，並<u>鬆開</u>他的領帶。
　　(A) **loosen** [3] ('lusn̩) *v.* 鬆開
　　(B) locate [2] ('loket , lo'ket) *v.* 使位於；找出…的位置
　　(C) nod [2] (nɑd) *v.* 點頭
　　(D) memorize [3] ('mɛmə,raɪz) *v.* 背誦；記憶

take off 脫掉　　jacket[2] 〔ˈdʒækɪt〕 *n.* 夾克
necktie[3] 〔ˈnɛkˌtaɪ〕 *n.* 領帶

5. (**D**) Due to <u>inflation</u>, the price of milk has more than tripled over the last year. 由於<u>通貨膨脹</u>，牛奶的價格在去年已經漲了超過三倍。

(A) impression[4] 〔ɪmˈprɛʃən〕 *n.* 印象
(B) illustration[4] 〔ˌɪləsˈtreʃən〕 *n.* 圖解說明；說明
(C) instruction[3] 〔ɪnˈstrʌkʃən〕 *n.* 教導
(D) *inflation*[4] 〔ɪnˈfleʃən〕 *n.* 通貨膨脹

due to 由於　　price[1] 〔praɪs〕 *n.* 價格
triple[5] 〔ˈtrɪpḷ〕 *v.* 成為三倍

6. (**C**) The seminar was very <u>informative</u>. It told us everything we need to know about starting a small business. 那場座談會<u>提供非常多的資訊</u>。它告訴我們創立小型企業必須知道的一切。

(A) mental[3] 〔ˈmɛntḷ〕 *adj.* 心理的；精神的
(B) negative[2] 〔ˈnɛgətɪv〕 *adj.* 負面的
(C) *informative*[4] 〔ɪnˈfɔrmətɪv〕 *adj.* 知識性的；提供很多資訊的
(D) intense[4] 〔ɪnˈtɛns〕 *adj.* 強烈的

*seminar[6] 〔ˈsɛməˌnɑr〕 *n.* 座談會　　start[1] 〔stɑrt〕 *v.* 創辦
business[2] 〔ˈbɪznɪs〕 *n.* 生意；事業；企業

7. (**B**) <u>Lay</u> the cloth over the table and I'll get the dishes and silverware. 把那塊布<u>放</u>在桌上，我會去拿碗盤和銀製餐具。

(A) lie[1] 〔laɪ〕 *v.* 躺【三態：lie-lay-lain】；說謊【三態：lie-lied-lied】
(B) *lay*[1] 〔le〕 *v.* 下（蛋）；放置；奠定【三態：lay-laid-laid】
(C) lick[2] 〔lɪk〕 *v.* 舔
(D) link[2] 〔lɪŋk〕 *v.* 連結

*cloth[2] 〔klɔθ〕 *n.* 布　　dishes[1] 〔ˈdɪʃɪz〕 *n. pl.* 碗盤
silverware 〔ˈsɪlvɚˌwɛr〕 *n.* 銀製餐具【集合名詞】

8. (**B**) The man fell from the seventh floor and died on <u>impact</u>. 那名男子從七樓墜落，並且因為<u>撞擊</u>而死亡。

(A) miracle[3] 〔ˈmɪrəkḷ〕 *n.* 奇蹟

(B) **impact**[4] (ˈɪmpækt) *n.* 影響；衝擊；撞擊 (力)
on impact 由於撞擊；相撞時
(C) harmony[4] (ˈhɑrmənɪ) *n.* 和諧
(D) liberty[3] (ˈlɪbɚtɪ) *n.* 自由   the Statue of Liberty 自由女神像
*floor[1] (flor) *n.* 樓層

9. (**C**) If Oscar is busy, why don't you ask George <u>instead</u>?
如果奧斯卡在忙，你何不<u>改</u>問喬治？
(A) however[2] (haʊˈɛvɚ) *adv.* 然而
(B) moreover[4] (morˈovɚ) *adv.* 此外
(C) **instead**[3] (ɪnˈstɛd) *adv.* 作為代替；改換
(D) namely[4] (ˈnemlɪ) *adv.* 也就是

10. (**B**) The country has obtained the technology to <u>launch</u> a nuclear missile.
這個國家已經獲得了<u>發射</u>核子飛彈的科技。
(A) lean[4] (lin) *v.* 倚靠 < *against* >；傾斜
(B) **launch**[4] (lɔntʃ) *v.* 發射；發動
(C) kneel[3] (nil) *v.* 跪下 【比較】knee[1] (ni) *n.* 膝蓋
(D) motivate[4] (ˈmotə,vet) *v.* 激勵；使有動機
*obtain[4] (əbˈten) *v.* 獲得   technology[3] (tɛkˈnɑlədʒɪ) *n.* 科技
nuclear[4] (ˈnjuklɪr) *adj.* 核子的   missile[3] (ˈmɪsḷ) *n.* 飛彈

11. (**D**) When Freddie gets depressed, he tends to <u>isolate</u> himself from his friends and family.
當佛萊迪覺得沮喪時，往往會<u>把</u>自己和家人及朋友<u>隔離</u>。
(A) murmur[4] (ˈmɝmɚ) *v.* 喃喃自語；低聲說
(B) measure[2,4] (ˈmɛʒɚ) *v.* 測量   *n.* 措施
(C) investigate[3] (ɪnˈvɛstə,get) *v.* 調查
(D) **isolate**[4] (ˈaɪsḷ,et) *v.* 使隔離
*depressed[4] (dɪˈprɛst) *adj.* 沮喪的   *tend to V.* 易於…；傾向於…

12. (**C**) The wife of an Italian nobleman was Da Vinci's <u>inspiration</u> for the *Mona Lisa*.
一名義大利貴族的妻子給了達文西靈感，畫出《蒙娜麗莎》。

(A) interaction [4] 〔͵ɪntə·ˈækʃən 〕 *n.* 相互作用

(B) intention [4] 〔 ɪnˈtɛnʃən 〕 *n.* 意圖

(C) *inspiration* [4] 〔͵ɪnspəˈreʃən 〕 *n.* 靈感；鼓舞

(D) interruption [4] 〔͵ɪntəˈrʌpʃən 〕 *n.* 打斷

*Italian 〔 ɪˈtæljən 〕 *adj.* 義大利的　　nobleman 〔ˈnobḷmən 〕 *n.* 貴族
Da Vinci 〔 də ˈvɪntʃɪ 〕 *n.* 達文西【1452-1519，義大利的畫家、雕刻家、
建築家、科學家】　　Mona Lisa 〔ˈmonə ˈlizə 〕 *n.* 蒙娜麗莎

13. (**A**) Only <u>intimate</u> friends were invited to their wedding.
只有<u>親密的</u>朋友獲邀參加他們的婚禮。

(A) *intimate* [4] 〔ˈɪntəmɪt 〕 *adj.* 親密的

(B) magical [3] 〔ˈmædʒɪkḷ 〕 *adj.* 神奇的

(C) mature [3] 〔 məˈtʃur 〕 *adj.* 成熟的

(D) luxurious [4] 〔 lʌgˈʒurɪəs , lʌkˈʃurɪəs 〕 *adj.* 奢侈的；豪華的

*wedding [1] 〔ˈwɛdɪŋ 〕 *n.* 婚禮

14. (**A**) It became clear that Mr. Irving needed <u>immediate</u> treatment for his
injuries. 很顯然歐文先生的傷需要<u>立刻</u>治療。

(A) *immediate* [3] 〔 ɪˈmidɪɪt 〕 *adj.* 立刻的

(B) nervous [3] 〔ˈnɝvəs 〕 *adj.* 緊張的

(C) identical [4] 〔 aɪˈdɛntɪkḷ 〕 *adj.* 完全相同的

(D) humble [2] 〔ˈhʌmbḷ 〕 *adj.* 謙虛的

*clear [1] 〔 klɪr 〕 *adj.* 清楚的；明顯的　　Irving 〔ˈɝvɪŋ 〕 *n.* 歐文
treatment [5] 〔ˈtritmənt 〕 *n.* 治療　　injury [3] 〔ˈɪndʒərɪ 〕 *n.* 傷害；損傷

15. (**D**) Dad was on his way home and Mom was in the kitchen. <u>Meanwhile</u>,
my sister was chatting on her phone.
爸爸正在回家的路上，而媽媽在廚房。<u>同時</u>，我姊姊正在打電話聊天。

(A) hardly [2] 〔ˈhɑrdlɪ 〕 *adv.* 幾乎不

(B) lately [4] 〔ˈletlɪ 〕 *adv.* 最近 (= *recently* [2])

(C) mostly [4] 〔ˈmostlɪ 〕 *adv.* 大多 (= *largely* [4])

(D) *meanwhile* [3] 〔ˈmin͵hwaɪl 〕 *adv.* 同時 (= *at the same time*)

*on one's *way home* 在某人回家的路上　　chat [3] 〔 tʃæt 〕 *v.* 聊天

TEST 19

【命題範圍：「高中生必背 4500 字」
p.151-160，noisy～passive】

Directions: *Choose the one word that best completes the sentence.*

1. Don't listen to him. Most of what he says is complete _____.

    (A) obedience   (B) parade

    (C) objection   (D) nonsense   (　　)

2. He _____ a slip of paper on his desk that hadn't been there the day before.

    (A) objected   (B) obeyed

    (C) occurred   (D) noticed   (　　)

3. She had _____ errands to run before heading to the airport.

    (A) numerous   (B) nuclear

    (C) obvious   (D) obedient   (　　)

4. She asked for my _____ opinion of her painting.

    (A) occasional   (B) noisy

    (C) objective   (D) opposite   (　　)

5. A license to carry a firearm is very difficult to _____.

    (A) occupy   (B) obtain

    (C) participate   (D) observe   (　　)

6. In his _____ as a salesman, constant travel is a part of the job.

    (A) occupation   (B) obstacle

    (C) participation   (D) offense   (　　)

7. The novel was censored for its use of _____ racial stereotypes.

    (A) odd   (B) oral

    (C) offensive   (D) outstanding   (　　)

8. We are not overly _____ about the future of the company.

   (A) ordinary   (B) outdoor
   (C) original   (D) optimistic   ( )

9. Her family's _____ can be traced back to 16th century England.

   (A) orbits   (B) origins
   (C) orders   (D) organs   ( )

10. He had to _____ many obstacles in his quest to break the record.

    (A) offend   (B) offer
    (C) omit   (D) overcome   ( )

11. The rebels sought to _____ the brutal dictatorship.

    (A) operate   (B) note
    (C) overthrow   (D) organize   ( )

12. He prefers to work at his own _____.

    (A) outcome   (B) pace
    (C) passion   (D) outline   ( )

13. Her face turned _____ when she saw a pool of blood.

    (A) outer   (B) pale
    (C) oval   (D) organic   ( )

14. The fire alarm sounded and people started to _____.

    (A) overtake   (B) owe
    (C) panic   (D) pack   ( )

15. The Indians of the remote village are considered to be _____ and unlikely to attack outsiders without reason.

    (A) passive   (B) painful
    (C) partial   (D) particular   ( )

TEST 19 詳解

1. (**D**) Don't listen to him. Most of what he says is complete <u>nonsense</u>.
別聽他的。他大部分都在<u>胡說</u>。
(A) obedience⁴〔ə'bidɪəns〕*n.* 服從（= *compliance*）
(B) parade³〔pə'red〕*n. v.* 遊行
(C) objection⁴〔əb'dʒɛkʃən〕*n.* 反對（= *opposition*）
(D) ***nonsense***⁴〔'nɑnsɛns〕*n.* 胡說（= *foolish words*）；無意義的話
*complete²〔kəm'plit〕*adj.* 完全的

2. (**D**) He <u>noticed</u> a slip of paper on his desk that hadn't been there the day
before. 他<u>注意到</u>書桌上有一條前一天沒有的紙片。
(A) object²〔əb'dʒɛkt〕*v.* 反對 < *to* >
(B) obey²〔ə'be〕*v.* 服從（= *give in*）；遵守（= *follow* = *observe*）
(C) occur²〔ə'kɝ〕*v.* 發生（= *happen*）
(D) ***notice***¹〔'notɪs〕*v.* 注意到（= *note*）
*slip²〔slɪp〕*n.* 紙片　　***the day before*** 前一天

3. (**A**) She had <u>numerous</u> errands to run before heading to the airport.
她去機場前有<u>很多</u>事要辦。
(A) ***numerous***⁴〔'njumərəs〕*adj.* 許多的（= *many*）
(B) nuclear⁴〔'njuklɪɚ〕*adj.* 核子的
(C) obvious³〔'ɑbvɪəs〕*adj.* 明顯的（= *apparent* = *evident*）
(D) obedient⁴〔ə'bidɪənt〕*adj.* 服從的（= *compliant*）
*errand⁴〔'ɛrənd〕*n.* 差事；跑腿　　***run an errand*** 辦事；跑腿
head to 動身前往　　airport¹〔'ɛr,port〕*n.* 機場

4. (**C**) She asked for my <u>objective</u> opinion of her painting.
她向我徵求關於她畫作的<u>客觀</u>意見。
(A) occasional⁴〔ə'keʒənḷ〕*adj.* 偶爾的（= *infrequent*）
(B) noisy¹〔'nɔɪzɪ〕*adj.* 吵鬧的
(C) ***objective***⁴〔əb'dʒɛktɪv〕*adj.* 客觀的（= *neutral*）
(D) opposite³〔'ɑpəzɪt〕*adj.* 相反的（= *contrary*）
***ask for** 要求；徵求　　opinion²〔ə'pɪnjən〕*n.* 意見

5. (**B**) A license to carry a firearm is very difficult to <u>obtain</u>.
攜帶槍枝的執照是很難<u>取得</u>的。

    (A) occupy[4] 〔'akjə,paɪ〕 *v.* 使忙碌；佔領 (= *take over*)

    (B) ***obtain***[4] 〔əb'ten〕 *v.* 獲得 (= *gain*)

    (C) participate[3] 〔par'tɪsə,pet〕 *v.* 參加 (= *take part*) < *in* >

    (D) observe[3] 〔əb's3v〕 *v.* 觀察；遵守 (= *obey*)

    *license[4] 〔'laɪsns〕 *n.* 許可；執照　　carry[1] 〔'kærɪ〕 *v.* 攜帶
     firearm 〔'faɪr,arm〕 *n.* 槍枝

6. (**A**) In his <u>occupation</u> as a salesman, constant travel is a part of the job.
在他擔任業務員的<u>職業</u>時，工作的一部份就是常常出差。

    (A) ***occupation***[4] 〔,akjə'peʃən〕 *n.* 職業 (= *job* = *vocation*)；佔領

    (B) obstacle[4] 〔'abstəkḷ〕 *n.* 阻礙；障礙 (= *barrier*)

    (C) participation[4] 〔pə,tɪsə'peʃən〕 *n.* 參與

    (D) offense[4] 〔ə'fɛns〕 *n.* 攻擊；生氣

    *salesman[4] 〔'selzmən〕 *n.* 銷售員；業務員
     constant[3] 〔'kanstənt〕 *adj.* 不斷的；時常的
     travel[2] 〔'trævḷ〕 *n.* 旅行

7. (**C**) The novel was censored for its use of <u>offensive</u> racial stereotypes.
這本小說受到審查，因為裡面使用了<u>冒犯性的</u>種族刻板印象。

    (A) odd[3] 〔ad〕 *adj.* 奇怪的 (= *strange*)；奇數的

    (B) oral[4] 〔'ɔrəl〕 *adj.* 口頭的 (= *spoken*)；口部的

    (C) ***offensive***[4] 〔ə'fɛnsɪv〕 *adj.* 無禮的 (= *insulting*)；冒犯的

    (D) outstanding[4] 〔'aʊt'stændɪŋ〕 *adj.* 傑出的 (= *excellent*)

    *novel[2] 〔'navḷ〕 *n.* 小說　　censor 〔'sɛnsə〕 *v.* 審查
     racial[3] 〔'reʃəl〕 *adj.* 種族的
     stereotype[5] 〔'stɛrɪə,taɪp〕 *n.* 刻板印象

8. (**D**) We are not overly <u>optimistic</u> about the future of the company.
我們對於這家公司的未來不太<u>樂觀</u>。

    (A) ordinary[2] 〔'ɔrdṇ,ɛrɪ〕 *adj.* 普通的 (= *usual*)；平淡的

    (B) outdoor[3] 〔'aʊt,dor〕 *adj.* 戶外的 (= *open-air*)

    (C) original[3] 〔ə'rɪdʒənḷ〕 *adj.* 最初的 (= *first*)；原本的

    (D) ***optimistic***[3] 〔,aptə'mɪstɪk〕 *adj.* 樂觀的 (= *hopeful*)

＊overly¹〔ˋovəlɪ〕*adv.* 過度地；非常

company²〔ˋkʌmpənɪ〕*n.* 公司

9. (**B**) Her family's <u>origins</u> can be traced back to 16th century England.
她家族的<u>起源</u>可以追溯到十六世紀的英國。

(A) orbit⁴〔ˋɔrbɪt〕*n.* 軌道；勢力範圍

(B) ***origin***³〔ˋɔrədʒɪn〕*n.* 起源（= *beginning*）；出身

(C) order¹〔ˋɔrdə〕*n.* 命令（= *command*）；順序

(D) organ²〔ˋɔrgən〕*n.* 器官

＊***be traced back to***　追溯到（= *go back to*）

century²〔ˋsɛntʃərɪ〕*n.* 一世紀

10. (**D**) He had to <u>overcome</u> many obstacles in his quest to break the record.
追求破紀錄的過程中，他必須<u>克服</u>許多障礙。

(A) offend⁴〔əˋfɛnd〕*v.* 得罪；觸怒（= *irritate*）

(B) offer²〔ˋɔfə〕*v.* 提供（= *give*）；提議

(C) omit²〔oˋmɪt〕*v.* 遺漏（= *leave out*）

(D) ***overcome***⁴〔͵ovəˋkʌm〕*v.* 克服（= *beat*）；戰勝（= *defeat*）

＊obstacle⁴〔ˋabstəkḷ〕*n.* 障礙　　quest⁵〔kwɛst〕*n.* 追求

break the record　破紀錄

11. (**C**) The rebels sought to <u>overthrow</u> the brutal dictatorship.
叛亂份子試圖<u>推翻</u>殘忍的獨裁制度。

(A) operate²〔ˋapə͵ret〕*v.* 操作（= *run*）；動手術（= *perform surgery*）

(B) note¹〔not〕*v.* 注意　　*n.* 筆記

(C) ***overthrow***⁴〔͵ovəˋθro〕*v.* 打翻；推翻（= *overturn*）

(D) organize²〔ˋɔrgən͵aɪz〕*v.* 組織（= *form*）；安排；籌辦

＊rebel⁴〔ˋrɛbḷ〕*n.* 叛徒；反抗者

sought³〔sɔt〕*v.* 試圖；嘗試【seek 的過去式】

brutal⁴〔ˋbrutḷ〕*adj.* 殘忍的；嚴厲的

dictatorship〔dɪkˋtetə͵ʃɪp〕*n.* 獨裁；專制

12. (**B**) He prefers to work at his own <u>pace</u>.
他偏好用自己的<u>步調</u>工作。

(A) outcome⁴〔ˋaʊt͵kʌm〕*n.* 結果（= *result*）

(B) ***pace*** ⁴ 〔 pes 〕 *n.* 步調 (= *speed of movement*)

(C) passion ³ 〔ˈpæʃən 〕 *n.* 熱情 (= *affection*)

(D) outline ³ 〔ˈaʊtˌlaɪn 〕 *n.* 輪廓；大綱 (= *summary*)

*prefer ² 〔 prɪˈfɝ 〕 *v.* 偏好

13. (**B**) Her face turned <u>pale</u> when she saw a pool of blood.
    當她看到一灘血，她臉色變得<u>蒼白</u>。

    (A) outer ³ 〔ˈaʊtɚ 〕 *adj.* 外部的 (= *external*)

    (B) ***pale*** ³ 〔 pel 〕 *adj.* 蒼白的

    (C) oval ⁴ 〔ˈovḷ 〕 *adj.* 橢圓形的 (= *egg-shaped*)

    (D) organic ⁴ 〔 ɔrˈgænɪk 〕 *adj.* 有機的；天然的 (= *natural*)

    *turn ¹ 〔 tɝn 〕 *v.* 變得   pool ¹ 〔 pul 〕 *n.* 一灘液體
    blood ¹ 〔 blʌd 〕 *n.* 血

14. (**C**) The fire alarm sounded and people started to <u>panic</u>.
    消防警報器響起，人們開始感到<u>恐慌</u>。

    (A) overtake ⁴ 〔ˌovɚˈtek 〕 *v.* 趕上 (= *catch up with*)；超越；超車

    (B) owe ³ 〔 o 〕 *v.* 欠 (= *be in debt to*)

    (C) ***panic*** ³ 〔ˈpænɪk 〕 *v.* 恐慌

    (D) pack ² 〔 pæk 〕 *v.* 打包；包裝

    ****fire alarm*** 消防警報器   sound ¹ 〔 saʊnd 〕 *v.* 響；鳴響

15. (**A**) The Indians of the remote village are considered to be <u>passive</u> and
    unlikely to attack outsiders without reason.
    偏遠村莊的印地安人被認為是很<u>被動的</u>，且不可能平白無故攻擊外人。

    (A) ***passive*** ⁴ 〔ˈpæsɪv 〕 *adj.* 被動的 (= *inactive*)；消極的

    (B) painful ² 〔ˈpenfəl 〕 *adj.* 疼痛的 (= *agonizing*)；痛苦的

    (C) partial ⁴ 〔ˈpɑrʃəl 〕 *adj.* 部分的；偏袒的

    (D) particular ² 〔 pɚˈtɪkjəlɚ 〕 *adj.* 特別的 (= *special*)

    *Indian 〔ˈɪndɪən 〕 *n.* 美國印地安人
    remote ³ 〔 rɪˈmot 〕 *adj.* 遙遠的；偏僻的   village ² 〔ˈvɪlɪdʒ 〕 *n.* 村莊
    consider ² 〔 kənˈsɪdɚ 〕 *v.* 認為   unlikely ¹ 〔 ʌnˈlaɪklɪ 〕 *adj.* 不可能的
    attack ² 〔 əˈtæk 〕 *v.* 攻擊   outsider ⁵ 〔ˌaʊtˈsaɪdɚ 〕 *n.* 外人
    without reason 毫無理由；平白無故

TEST 20

【命題範圍：「高中生必背4500字」
p.161-170，passport～practical】

Directions: Choose the one word that best completes the sentence.

1. All four robberies followed the same _____.
   (A) pattern   (B) pioneer
   (C) password   (D) pirate   (　)

2. She _____ for a moment before saying her name.
   (A) patted   (B) paused
   (C) peeled   (D) paved   (　)

3. They did wrong and will have to pay the _____.
   (A) patience   (B) pavement
   (C) penalty   (D) payment   (　)

4. He has a warm smile and pleasing _____.
   (A) perfection   (B) pebble
   (C) personality   (D) percentage   (　)

5. They were _____ about their chances of winning the lottery.
   (A) pessimistic   (B) percent
   (C) permanent   (D) personal   (　)

6. After a great deal of nagging, the woman finally _____ her husband to replace the broken window.
   (A) performed   (B) permitted
   (C) peeped   (D) persuaded   (　)

7. Less than a century ago, carrier _____ were used to relay messages across great distances.
   (A) penguins   (B) pigeons
   (C) ponies   (D) poultries   (　)

8. The white, puffy clouds look like floating _____.

   (A) pillows   (B) periods

   (C) petals   (D) pedals   (   )

9. The desktop was covered by a thin layer of fine white _____.

   (A) power   (B) pottery

   (C) powder   (D) postage   (   )

10. The government has banned the sale and use of _____ bags.

   (A) plastic   (B) powerful

   (C) positive   (D) practical   (   )

11. Bananas are _____ in this part of the world.

   (A) philosophical   (B) plentiful

   (C) physical   (D) persuasive   (   )

12. A large _____ of his grandfather hangs in the library.

   (A) platform   (B) portrait

   (C) phenomenon   (D) perfume   (   )

13. Since he's looking for a new job, Sean should probably _____ his resume and bring it up to date.

   (A) postpone   (B) pollute

   (C) polish   (D) portray   (   )

14. The concert promoter brought in dozens of _____ restrooms for attendees of the music festival.

   (A) pleasant   (B) poisonous

   (C) political   (D) portable   (   )

15. Stephen Hawking is still the most famous _____ in the world.

   (A) pilgrim   (B) plumber

   (C) physician   (D) physicist   (   )

TEST 20 詳解

1. (**A**) All four robberies followed the same <u>pattern</u>.
   這四起搶案都遵循一樣的<u>模式</u>。
   (A) ***pattern*** [2] 〔'pætən 〕 *n.* 模式 (= *order*)；圖案；典範
   (B) pioneer [4] 〔ˌpaɪə'nɪr 〕 *n.* 先驅 (= *starter*)；先鋒 (= *forerunner*)
   (C) password [3] 〔'pæsˌwɝd 〕 *n.* 密碼
   (D) pirate [4] 〔'paɪrət 〕 *n.* 海盜
   *robbery [3] 〔'rɑbərɪ 〕 *n.* 搶劫；搶案　　follow [1] 〔'falo 〕 *v.* 遵循

2. (**B**) She <u>paused</u> for a moment before saying her name.
   她在說出她的名字前<u>停頓</u>了一下。
   (A) pat [2] 〔 pæt 〕 *v.* 輕拍 (= *tap*)
   (B) ***pause*** [3] 〔 pɔz 〕 *v.* 暫停
   (C) peel [3] 〔 pil 〕 *v.* 剝 (皮) (= *skin*)；剝；脫落
   (D) pave [3] 〔 pev 〕 *v.* 鋪 (路)
   *moment [1] 〔'momənt 〕 *n.* 瞬間；一會兒

3. (**C**) They did wrong and will have to pay the <u>penalty</u>.
   他們做錯了事，而將得付<u>罰款</u>。
   (A) patience [3] 〔'peʃəns 〕 *n.* 耐心
   (B) pavement [3] 〔'pevmənt 〕 *n.* 人行道 (= *sidewalk*)；路面
   (C) ***penalty*** [4] 〔'pɛnḷtɪ 〕 *n.* 處罰；罰款
   (D) payment [1] 〔'pemənt 〕 *n.* 付款 (= *expense*)
   *do wrong 做錯事

4. (**C**) He has a warm smile and pleasing <u>personality</u>.
   他的微笑很溫暖，<u>個性</u>討人喜歡。
   (A) perfection [4] 〔 pə'fɛkʃən 〕 *n.* 完美 (= *flawlessness*)
   (B) pebble [4] 〔'pɛbḷ 〕 *n.* 小圓石；鵝卵石
   (C) ***personality*** [3] 〔ˌpɝsṇ'ælətɪ 〕 *n.* 個性 (= *individuality* = *character*)
   (D) percentage [4] 〔 pə'sɛntɪdʒ 〕 *n.* 百分比
   *smile [1] 〔 smaɪl 〕 *n.* 微笑　　pleasing [1] 〔'plizɪŋ 〕 *adj.* 令人愉快的

5. (**A**) They were <u>pessimistic</u> about their chances of winning the lottery.
他們對於贏得樂透的機會感到<u>悲觀</u>。

    (A) ***pessimistic***[4] 〔͵pɛsə'mɪstɪk 〕 *adj.* 悲觀的（= *gloomy*）

    (B) percent[4] 〔 pə'sɛnt 〕 *adj.* 百分之⋯的

    (C) permanent[4] 〔'pɝmənənt 〕 *adj.* 永久的（= *eternal*）

    (D) personal[2] 〔'pɝsn̩l 〕 *adj.* 個人的（= *individual*）

    * chance[1] 〔 tʃæns 〕 *n.* 機會   lottery[5] 〔'lɑtərɪ 〕 *n.* 樂透；抽獎

6. (**D**) After a great deal of nagging, the woman finally <u>persuaded</u> her husband to replace the broken window.
嘮叨許久後，女士終於<u>說服</u>她的丈夫去替換破裂的窗戶。

    (A) perform[3] 〔 pə'fɔrm 〕 *v.* 表演（= *appear on stage*）；執行

    (B) permit[3] 〔 pə'mɪt 〕 *v.* 允許（= *allow*）

    (C) peep[3] 〔 pip 〕 *v.* 偷窺

    (D) ***persuade***[3] 〔 pə'swed 〕 *v.* 說服（= *convince*）

    * ***a great deal of*** 大量的；許多   nag[5] 〔 næg 〕 *v.* 嘮叨不休；責罵
    husband[1] 〔'hʌzbənd 〕 *n.* 丈夫   replace[3] 〔 rɪ'ples 〕 *v.* 替換
    broken[4] 〔'brokən 〕 *adj.* 破裂的

7. (**B**) Less than a century ago, carrier <u>pigeons</u> were used to relay messages across great distances.
不到一百年前，信<u>鴿</u>被用來轉送遠距離的書信。

    (A) penguin[2] 〔'pɛngwɪn 〕 *n.* 企鵝

    (B) ***pigeon***[2] 〔'pɪdʒɪn 〕 *n.* 鴿子（= *dove*）

    (C) pony[3] 〔'ponɪ 〕 *n.* 小馬（= *little horse*）

    (D) poultry[4] 〔'poltrɪ 〕 *n.* 家禽（= *domesticated birds*）

    * century[2] 〔'sɛntʃərɪ 〕 *n.* 一世紀   carrier[4] 〔'kærɪɚ 〕 *n.* 郵差；信差
    relay[6] 〔 rɪ'le 〕 *v.* 轉送   message[2] 〔'mɛsɪdʒ 〕 *n.* 訊息；書信
    distance[2] 〔'dɪstəns 〕 *n.* 距離

8. (**A**) The white, puffy clouds look like floating <u>pillows</u>.
朵朵白色的雲看起來像是漂浮的<u>枕頭</u>。

    (A) ***pillow***[2] 〔'pɪlo 〕 *n.* 枕頭（= *cushion*）

    (B) period[2] 〔'pɪrɪəd 〕 *n.* 期間；句點

    (C) petal[4] 〔'pɛtl̩ 〕 *n.* 花瓣

(D) pedal⁴〔'pɛdl̩〕*n.* 踏板；腳踏板

*puffy⁵〔'pʌfɪ〕*adj.* 膨脹的；白色棉團狀的　　float³〔flot〕*v.* 漂浮

9. (**C**) The desktop was covered by a thin layer of fine white <u>powder</u>.
桌面覆蓋著一層薄薄的白色細<u>粉</u>。

(A) power¹〔'pauɚ〕*n.* 力量（= *ability*）

(B) pottery³〔'patərɪ〕*n.* 陶器（= *ceramic*）；陶藝

(C) ***powder***³〔'paudɚ〕*n.* 粉末

(D) postage³〔'postɪdʒ〕*n.* 郵資（= *postal fees*）

*desktop〔'dɛsk,tap〕*n.* 桌子表面　　cover¹〔'kʌvɚ〕*v.* 覆蓋
thin²〔θɪn〕*adj.* 薄的　　layer⁵〔'leɚ〕*n.* 一層

10. (**A**) The government has banned the sale and use of <u>plastic</u> bags.
政府已經禁<u>止</u>塑膠袋的販賣和使用。

(A) ***plastic***³〔'plæstɪk〕*adj.* 塑膠的

(B) powerful²〔'pauɚfəl〕*adj.* 強而有力的（= *strong*）

(C) postive²〔'pazətɪv〕*adj.* 肯定的（= *certain*）；樂觀的（= *optimistic*）

(D) practical³〔'præktɪkl̩〕*adj.* 實際的（= *realistic*）

*government²〔'gʌvənmənt〕*n.* 政府　　ban⁵〔bæn〕*v.* 禁止
sale¹〔sel〕*n.* 銷售；販賣　　use¹〔jus〕*n.* 使用

11. (**B**) Bananas are <u>plentiful</u> in this part of the world.
香蕉在這裡<u>很豐富</u>。

(A) philosophical⁴〔,fɪlə'safɪkl̩〕*adj.* 哲學的

(B) ***plentiful***⁴〔'plɛntəfəl〕*adj.* 豐富的（= *abundant*）

(C) physical⁴〔'fɪzɪkl̩〕*adj.* 身體的

(D) persuasive⁴〔pɚ'swesɪv〕*adj.* 有說服力的（= *convincing*）

*banana¹〔bə'nænə〕*n.* 香蕉
this part of the world 這裡（= *where we live*）

12. (**B**) A large <u>portrait</u> of his grandfather hangs in the library.
他祖父一個大大的<u>肖像畫</u>掛在圖書館裡。

(A) platform²〔'plæt,fɔrm〕*n.* 月台

(B) ***portrait***³〔'portret〕*n.* 肖像（畫）（= *image*）

(C) phenomenon⁴〔fə'namə,nan〕*n.* 現象（= *happening*）

(D) perfume [4] (pəˈfjum) *n.* 香水 (= *fragrance*)

*hang [2] (hæŋ) *v.* 掛

13. (C) Since he's looking for a new job, Sean should probably <u>polish</u> his resume and bring it up to date.

因爲西恩正在找新工作，他可能應該會<u>潤飾</u>並更新他的履歷。

(A) postpone [3] (postˈpon) *v.* 延期 (= *delay* = *put off*)；延後

(B) pollute [3] (pəˈlut) *v.* 污染 (= *contaminate*)

(C) ***polish*** [4] (ˈpɑlɪʃ) *v.* 擦亮 (= *shine*)；加強；潤飾

(D) portray [4] (porˈtre) *v.* 描繪；描寫

* ***look for*** 尋找   probably [3] (ˈprɑbəblɪ) *adv.* 可能

resume [5] (ˈrɛzuˌme) *n.* 履歷   ***bring*** sth. ***up to date*** 更新

14. (D) The concert promoter brought in dozens of <u>portable</u> restrooms for attendees of the music festival.

演唱會的承辦人員引入許多<u>流動</u>廁所給音樂季在場的人使用。

(A) pleasant [2] (ˈplɛzn̩t) *adj.* 令人愉快的 (= *agreeable*)

(B) poisonous [4] (ˈpɔɪznəs) *adj.* 有毒的 (= *toxic*)

(C) political [3] (pəˈlɪtɪkl̩) *adj.* 政治的

(D) ***portable*** [4] (ˈportəbl̩) *adj.* 手提的；可搬運的

portable restroom 流動廁所

*concert [3] (ˈkɑnsɚt) *n.* 音樂會；演唱會

promoter [4] (prəˈmotɚ) *n.* 承辦者   ***dozens of*** 很多的

restroom [2] (ˈrɛstˌrum) *n.* 公共廁所；洗手間

attendee [2] (ətɛnˈdi) *n.* 參加者   festival [2] (ˈfɛstəvl̩) *n.* 節慶；表演

15. (D) Stephen Hawking is still the most famous <u>physicist</u> in the world.

史蒂芬・霍金仍然是世界上最知名的<u>物理學家</u>。

(A) pilgrim [4] (ˈpɪlgrɪm) *n.* 朝聖者 (= *palmer*)

(B) plumber [3] (ˈplʌmɚ) *n.* 水管工人 (= *pipe fitter*)

(C) physician [4] (fəˈzɪʃən) *n.* 內科醫生

(D) ***physicist*** [4] (ˈfɪzəsɪst) *n.* 物理學家

*Stephen Hawking (ˈstivən ˈhɔkɪŋ) *n.* 史蒂芬・霍金【英國著名物理學家】

famous [2] (ˈfeməs) *adj.* 有名的

TEST 21

【命題範圍：「高中生必背 4500 字」
p.171-180，practice～raise】

Directions: *Choose the one word that best completes the sentence.*

1. The outcome of the game is impossible to _____.
   (A) practice　　　　　(B) pray
   (C) predict　　　　　(D) prefer　　　　　(　　)

2. We must work hard to _____ our natural resources.
   (A) preserve　　　　　(B) prepare
   (C) praise　　　　　(D) pretend　　　　　(　　)

3. When did _____ life forms first appear on earth?
   (A) prime　　　　　(B) primary
   (C) primitive　　　　　(D) pregnant　　　　　(　　)

4. His medical _____ will not be covered by insurance.
   (A) preparation　　　　　(B) procedure
   (C) pressure　　　　　(D) presentation　　　　　(　　)

5. They have made considerable _____ in cleaning up the river.
   (A) presence　　　　　(B) principle
   (C) progress　　　　　(D) privilege　　　　　(　　)

6. I've never been to this restaurant but the menu looks _____.
   (A) precise　　　　　(B) previous
   (C) precious　　　　　(D) promising　　　　　(　　)

7. They were hoping for a _____ reply from the agency but still haven't heard anything.
   (A) prompt　　　　　(B) principal
   (C) private　　　　　(D) probable　　　　　(　　)

8. He _____ that we open the store on Saturdays.
   (A) produced
   (B) promised
   (C) proposed
   (D) presented ( )

9. She has developed a _____ consulting business.
   (A) psychological
   (B) proud
   (C) prosperous
   (D) purple ( )

10. The boy was told to sit down, and for once he didn't _____.
    (A) protest
    (B) promote
    (C) prosper
    (D) pronounce ( )

11. She was _____ by his reaction to the joke.
    (A) protected
    (B) provided
    (C) puzzled
    (D) quoted ( )

12. The pop star is hungry for _____ and will do anything to stay in the headlines.
    (A) production
    (B) publicity
    (C) profession
    (D) publication ( )

13. Some retailers will give you a discount for buying a large _____ of a particular item.
    (A) prosperity
    (B) property
    (C) quantity
    (D) quality ( )

14. Direct _____ from academic sources will help support the argument of your thesis.
    (A) proverbs
    (B) quotations
    (C) proposals
    (D) protections ( )

15. Due to new tax laws, the shop was forced to _____ its prices on imported goods.
    (A) pursue
    (B) punch
    (C) raise
    (D) punish ( )

TEST 21 詳解

1. (**C**) The outcome of the game is impossible to <u>predict</u>.
比賽的結果是不可能<u>預測</u>到的。

    (A) practice [1] (ˈpræktɪs) *v., n.* 練習

    (B) pray [2] (pre) *v.* 祈禱

    (C) ***predict*** [4] (prɪˈdɪkt) *v.* 預測

    (D) prefer [2] (prɪˈfɝ) *v.* 比較喜歡

    *outcome [4] (ˈaʊtˌkʌm) *n.* 結果

2. (**A**) We must work hard to <u>preserve</u> our natural resources.
我們必須努力<u>保存</u>我們的天然資源。

    (A) ***preserve*** [4] (prɪˈzɝv) *v.* 保存

    (B) prepare [1] (prɪˈpɛr) *v.* 準備

    (C) praise [2] (prez) *v.* 稱讚

    (D) pretend [3] (prɪˈtɛnd) *v.* 假裝

    *natural [2] (ˈnætʃərəl) *adj.* 天然的   resource [3] (rɪˈsors) *n.* 資源

3. (**C**) When did <u>primitive</u> life forms first appear on earth?
<u>原始的</u>生物最早出現在地球上是什麼時候呢？

    (A) prime [4] (praɪm) *adj.* 主要的；上等的

    (B) primary [3] (ˈpraɪˌmɛrɪ) *adj.* 主要的；基本的

    (C) ***primitive*** [4] (ˈprɪmətɪv) *adj.* 原始的

    (D) pregnant [4] (ˈprɛgnənt) *adj.* 懷孕的

    life form 生命型態；生物   appear [1] (əˈpɪr) *v.* 出現

4. (**B**) His medical <u>procedure</u> will not be covered by insurance.
他的醫療<u>程序</u>並沒有涵蓋在保險裡。

    (A) preparation [3] (ˌprɛpəˈreʃən) *n.* 準備

    (B) ***procedure*** [4] (prəˈsidʒɚ) *n.* 程序

    (C) pressure [3] (ˈprɛʃɚ) *n.* 壓力

    (D) presentation [4] (ˌprɛznˈteʃən) *n.* 報告；演出

    *medical [3] (ˈmɛdɪkl̩) *adj.* 醫學的；醫療的

    cover [1] (ˈkʌvɚ) *v.* 涵蓋   insurance [4] (ɪnˈʃʊrəns) *n.* 保險

5. (**C**) They have made considerable <u>progress</u> in cleaning up the river.
他們清理這條河已經有了相當大的<u>進步</u>。
　　(A) presence[2]〔'prɛzns 〕 *n.* 出席
　　(B) principle[2] 〔'prɪnsəpl 〕 *n.* 原則
　　(C) ***progress***[2] 〔'prɑgrɛs 〕 *n.* 進步
　　(D) privilege[4] 〔'prɪvl̩ɪdʒ 〕 *n.* 特權
　　*considerable[3] 〔 kən'sɪdərəbl 〕 *adj.* 相當大的　　***clean up*** 清理

6. (**D**) I've never been to this restaurant but the menu looks <u>promising</u>.
我從來沒有去過這家餐廳，但是菜單看起來<u>很不錯</u>。
　　(A) precise[4] 〔 prɪ'saɪs 〕 *adj.* 精確的
　　(B) previous[3] 〔'priviəs 〕 *adj.* 先前的；以前的
　　(C) precious[3] 〔'prɛʃəs 〕 *adj.* 珍貴的
　　(D) ***promising***[4] 〔'prɑmɪsɪŋ 〕 *adj.* 有希望的；有前途的
　　*menu[2] 〔'mɛnju 〕 *n.* 菜單

7. (**A**) They were hoping for a <u>prompt</u> reply from the agency but still haven't heard anything.
他們希望<u>迅速</u>得到代理商的回應，但是還沒聽到任何消息。
　　(A) ***prompt***[4] 〔 prɑmpt 〕 *adj.* 迅速的；敏捷的
　　(B) principal[2] 〔'prɪnsəpl 〕 *adj.* 主要的　　*n.* 校長
　　(C) private[2] 〔'praɪvɪt 〕 *adj.* 私人的
　　(D) probable[3] 〔'prɑbəbl 〕 *adj.* 可能的
　　*reply[2] 〔 rɪ'plaɪ 〕 *n., v.* 回答
　　 agency[4] 〔'edʒənsɪ 〕 *n.* 代辦處；代理商

8. (**C**) He <u>proposed</u> that we open the store on Saturdays.
他<u>提議</u>我們每週六開店。
　　(A) produce[2] 〔 prə'djus 〕 *v.* 生產；製造
　　(B) promise[2] 〔'prɑmɪs 〕 *v., n.* 保證；答應；承諾
　　(C) ***propose***[2] 〔 prə'poz 〕 *v.* 提議；求婚
　　(D) present[2] 〔 prɪ'zɛnt 〕 *v.* 展示；呈現

9. (**C**) She has developed a <u>prosperous</u> consulting business.
　　她的諮商事業發展得非常<u>興盛</u>。

　　(A) psychological [4] ﹝͵saɪkə'lɑdʒɪkḷ﹞ *adj.* 心理的

　　(B) proud [2] ﹝praʊd﹞ *adj.* 驕傲的；自豪的

　　(C) ***prosperous*** [4] ﹝'prɑspərəs﹞ *adj.* 繁榮的；興盛的

　　(D) purple [1] ﹝'pɝpḷ﹞ *adj.* 紫色的

　　＊develop [2] ﹝dɪ'vɛləp﹞ *v.* 發展　　consult [4] ﹝kən'sʌlt﹞ *v.* 請教；諮詢

10. (**A**) The boy was told to sit down, and for once he didn't <u>protest</u>.
　　男孩被叫坐下，這一次他沒有<u>抗議</u>。

　　(A) ***protest*** [4] ﹝prə'tɛst﹞ *v.* 抗議　﹝'protɛst﹞ *n.* 抗議

　　(B) promote [3] ﹝prə'mot﹞ *v.* 升遷；提倡；促銷

　　(C) prosper [4] ﹝'prɑspɚ﹞ *v.* 繁榮；興盛

　　(D) pronounce [2] ﹝prə'naʊns﹞ *v.* 發音

　　＊***for once*** 至少一次；這一次

11. (**C**) She was <u>puzzled</u> by his reaction to the joke.
　　他對這個笑話的反應<u>使</u>她很<u>困惑</u>。

　　(A) protect [2] ﹝prə'tɛkt﹞ *v.* 保護

　　(B) provide [2] ﹝prə'vaɪd﹞ *v.* 提供

　　(C) ***puzzle*** [2] ﹝'pʌzḷ﹞ *v.* 使困惑

　　(D) quote [3] ﹝kwot﹞ *v.* 引用

　　＊reaction [3] ﹝rɪ'ækʃən﹞ *n.* 反應　　joke [1] ﹝dʒok﹞ *n.* 玩笑

12. (**B**) The pop star is hungry for <u>publicity</u> and will do anything to stay in the headlines.
　　這位流行樂的明星渴望<u>出名</u>，他會盡一切努力持續上新聞標題。

　　(A) production [4] ﹝prə'dʌkʃən﹞ *n.* 生產

　　(B) ***publicity*** [4] ﹝pʌb'lɪsətɪ﹞ *n.* 出名；知名度

　　(C) profession [4] ﹝prə'fɛʃən﹞ *n.* 職業

　　(D) publication [4] ﹝͵pʌblɪ'keʃən﹞ *n.* 出版（品）

　　＊pop [3] ﹝pɑp﹞ *adj.* 流行的　　***be hungry for*** 渴望
　　headline [3] ﹝'hɛd͵laɪn﹞ *n.* （新聞報導的）標題

13. (**C**) Some retailers will give you a discount for buying a large <u>quantity</u> of a particular item.

　　　某些零售商對於你大量購買某項商品會給你折扣。

　　　(A) prosperity⁴〔prɑsˈpɛrətɪ〕*n.* 繁榮

　　　(B) property³〔ˈprɑpətɪ〕*n.* 財產；特性

　　　(C) *quantity*²〔ˈkwɑntətɪ〕*n.* 量　　*a large quantity of* 大量的

　　　(D) quality²〔ˈkwɑlətɪ〕*n.* 品質；特質

　　　＊retailer⁶〔rɪˈtelə〕*n.* 零售商　　discount³〔ˈdɪskaʊnt〕*n.* 折扣

　　　particular²〔pəˈtɪkjələ〕*adj.* 特別的；特定的

　　　item²〔ˈaɪtəm〕*n.* 項目；物品

14. (**B**) Direct <u>quotations</u> from academic sources will help support the argument of your thesis.

　　　直接引用學術來源有助於支持你論文中的論點。

　　　(A) proverb⁴〔ˈprɑvɝb〕*n.* 諺語；格言

　　　(B) *quotation*⁴〔kwoˈteʃən〕*n.* 引用的文句

　　　(C) proposal³〔prəˈpozl̩〕*n.* 提議；求婚

　　　(D) protection³〔prəˈtɛkʃən〕*n.* 保護

　　　＊direct¹〔dəˈrɛkt〕*adj.* 直接的

　　　academic⁴〔ˌækəˈdɛmɪk〕*adj.* 學術的

　　　source²〔sors〕*n.* 來源　　support²〔səˈport〕*v.* 支持

　　　argument²〔ˈɑrgjəmənt〕*n.* 爭論；論點

　　　thesis〔ˈθisɪs〕*n.* 論文

15. (**C**) Due to new tax laws, the shop was forced to <u>raise</u> its prices on imported goods.

　　　由於新的稅法，這家商店被迫提高進口商品的售價。

　　　(A) pursue³〔pəˈsu〕*v.* 追求

　　　(B) punch³〔pʌntʃ〕*v.* 用拳頭打

　　　(C) *raise*¹〔rez〕*v.* 提高；舉起；養育

　　　(D) punish²〔ˈpʌnɪʃ〕*v.* 處罰

　　　＊*due to* 因為　　tax³〔tæks〕*n.* 稅　　force¹〔fors〕*v.* 強迫

　　　imported³〔ɪmˈportɪd〕*adj.* 進口的　　goods⁴〔gʊdz〕*n. pl.* 商品

TEST 22

【命題範圍：「高中生必背 4500 字」
p.181-190，raisin～retain】

Directions: *Choose the one word that best completes the sentence.*

1. The politician said he did not _____ meeting with a prostitute.
   (A) rebel
   (B) recite
   (C) recall
   (D) react （　）

2. The _____ time from this type of surgery is usually two weeks.
   (A) reservation
   (B) recreation
   (C) recovery
   (D) reduction （　）

3. Sunlight _____ off the surface of the ocean.
   (A) recognized
   (B) referred
   (C) reduced
   (D) reflected （　）

4. The war has caused over a million _____ to flee the country.
   (A) refugees
   (B) reporters
   (C) researchers
   (D) relatives （　）

5. My family's _____ for lasagna has been passed down for generations.
   (A) rectangle
   (B) recipe
   (C) receiver
   (D) reception （　）

6. The hometown fans went through a _____ of emotions during the exciting match.
   (A) raisin
   (B) rank
   (C) range
   (D) razor （　）

7. Being completely _____, a student like Ben has no chance of ever attending Harvard.
   (A) realistic
   (B) rapid
   (C) reasonable
   (D) recent （　）

8. Though he used to be a terrible drunk, John doesn't drink on a
_____ basis anymore.

  (A) regional   (B) responsible

  (C) regular   (D) reliable   (   )

9. Let's get together after class and _____ our speeches. We can be
each other's audience.

  (A) refresh   (B) regard

  (C) rehearse   (D) register   (   )

10. He made a _____ never to see her again.

  (A) resolution   (B) resistance

  (C) reservation   (D) resignation   (   )

11. Aging is a disease without _____.

  (A) religion   (B) remedy

  (C) resource   (D) rejection   (   )

12. You will be _____ to present a valid ID in order to enter the
building.

  (A) regulated   (B) retained

  (C) required   (D) restricted   (   )

13. Oddly enough, the boy doesn't _____ either of his parents.

  (A) reject   (B) relax

  (C) resemble   (D) release   (   )

14. When dealing with the police, always be _____ and cooperative.

  (A) reluctant   (B) respectful

  (C) remarkable   (D) respectable   (   )

15. I've just received her _____. She can't make it tonight.

  (A) repetition   (B) requirement

  (C) response   (D) reputation   (   )

TEST 22 詳解

1. (**C**) The politician said he did not <u>recall</u> meeting with a prostitute.
這名政客說，他想不起來有和娼妓見過面。

 (A) rebel [4] 〔rɪ'bɛl〕 v. 反叛

 (B) recite [4] 〔rɪ'saɪt〕 v. 背誦；朗誦

 (C) ***recall*** [4] 〔rɪ'kɔl〕 v. 回想；想起；召回

 (D) react [3] 〔rɪ'ækt〕 v. 反應

 *politician [3] 〔ˌpɑlə'tɪʃən〕 n. 政客　　prostitute〔'prɑstə,tjut〕 n. 娼妓

2. (**C**) The <u>recovery</u> time from this type of surgery is usually two weeks.
這種手術的復原期通常約兩週。

 (A) reservation [4] 〔ˌrɛzɚ'veʃən〕 n. 預訂

 (B) recreation [4] 〔ˌrɛkrɪ'eʃən〕 n. 娛樂

 (C) ***recovery*** [4] 〔rɪ'kʌvərɪ〕 n. 恢復；復原

 (D) reduction [4] 〔rɪ'dʌkʃən〕 n. 減少

 *surgery [4] 〔'sɝdʒərɪ〕 n. 手術

3. (**D**) Sunlight <u>reflected</u> off the surface of the ocean.
陽光會從海洋表面反射開來。

 (A) recognize [3] 〔'rɛkəg,naɪz〕 v. 認得

 (B) refer [4] 〔rɪ'fɝ〕 v. 提到；參考；委託；指

 (C) reduce [3] 〔rɪ'djus〕 v. 減少

 (D) ***reflect*** [4] 〔rɪ'flɛkt〕 v. 反射；反映

 *sunlight〔'sʌn,laɪt〕 n. 陽光　　surface [2] 〔'sɝfɪs〕 n. 表面

4. (**A**) The war has caused over a million <u>refugees</u> to flee the country.
這場戰爭已經使得超過一百萬的難民逃離該國。

 (A) ***refugee*** [4] 〔ˌrɛfju'dʒi〕 n. 難民

 (B) reporter [2] 〔rɪ'portɚ〕 n. 記者

 (C) researcher [4] 〔rɪ'sɝtʃɚ〕 n. 研究人員

 (D) relative [4] 〔'rɛlətɪv〕 n. 親戚

 *flee [4] 〔fli〕 n. 逃離

5. (**B**) My family's <u>recipe</u> for lasagna has been passed down from generations. 我家這道千層麵食譜已經傳了好幾代了。

    (A) rectangle[2]〔ˈrɛktæŋgl̩〕 *n.* 長方形

    (B) ***recipe***[4] 〔ˈrɛsəpɪ〕 *n.* 食譜；祕訣

    (C) receiver[3] 〔rɪˈsivɚ〕 *n.* 聽筒

    (D) reception[4] 〔rɪˈsɛpʃən〕 *n.* 歡迎（會）；接待

    ＊lasagna 〔ləˈzænjə , ləˈzɑnjə〕 *n.* 義式寬麵條；義式千層麵

    pass down 傳遞   generation[4] 〔ˌdʒɛnəˈreʃən〕 *n.* 世代

6. (**C**) The hometown fans went through a <u>range</u> of emotions during the exciting match.

家鄉的粉絲在這場令人興奮的遊行中，經歷到了<u>各種</u>情緒。

    (A) raisin[3] 〔ˈrezn̩〕 *n.* 葡萄乾

    (B) rank[3] 〔ræŋk〕 *n.* 階級；地位

    (C) ***range***[2] 〔rendʒ〕 *n.* 範圍；種類   ***a range of*** 各種的

    (D) razor[3] 〔ˈrezɚ〕 *n.* 刮鬍刀；剃刀

    ＊hometown[3] 〔ˈhomˌtaʊn〕 *n.* 家鄉   fan[4] 〔fæn〕 *n.* 迷；粉絲

    go through 經歷；歷經   emotion[2] 〔ɪˈmoʃən〕 *n.* 情感；情緒

    march[3] 〔mɑrtʃ〕 *n.* 行軍；行進

7. (**A**) Being completely <u>realistic</u>, a student like Ben has no chance of ever attending Harvard.

完全<u>現實</u>來看，像班這樣的學生絕對不可能唸哈佛大學。

    (A) ***realistic***[4] 〔ˌriəˈlɪstɪk〕 *adj.* 寫實的；現實的

    (B) rapid[2] 〔ˈræpɪd〕 *adj.* 迅速的；快速的

    (C) reasonable[3] 〔ˈriznəbl̩〕 *adj.* 合理的

    (D) recent[2] 〔ˈrisn̩t〕 *adj.* 最近的

    ＊completely[2] 〔kəmˈplitlɪ〕 *adv.* 完全地   chance[1] 〔tʃæns〕 *n.* 機會

    attend[2] 〔əˈtɛnd〕 *v.* 上（學）   Harvard 〔ˈhɑrvɚd〕 *n.* 哈佛大學

8. (**C**) Though he used to be a terrible drunk, John doesn't drink on a <u>regular</u> basis anymore.

雖然約翰過去曾經是個酒鬼，但他現在不再<u>經常</u>喝酒了。

    (A) regional[3] 〔ˈridʒənl̩〕 *adj.* 區域性的

(B) responsible [2] 〔 rɪˋspɑnsəbḷ 〕 *adj.* 應負責任的

(C) ***regular*** [2] 〔ˋrɛgjələ 〕 *adj.* 規律的；定期的；經常的

　　on a regular basis 經常地 (= *regularly*)

(D) reliable [3] 〔 rɪˋlaɪəbḷ 〕 *adj.* 可靠的

*****used to V** 過去曾經　　　drunk [3] 〔 drʌŋk 〕 *adj.* 喝醉的　*n.* 酒醉者

　not...anymore 不再　　　basis [2] 〔ˋbesɪs 〕 *n.* 基礎；根據

9. (**C**) Let's get together after class and <u>rehearse</u> our speeches. We can be each other's audience. 我們放學之後聚一聚，<u>預演</u>一下我們的演講吧。我們可以當彼此的觀眾。

　　(A) refresh [4] 〔 rɪˋfrɛʃ 〕 *v.* 使提神；使神清氣爽

　　(B) regard [2] 〔 rɪˋgɑrd 〕 *v.* 認為；尊重

　　(C) ***rehearse*** [4] 〔 rɪˋhɝs 〕 *v.* 預演；排練

　　(D) register [4] 〔ˋrɛdʒɪstə 〕 *v.* 登記；註冊

　*****get together** 聚會　　audience [3] 〔ˋɔdɪəns 〕 *n.* 聽眾；觀眾

10. (**A**) He made a <u>resolution</u> never to see her again. 他<u>決定</u>永遠不再見她。

　　(A) ***resolution*** [4] 〔ˏrɛzəˋluʃən 〕 *n.* 解決；決心

　　(B) resistance [4] 〔 rɪˋzɪstəns 〕 *n.* 抵抗

　　(C) reservation [4] 〔ˏrɛzəˋveʃən 〕 *n.* 預訂

　　(D) resignation [4] 〔ˏrɛzɪgˋneʃən 〕 *n.* 辭職

11. (**B**) Aging is a disease without <u>remedy</u>. 老化是一種沒有<u>治療方法</u>的疾病。

　　(A) religion [3] 〔 rɪˋlɪdʒən 〕 *n.* 宗教

　　(B) ***remedy*** [4] 〔ˋrɛmədɪ 〕 *n.* 治療法

　　(C) resource [3] 〔 rɪˋsors 〕 *n.* 資源

　　(D) rejection [4] 〔 rɪˋdʒɛkʃən 〕 *n.* 拒絕

　*****age** [1] 〔 edʒ 〕 *v.* 變老；老化　　disease [3] 〔 dɪˋziz 〕 *n.* 疾病

12. (**C**) You will be <u>required</u> to present a valid ID in order to enter the building. 你<u>必須</u>出示有效的身分證明，才能進入這棟大樓。

　　(A) regulate [4] 〔ˋrɛgjəˏlet 〕 *v.* 管制；管理

　　(B) retain [4] 〔 rɪˋten 〕 *v.* 保留；抑制

(C) **require**[2] ﹝rɪ`kwaɪr﹞ v. 需要；要求

(D) restrict[3] ﹝rɪ`strɪkt﹞ v. 限制

* present[2] ﹝prɪ`zɛnt﹞ v. 提出；出示

valid[6] ﹝`vælɪd﹞ adj. 有效的

ID 身分證明 (= *identification*[4])　　　enter[1] ﹝`ɛntɚ﹞ v. 進入

13. (**C**) Oddly enough, the boy doesn't <u>resemble</u> either of his parents.

說也奇怪，這個男孩<u>長得</u>不像父母任何一位。

(A) reject[2] ﹝rɪ`dʒɛkt﹞ v. 拒絕

(B) relax[3] ﹝rɪ`læks﹞ v. 放鬆

(C) **resemble**[4] ﹝rɪ`zɛmbḷ﹞ v. 長得像

(D) release[3] ﹝rɪ`lis﹞ v. 釋放

* oddly[3] ﹝`ɑdlɪ﹞ adv. 奇怪地

oddly enough 說也奇怪；奇怪的是

either[1] ﹝`iðɚ﹞ pron. 兩者中任一

14. (**B**) When dealing with the police, always be <u>respectful</u> and cooperative.

與警方打交道時，一定要<u>有禮貌</u>，採取合作的態度。

(A) reluctant[4] ﹝rɪ`lʌktənt﹞ adj. 不願意的

(B) **respectful**[4] ﹝rɪ`spɛktfəl﹞ adj. 恭敬的；有禮貌的

(C) remarkable[4] ﹝rɪ`mɑrkəbḷ﹞ adj. 出色的；顯著的；極好的

(D) respectable[4] ﹝rɪ`spɛktəbḷ﹞ adj. 可敬的；值得尊敬的

* **deal with** 應付　　　cooperative[4] ﹝ko`ɑpəˏretɪv﹞ adj. 合作的

15. (**C**) I've just received her <u>response</u>. She can't make it tonight.

我剛剛收到她的<u>回覆</u>，她今天晚上不能來了。

(A) repetition[4] ﹝ˏrɛpɪ`tɪʃən﹞ n. 重複

(B) requirement[2] ﹝rɪ`kwaɪrmənt﹞ n. 必備條件；要求

(C) **response**[3] ﹝rɪ`spɑns﹞ n. 回答；回應

(D) reputation[4] ﹝ˏrɛpjə`teʃən﹞ n. 名聲

* receive[1] ﹝rɪ`siv﹞ v. 收到　　　**make it** 成功；做到

TEST 23

【命題範圍：「高中生必背 4500 字」
p.191-200，retire～shake】

Directions: Choose the one word that best completes the sentence.

1. Nothing short of a _____ will change our system of government.
   (A) satisfaction
   (B) selection
   (C) separation
   (D) revolution
   (　　)

2. You should dance to the _____ of the music.
   (A) rhythm
   (B) rhyme
   (C) reward
   (D) riddle
   (　　)

3. The winner of the contest will be _____ tomorrow at noon.
   (A) reviewed
   (B) revealed
   (C) retired
   (D) retreated
   (　　)

4. The bombing attack was _____ for the recent arrest of two dozen suspected terrorists.
   (A) reunion
   (B) responsibility
   (C) revision
   (D) revenge
   (　　)

5. She played some soft music and lit some candles to set a _____ mood.
   (A) revolutionary
   (B) rough
   (C) romantic
   (D) rotten
   (　　)

6. Your _____ gets longer as the sun sets.
   (A) satellite
   (B) shadow
   (C) screwdriver
   (D) saucer
   (　　)

7. Money was _____ in his childhood, so he learned to be frugal from a young age.
   (A) satisfactory
   (B) rude
   (C) scarce
   (D) rusty
   (　　)

8. The school offers a variety of _____ for underprivileged students.
   (A) schedules   (B) scholars
   (C) sculptures   (D) scholarships   (   )

9. She _____ him for eating all the ice cream.
   (A) screamed   (B) scolded
   (C) scattered   (D) scared   (   )

10. A number of dead _____ were washed up on the beach.
    (A) seagulls   (B) scarecrows
    (C) robots   (D) roosters   (   )

11. The article only _____ the surface of corruption in the current government.
    (A) scouts   (B) scrubs
    (C) separates   (D) scratches   (   )

12. Mr. Franklin failed to make his car payments, so the bank _____ the vehicle.
    (A) sought   (B) sealed
    (C) seized   (D) satisfied   (   )

13. It was _____ of you to go there without me.
    (A) secondary   (B) selfish
    (C) severe   (D) senior   (   )

14. With a _____ diet and regular exercise, you should be able to lose the weight in a month or so.
    (A) salty   (B) sensible
    (C) royal   (D) shady   (   )

15. Her _____ got caught in the revolving door, nearly choking her to death.
    (A) route   (B) rubber
    (C) scarf   (D) semester   (   )

TEST 23 詳解

1. (**D**) Nothing short of a <u>revolution</u> will change our system of government.
如果缺乏<u>重大的變革</u>，就無法改變我們政府的制度。
   - (A) satisfaction⁴ (ˌsætɪsˈfækʃən) *n.* 滿足
   - (B) selection² (səˈlɛkʃən) *n.* 選擇；精選集
   - (C) separation³ (ˌsɛpəˈreʃən) *n.* 分開
   - (D) ***revolution***⁴ (ˌrɛvəˈluʃən) *n.* 革命；重大的變革
   - ***be short of** 缺乏　　**system**³ (ˈsɪstəm) *n.* 系統；制度

2. (**A**) You should dance to the <u>rhythm</u> of the music.
你應該隨著音樂的<u>節奏</u>跳舞。
   - (A) ***rhythm***⁴ (ˈrɪðəm) *n.* 節奏
   - (B) rhyme⁴ (raɪm) *n.* 押韻詩　*v.* 押韻
   - (C) reward⁴ (rɪˈwɔrd) *n.* 報酬；獎賞
   - (D) riddle³ (ˈrɪdl̩) *n.* 謎語
   - ***dance to the music** 隨著音樂跳舞

3. (**B**) The winner of the contest will be <u>revealed</u> tomorrow at noon.
這場比賽的優勝者將會在明天中午<u>揭曉</u>。
   - (A) review² (rɪˈvju) *v.* 複習
   - (B) ***reveal***³ (rɪˈvil) *v.* 透露；顯示
   - (C) retire⁴ (rɪˈtaɪr) *v.* 退休
   - (D) retreat⁴ (rɪˈtrit) *v.* 撤退
   - ***winner**² (ˈwɪnə) *n.* 優勝者　　**contest**⁴ (ˈkɑntɛst) *n.* 比賽
   - **noon**¹ (nun) *n.* 正午

4. (**D**) The bombing attack was <u>revenge</u> for the recent arrest of two dozen suspected terrorists.
那場炸彈攻擊是要<u>報復</u>最近逮捕了二十四名疑似恐怖份子。
   - (A) reunion⁴ (riˈjunjən) *n.* 團聚
   - (B) responsibility³ (rɪˌspɑnsəˈbɪlətɪ) *n.* 責任
   - (C) revision⁴ (rɪˈvɪʒən) *n.* 修訂
   - (D) ***revenge***⁴ (rɪˈvɛndʒ) *n.* 報復
   - ***bomb**² (bɑm) *v.* 投下炸彈　　**attack**² (əˈtæk) *n.* 攻擊
   - **recent**² (ˈrisn̩t) *adj.* 最近的　　**arrest**² (əˈrɛst) *n.* 逮捕

　　　dozen[1] (ˈdʌzn̩) *n.* 一打；十二個
　　　suspected[3] (səˈspɛktɪd) *adj.* 涉嫌的；有…嫌疑的
　　　terrorist[4] (ˈtɛrərɪst) *n.* 恐怖份子

5. (**C**) She played some soft music and lit some candles to set a <u>romantic</u>
　　　mood. 她播放一些輕音樂，並點了一些蠟燭，以製造<u>浪漫的</u>氣氛。
　　　(A) revolutionary[4] (ˌrɛvəˈluʃənˌɛrɪ) *adj.* 革命性的
　　　(B) rough[4] (rʌf) *adj.* 粗糙的
　　　(C) **romantic**[2] (roˈmæntɪk) *adj.* 浪漫的
　　　(D) rotten[2] (ˈrɑtn̩) *adj.* 腐爛的
　　　*play[1] (ple) *v.* 播放　　soft[1] (sɔft) *adj.* 輕柔的
　　　light[1] (laɪt) *v.* 點燃【三態：light-lit-lit】　　candle[2] (ˈkændl̩) *n.* 蠟燭
　　　set[1] (sɛt) *v.* 佈置；安排　　mood[3] (mud) *n.* 心情；氣氛

6. (**B**) Your <u>shadow</u> gets longer as the sun sets.
　　　當太陽下山時，你的<u>影子</u>會變長。
　　　(A) satellite[4] (ˈsætl̩ˌaɪt) *n.* 衛星；人造衛星
　　　(B) **shadow**[3] (ˈʃædo) *n.* 影子
　　　(C) screwdriver[4] (ˈskruˌdraɪvɚ) *n.* 螺絲起子
　　　(D) saucer[3] (ˈsɔsɚ) *n.* 碟子
　　　*set[1] (sɛt) *v.* (太陽) 落下

7. (**C**) Money was <u>scarce</u> in his childhood, so he learned to be frugal from
　　　a young age. 他在童年時期錢<u>很少</u>，所以他從小就學會節儉。
　　　(A) satisfactory[3] (ˌsætɪsˈfæktərɪ) *adj.* 令人滿意的
　　　(B) rude[2] (rud) *adj.* 粗魯的；無禮的
　　　(C) **scarce**[3] (skɛrs) *adj.* 稀少的；不足的
　　　(D) rusty[3] (ˈrʌstɪ) *adj.* 生銹的
　　　*childhood[3] (ˈtʃaɪldˌhud) *n.* 童年時期　　frugal (ˈfrugl̩) *adj.* 節儉的
　　　young[2] (jʌŋ) *adj.* 年輕的；幼小的

8. (**D**) The school offers a variety of <u>scholarships</u> for underprivileged
　　　students. 學校提供各式各樣的<u>獎學金</u>給貧困的學生。
　　　(A) schedule[3] (ˈskɛdʒul) *n.* 時間表
　　　(B) scholar[3] (ˈskɑlɚ) *n.* 學者

(C) *sculpture* [4] ﹝'skʌlptʃə﹞ *n.* 雕刻

(D) *scholarship* [3] ﹝'skɑləˏʃɪp﹞ *n.* 獎學金

* offer [2] ﹝'ɔfə﹞ *v.* 提供　　*a variety of* 各式各樣的

underprivileged ﹝ˏʌndə'prɪvlˏɪdʒd﹞ *adj.* 所享權益較少的；社會地位
低下的；貧困的【privilege [4] *n.* 特權】

9. (**B**) She <u>scolded</u> him for eating all the ice cream.

她<u>責罵</u>他，因為他吃了所有的冰淇淋。

(A) scream [3] ﹝skrim﹞ *v.* 尖叫

(B) *scold* [4] ﹝skold﹞ *v.* 責罵

(C) scatter [3] ﹝'skætə﹞ *v.* 散播

(D) scare [1] ﹝skɛr﹞ *v.* 驚嚇

10. (**A**) A number of dead <u>seagulls</u> were washed up on the beach.

有一些死掉的<u>海鷗</u>被沖上海灘。

(A) *seagull* [4] ﹝'siˏgʌl﹞ *n.* 海鷗

(B) scarecrow [3] ﹝'skɛrˏkro﹞ *n.* 稻草人　【比較】crow [1,2] *n.* 烏鴉

(C) robot [1] ﹝'robət﹞ *n.* 機器人

(D) rooster [1] ﹝'rustə﹞ *n.* 公雞

* *a number of* 一些；許多　　wash [1] ﹝wɑʃ﹞ *v.* (海浪、河水等) 沖擊

11. (**D**) The article only <u>scratches</u> the surface of corruption in the current
government. 這篇文章只<u>觸及</u>目前政府貪污腐敗的皮毛。

(A) scout [3] ﹝skaut﹞ *v.* 偵察　　*n.* 童子軍

(B) scrub [3] ﹝skrʌb﹞ *v.* 刷洗

(C) separate [2] ﹝'sɛpəˏret﹞ *v.* 使分開

(D) *scratch* [4] ﹝skrætʃ﹞ *v.* 抓 (癢)；搔 (頭)；抓傷

scratch the surface of 僅觸及…的皮毛【未深入探討問題的核心】

* article [2,4] ﹝'ɑrtɪkl̩﹞ *n.* 文章　　surface [2] ﹝'sɝfɪs﹞ *n.* 表面

corruption [6] ﹝kə'rʌpʃən﹞ *n.* 貪污；腐敗

current [3] ﹝'kɝənt﹞ *adj.* 現在的　　government [2] ﹝'gʌvənmənt﹞ *n.* 政府

12. (**C**) Mr. Franklin failed to make his car payments, so the bank <u>seized</u> the
vehicle.

富蘭克林先生未能支付他車子的款項，所以銀行將那輛車<u>沒收</u>。

(A) seek³ 〔 sik 〕 *v.* 尋找【三態：seek-sought-sought】

(B) seal³ 〔 sil 〕 *v.* 密封　*n.* 印章；海豹

(C) *seize*³ 〔 siz 〕 *v.* 抓住；沒收

(D) satisfy² 〔'sætɪs,faɪ 〕 *v.* 使滿足

*fail to V. 未能⋯　payment¹ 〔'pemənt 〕 *n.* 支付；付款；支付的款項
make a payment 支付；繳納　vehicle³ 〔'viɪkḷ 〕 *n.* 車輛

13. (**B**) It was <u>selfish</u> of you to go there without me.
你不帶我而自己去那裡是<u>自私的</u>。

(A) secondary³ 〔'sɛkən,dɛrɪ 〕 *adj.* 次要的

(B) *selfish*¹ 〔'sɛlfɪʃ 〕 *adj.* 自私的

(C) severe⁴ 〔 sə'vɪr 〕 *adj.* 嚴格的；嚴重的

(D) senior⁴ 〔'sinjɚ 〕 *adj.* 年長的；資深的

14. (**B**) With a <u>sensible</u> diet and regular exercise, you should be able to lose
the weight in a month or so.
有<u>明智的</u>飲食和規律的運動，你應該大約一個月之內，就能減輕體重。

(A) salty² 〔'sɔltɪ 〕 *adj.* 鹹的　【比較】salt¹ 〔 sɔlt 〕 *n.* 鹽

(B) *sensible*³ 〔'sɛnsəbḷ 〕 *adj.* 明智的；理智的；合理的
【比較】sensitive³ 〔'sɛnsətɪv 〕 *adj.* 敏感的

(C) royal² 〔'rɔɪəl 〕 *adj.* 皇家的

(D) shady³ 〔'ʃedɪ 〕 *adj.* 陰涼的

**diet*³ 〔'daɪət 〕 *n.* 飲食　regular² 〔'rɛgjələ 〕 *adj.* 規律的
be able to V. 能夠⋯　weight¹ 〔 wet 〕 *n.* 體重
lose weight 減輕體重　*or so* 大約

15. (**C**) Her <u>scarf</u> got caught in the revolving door, nearly choking her to
death.　她的<u>圍巾</u>卡在旋轉門內，差點使她窒息而死。

(A) route⁴ 〔 rut 〕 *n.* 路線

(B) rubber¹ 〔'rʌbɚ 〕 *n.* 橡膠；橡皮擦

(C) *scarf*³ 〔 skɑrf 〕 *n.* 圍巾

(D) semester² 〔 sə'mɛstɚ 〕 *n.* 學期

**catch*¹ 〔 kætʃ 〕 *v.* 卡住；鉤住；絆住；纏住
revolving⁵ 〔 rɪ'vɑlvɪŋ 〕 *adj.* 旋轉的　*a revolving door* 旋轉門
nearly² 〔'nɪrlɪ 〕 *adv.* 幾乎　choke³ 〔 tʃok 〕 *v.* 使窒息

TEST 24

【命題範圍：「高中生必背 4500 字」
p.151-200，noisy～shake】

Directions: Choose the one word that best completes the sentence.

1. He was told _____ times to turn down the music.

(A) numerous   (B) objective

(C) occasional   (D) nuclear   ( )

2. He faced many challenges and _____ in his path to success.

(A) orphans   (B) obstacles

(C) overpasses   (D) orbits   ( )

3. They were willing to _____ his mistake if he sincerely apologized.

(A) overtake   (B) overcome

(C) overlook   (D) overthrow   ( )

4. The meeting was _____ until Wednesday.

(A) persuaded   (B) participated

(C) postponed   (D) possessed   ( )

5. Pat has a _____ way of speaking that sounds like she has food in her mouth.

(A) patient   (B) peaceful

(C) passive   (D) peculiar   ( )

6. Instead of hitting the brakes, the old lady stepped on the gas _____ and ran into a tree.

(A) pebble   (B) petal

(C) penalty   (D) pedal   ( )

7. Grant doesn't have any _____ experience in management, so it's surprising they promoted him to supervisor.

(A) previous   (B) portable

(C) primitive   (D) pregnant   ( )

8. He stood by his _____ and refused to accept the bribe.

    (A) principals   (B) processes

    (C) principles   (D) procedures   ( )

9. His family name is difficult to _____.

    (A) pronounce   (B) prosper

    (C) publish   (D) proceed   ( )

10. It was _____ that Sarah was angry, but she didn't say a word.

    (A) plentiful   (B) realistic

    (C) remote   (D) obvious   ( )

11. Nothing can _____ a mother's love.

    (A) restore   (B) resist

    (C) replace   (D) resolve   ( )

12. The actor's _____ has decreased in recent years, but his movies still make money.

    (A) popularity   (B) population

    (C) position   (D) possibility   ( )

13. It's hard to say how old he is, but I guess he's _____ 80 years old.

    (A) overnight   (B) overseas

    (C) otherwise   (D) roughly   ( )

14. A high _____ of the female staff are part-time workers.

    (A) percentage   (B) personality

    (C) opportunity   (D) photography   ( )

15. Ted is being quite _____ in saying the meeting will end before five o'clock.

    (A) ordinary   (B) tropical

    (C) religious   (D) optimistic   ( )

TEST 24 詳解

1. (**A**) He was told <u>numerous</u> times to turn down the music.
他被告知<u>很多次</u>，要把音樂關小聲。
 (A) ***numerous*** [4] [ˈnjumərəs] *adj.* 很多的【注意發音】
 (B) objective [4] [əbˈdʒɛktɪv] *adj.* 客觀的 (↔ subjective [6] *adj.* 主觀的)
 (C) occasional [4] [əˈkeʒən̩] *adj.* 偶爾的
 (D) nuclear [4] [ˈnjuklɪr] *adj.* 核子的
 *time [4] [taɪm] *n.* 次　　***turn down*** 把…關小聲

2. (**B**) He faced many challenges and <u>obstacles</u> in his path to success.
在通往成功的道路上，他面臨許多挑戰和<u>阻礙</u>。
 (A) orphan [3] [ˈɔrfən] *n.* 孤兒
 (B) ***obstacle*** [4] [ˈabstək̩l] *n.* 阻礙
 (C) overpass [2] [ˈovəˌpæs] *n.* 天橋
 (D) orbit [4] [ˈɔrbɪt] *n.* 軌道
 *face [1] [fes] *v.* 面對　　challenge [3] [ˈtʃælɪndʒ] *n.* 挑戰
 path [2] [pæθ] *n.* 小徑；道路；前進的路線

3. (**C**) They were willing to <u>overlook</u> his mistake if he sincerely apologized.
如果他真心道歉，他們願意<u>忽視</u>他的錯誤。
 (A) overtake [4] [ˌovəˈtek] *v.* 趕上
 (B) overcome [4] [ˌovəˈkʌm] *v.* 克服
 (C) ***overlook*** [4] [ˌovəˈluk] *v.* 忽視
 (D) overthrow [4] [ˌovəˈθro] *v.* 推翻；打翻
 *willing [2] [ˈwɪlɪŋ] *adj.* 願意的　　sincerely [3] [sɪnˈsɪrlɪ] *adv.* 真誠地
 apologize [4] [əˈpɑləˌdʒaɪz] *v.* 道歉

4. (**C**) The meeting was <u>postponed</u> until Wednesday.
那場會議被<u>延</u>至星期三。
 (A) persuade [3] [pəˈswed] *v.* 說服
 (B) participate [3] [pɑrˈtɪsəˌpet] *v.* 參加

(C) ***postpone***[3] ﹝ post'pon ﹞ *v.* 延期；延後；拖延

(D) possess[4] ﹝ pə'zɛs ﹞ *v.* 擁有

＊meeting[4] ﹝'mitɪŋ﹞ *n.* 會議

5. (**D**) Pat has a <u>peculiar</u> way of speaking that sounds like she has food in her mouth. 派特說話的方式很<u>獨特</u>，聽起來好像有食物在嘴巴裡。

(A) patient[2] ﹝'peʃənt﹞ *adj.* 有耐心的　*n.* 病人

(B) peaceful[2] ﹝'pisfəl﹞ *adj.* 和平的；平靜的；寧靜的

(C) passive[4] ﹝'pæsɪv﹞ *adj.* 被動的（↔ *active*）

(D) ***peculiar***[4] ﹝ pɪ'kjuljɚ ﹞ *adj.* 獨特的；特有的

＊sound[1] ﹝ saʊnd ﹞ *v.* 聽起來　　mouth[1] ﹝ maʊθ ﹞ *n.* 嘴巴

6. (**D**) Instead of hitting the brakes, the old lady stepped on the gas <u>pedal</u> and ran into a tree.
那位老太太不是緊急煞車，而是踩了油門的<u>踏板</u>，然後撞到樹。

(A) pebble[4] ﹝'pɛbḷ﹞ *n.* 小圓石；鵝卵石

(B) petal[4] ﹝'pɛtḷ﹞ *n.* 花瓣

(C) penalty[4] ﹝'pɛnḷtɪ﹞ *n.* 刑罰

(D) ***pedal***[4] ﹝'pɛdḷ﹞ *n.* 踏板；腳踏板

＊***instead of*** 不…而～　　hit[1] ﹝ hɪt ﹞ *v.* 煞（車）
brake[3] ﹝ brek ﹞ *n.* 煞車　　***hit the brakes*** 緊急煞車
step[1] ﹝ stɛp ﹞ *v.* 踩　　gas[1] ﹝ gæs ﹞ *n.* 汽油；（汽車的）油門
run into 開車意外撞上

7. (**A**) Grant doesn't have any <u>previous</u> experience in management, so it's surprising they promoted him to supervisor. 格蘭特<u>之前</u>沒有任何管理方面的經驗，所以他們把他升為主管，令人十分驚訝。

(A) ***previous***[3] ﹝'privɪəs﹞ *adj.* 先前的；以前的

(B) portable[4] ﹝'portəbḷ﹞ *adj.* 手提的

(C) primitive[4] ﹝'prɪmətɪv﹞ *adj.* 原始的

(D) pregnant[4] ﹝'prɛgnənt﹞ *adj.* 懷孕的

＊management[3] ﹝'mænɪdʒmənt﹞ *n.* 管理
promote[3] ﹝ prə'mot ﹞ *v.* 使升遷　　supervisor[5] ﹝ˌsupɚ'vaɪzɚ﹞ *n.* 主管

8. (**C**) He stood by his <u>principles</u> and refused to accept the bribe.
他遵守他的<u>原則</u>，拒絕接受賄賂。

    (A) principal [2]〔'prɪnsəpḷ〕*n.* 校長　*adj.* 主要的

    (B) process [3]〔'prɑsɛs〕*n.* 過程

    (C) ***principle*** [2]〔'prɪnsəpḷ〕*n.* 原則

    (D) procedure [4]〔prə'sidʒɚ〕*n.* 程序

    ***stand by** 遵守　　refuse [2]〔rɪ'fjuz〕*v.* 拒絕

    accept [2]〔ək'sɛpt〕*v.* 接受　　bribe [5]〔braɪb〕*n.* 賄賂

9. (**A**) His family name is difficult to <u>pronounce</u>.
他的姓很難<u>唸</u>。

    (A) ***pronounce*** [2]〔prə'naʊns〕*v.* 發音

    (B) prosper [4]〔'prɑspɚ〕*v.* 繁榮；興盛

    (C) publish [4]〔'pʌblɪʃ〕*v.* 出版

    (D) proceed [4]〔prə'sid〕*v.* 前進

    ***family name** 姓 (= *last name* = *surname*)

10. (**D**) It was <u>obvious</u> that Sarah was angry, but she didn't say a word.
很<u>顯然</u>莎拉在生氣，但是她一句話也沒說。

    (A) plentiful [4]〔'plɛntɪfəl〕*adj.* 豐富的

    (B) realistic [4]〔ˌriə'lɪstɪk〕*adj.* 寫實的

    (C) remote [3]〔rɪ'mot〕*adj.* 遙遠的；偏僻的

       remote control 遙控

    (D) ***obvious*** [3]〔'ɑbvɪəs〕*adj.* 明顯的

    *word [1]〔wɝd〕*n.* 字；話

1. (**C**) Nothing can <u>replace</u> a mother's love.
什麼都無法<u>取代</u>母愛。

    (A) restore [4]〔rɪ'stor〕*v.* 恢復

    (B) resist [3]〔rɪ'zɪst〕*v.* 抵抗；抗拒

    (C) ***replace*** [4]〔rɪ'ples〕*v.* 取代

    (D) resolve [4]〔rɪ'zɑlv〕*v.* 決定；決心；解決

12. (**A**) The actor's <u>popularity</u> has decreased in recent years, but his movies still make money.
那名演員在最近幾年較不<u>受歡迎</u>，但他的電影仍然很賺錢。

(A) ***popularity***⁴〔͵pɑpjə'lærətɪ〕*n.* 受歡迎
(B) population²〔͵pɑpjə'leʃən〕*n.* 人口
(C) position¹〔pə'zɪʃən〕*n.* 位置
(D) possibility²〔͵pɑsə'bɪlətɪ〕*n.* 可能性

＊actor¹〔'æktɚ〕*n.* 演員　　decrease⁴〔dɪ'kris〕*v.* 減少
recent²〔'risn̩t〕*adj.* 最近的　　***make money*** 賺錢

13. (**D**) It's hard to say how old he is, but I guess he's <u>roughly</u> 80 years old.　很難說他年紀有多大，但我猜他<u>大約</u>八十歲。

(A) overnight⁴〔'ovɚ'naɪt〕*adv.* 一夜之間
(B) overseas²〔'ovɚ'siz〕*adv.* 在海外
(C) otherwise⁴〔'ʌðɚ͵waɪz〕*adv.* 否則
(D) ***roughly***⁴〔'rʌflɪ〕*adv.* 大約

14. (**A**) A high <u>percentage</u> of the female staff are part-time workers.
在女職員中，兼職工作的人佔很高的<u>比例</u>。

(A) ***percentage***⁴〔pɚ'sɛntɪdʒ〕*n.* 百分比；比例
(B) personality³〔͵pɝsn̩'ælətɪ〕*n.* 個性
(C) opportunity³〔͵ɑpɚ'tjunətɪ〕*n.* 機會
(D) photography⁴〔fə'tɑgrəfɪ〕*n.* 攝影

＊female²〔'fimel〕*adj.* 女性的　　staff³〔stæf〕*n.* 職員【集合名詞】
part-time〔͵pɑrt'taɪm〕*adj.* 兼職的

15. (**D**) Ted is being quite <u>optimistic</u> in saying the meeting will end before five o'clock.　泰德相當<u>樂觀</u>地說，會議會在五點之前結束。

(A) ordinary²〔'ɔrdn̩͵ɛrɪ〕*adj.* 普通的
(B) tropical³〔'trɑpɪkl̩〕*adj.* 熱帶的
(C) religious³〔rɪ'lɪdʒəs〕*adj.* 宗教的；虔誠的
(D) ***optimistic***³〔͵ɑptə'mɪstɪk〕*adj.* 樂觀的（↔ pessimistic⁴ *adj.* 悲觀的

TEST 25

【命題範圍：「高中生必背 4500 字」
p.201-210，shall～spoil】

Directions: *Choose the one word that best completes the sentence.*

1. The river is too _____ to accommodate large boats and ships.
   (A) shameful
   (B) sharp
   (C) significant
   (D) shallow （　）

2. As it started to rain, the hikers took _____ beneath an oak tree.
   (A) shovel
   (B) shaver
   (C) shuttle
   (D) shelter （　）

3. When I asked what happened, he _____ and said he didn't know.
   (A) shifted
   (B) shrunk
   (C) shrugged
   (D) shocked （　）

4. "Your father is working late again tonight," Mother _____.
   (A) shortened
   (B) sighed
   (C) shut
   (D) shined （　）

5. His plan is _____ and ignores the long-term needs of the community.
   (A) shortsighted
   (B) sorrowful
   (C) skinny
   (D) slight （　）

6. There's a remarkable _____ between the boy and his cousin. They almost look like twins.
   (A) similarity
   (B) significance
   (C) sincerity
   (D) signature （　）

7. She hoped to lose weight by _____ meals and cutting down on snacks.
   (A) splitting
   (B) sparkling
   (C) skipping
   (D) snapping （　）

8. These boots provide extra traction on _____ surfaces.
   (A) shiny   (B) slippery
   (C) smooth   (D) sincere   ( )

9. It took the boy less than five minutes to _____ the puzzle.
   (A) spoil   (B) splash
   (C) solve   (D) spare   ( )

10. The Buddha's main message is: Desire is the cause of all _____.
    (A) source   (B) sorrow
    (C) silence   (D) solution   ( )

11. Advances in construction techniques have allowed _____ to narrow in width, while increasing in height.
    (A) sleeves   (B) slopes
    (C) sidewalks   (D) skyscrapers   ( )

12. "Girl power" is a _____ that encourages and celebrates women's independence and confidence.
    (A) sketch   (B) snack
    (C) shampoo   (D) slogan   ( )

13. The rules of badminton are _____ similar to those for tennis, but with several modifications.
    (A) someday   (B) somehow
    (C) somewhere   (D) somewhat   ( )

14. Lifeguards ordered everyone out of the water after a _____ was spotted in shallow water near the beach.
    (A) shrimp   (B) snail
    (C) shark   (D) spider   ( )

15. The most remarkable feature of the palace is its _____ series of balconies.
    (A) splendid   (B) spiritual
    (C) solid   (D) specific   ( )

TEST 25 詳解

1. (**D**) The river is too <u>shallow</u> to accommodate large boats and ships.
   這河流水太淺，無法容納大型的船隻。
   (A) shameful [4] 〔ˈʃemfʊl 〕 *adj.* 可恥的
   (B) sharp [1] 〔 ʃɑrp 〕 *adj.* 銳利的；急轉的；鮮明的
   (C) significant [3] 〔 sɪɡˈnɪfəkənt 〕 *adj.* 意義重大的
   (D) ***shallow*** [3] 〔ˈʃælo 〕 *adj.* 淺的；膚淺的
   *accommodate [6] 〔 əˈkɑməˌdet 〕 *v.* 容納；裝載

2. (**D**) As it started to rain, the hikers took <u>shelter</u> beneath an oak tree.
   因為開始下雨了，遠足的人到橡樹下躲雨。
   (A) shovel [3] 〔ˈʃʌvl 〕 *n.* 鏟子 (= *spade*)
   (B) shaver [4] 〔ˈʃevɚ 〕 *n.* 電動刮鬍刀 (= *electric razor*)
   (C) shuttle [4] 〔ˈʃʌtl̩ 〕 *n.* 來回行駛；太空梭
   (D) ***shelter*** [4] 〔ˈʃɛltɚ 〕 *n.* 避難所；庇護
   *hiker [3] 〔ˈhaɪkɚ 〕 *n.* 遠足者　　beneath [3] 〔 bɪˈniθ 〕 *prep.* 在…下
   oak [3] 〔 ok 〕 *n.* 橡樹

3. (**C**) When I asked what happened, he <u>shrugged</u> and said he didn't know.
   當我問發生什麼事了，他聳肩說他不知道。
   (A) shift [4] 〔 ʃɪft 〕 *v.* 改變 (= *change*)；換檔
   (B) shrink [3] 〔 ʃrɪŋk 〕 *v.* 收縮；減少
   　　【三態變化：shrink–shrunk/shrank–shrunk】
   (C) ***shrug*** [4] 〔 ʃrʌɡ 〕 *v.* 聳 (肩)
   (D) shock [2] 〔 ʃɑk 〕 *v.* 震驚

4. (**B**) "Your father is working late again tonight," Mother <u>sighed</u>.
   「你父親今晚又加班了，」媽媽嘆氣著說。
   (A) shorten [3] 〔ˈʃɔrtn̩ 〕 *v.* 縮短　　(B) ***sigh*** [3] 〔 saɪ 〕 *v.* 嘆息；(風) 呼嘯
   (C) shut [1] 〔 ʃʌt 〕 *v.* 關；閉 (= *close*)
   (D) shine [1] 〔 ʃaɪn 〕 *v.* 照耀【三態變化：shine–shone–shone 】；
   　　擦亮【三態變化：shined–shined–shined 】

5. (**A**) His plan is <u>shortsighted</u> and ignores the long-term needs of the
   community. 他的計畫短視近利，而且忽略的社區長期的需求。

(A) ***shortsighted*** [4]〔'ʃɔrt'saɪtɪd 〕*adj.* 近視的；短視近利的

(B) sorrowful [4] 〔'sɑrofəl 〕*adj.* 悲傷的（ = *sad* ）

(C) skinny [2] 〔'skɪnɪ 〕*adj.* 皮包骨的（ = *very thin* ）

(D) slight [4] 〔 slaɪt 〕*adj.* 輕微的

*ignore [2]〔 ɪg'nɔr 〕*v.* 忽視   long-term〔,lɔŋ 'tɝm 〕*adj.* 長期的
community [4]〔 kə'mjunətɪ 〕*n.* 社區；社會

6. (**A**) There's a remarkable <u>similarity</u> between the boy and his cousin.
They almost look like twins.
男孩和他的堂弟非常<u>相似</u>。他們簡直像雙胞胎。

(A) ***similarity*** [3]〔,sɪmə'lærətɪ 〕*n.* 相似之處（ = *resemblance* ）

(B) significance [4]〔 sɪg'nɪfəkəns 〕*n.* 意義；重要性（ = *importance* ）

(C) sincerity [4]〔 sɪn'sɛrətɪ 〕*n.* 眞誠；誠意（ = *earnestness* ）

(D) signature [4]〔'sɪgnətʃɚ 〕*n.* 簽名

*remarkable [4]〔 rɪ'mɑrkəbl 〕*adj.* 顯著的；引人注目的
twin [3]〔 twɪn 〕*n.* 雙胞胎

7. (**C**) She hoped to lose weight by <u>skipping</u> meals and cutting down on
snacks. 她希望藉由<u>不吃飯</u>和減少吃點心來減重。

(A) split [4]〔 splɪt 〕*v.* 使分裂（ = *divide* ）；分攤

(B) sparkle [4]〔'spɑrkl 〕*v.* 閃耀

(C) ***skip*** [3]〔 skɪp 〕*v.* 跳過；翹（課）；不喝；不吃

(D) snap [3]〔 snæp 〕*v.* 啪的一聲折斷

lose weight 減重   meal [2]〔 mil 〕*n.* 一餐
cut down on 減少   snack [2]〔 snæk 〕*n.* 點心

8. (**B**) These boots provide extra traction on <u>slippery</u> surfaces.
這靴子在<u>滑溜的</u>表面上給予額外的摩擦力。

(A) shiny [3]〔'ʃaɪnɪ 〕*adj.* 閃亮的

(B) ***slippery*** [3]〔'slɪpərɪ 〕*adj.* 滑的；滑溜的

(C) smooth [3]〔 smuð 〕*adj.* 平滑的

(D) sincere [3]〔 sɪn'sɪr 〕*adj.* 眞誠的（ = *earnest* ）

*boots [3]〔 buts 〕*n. pl.* 靴子   provide [2]〔 prə'vaɪd 〕*v.* 提供；給予
extra [2]〔'ɛkstrə 〕*adj.* 額外的
traction〔'trækʃən 〕*n.*（防止在路面滑動的）附著摩擦力
surface [2]〔'sɝfɪs 〕*n.* 表面

9. (**C**) It took the boy less than five minutes to <u>solve</u> the puzzle.
男孩花了不到五分鐘<u>解開</u>這謎題。

(A) spoil [3] 〔spɔɪl〕 *v.* 破壞（= *make worse*）；寵壞

(B) splash [3] 〔splæʃ〕 *v.* 濺起

(C) ***solve*** [2] 〔sɑlv〕 *v.* 解決；解答

(D) spare [4] 〔spɛr〕 *v.* 騰出（時間）；吝惜

* take [1] 〔tek〕 *v.* 花（時間）　　puzzle [2] 〔'pʌzl〕 *n.* 謎；難題

10. (**B**) The Buddha's main message is: Desire is the cause of all <u>sorrow</u>.
佛陀的主要思想就是：慾望是所有悲傷的根源。

(A) source [2] 〔sors〕 *n.* 來源

(B) ***sorrow*** [3] 〔'sɑro〕 *n.* 悲傷（= *great sadness* = *grief*）

(C) silence [2] 〔'saɪləns〕 *n.* 沈默

(D) solution [2] 〔sə'kuʃən〕 *n.* 解決之道

* Buddha 〔'budə〕 *n.* 佛；佛陀　　main [2] 〔men〕 *adj.* 主要的
message [5] 〔'mɛsɪdʒ〕 *n.* 訊息；中心思想
desire [2] 〔dɪ'zaɪr〕 *n.* 慾望　　cause [1] 〔kɔz〕 *n.* 原因

11. (**D**) Advances in construction techniques have allowed <u>skyscrapers</u> to narrow in width, while increasing in height.
建築技術的進步讓<u>摩天大樓</u>得以更狹長，同時更高。

(A) sleeve [3] 〔sliv〕 *n.* 袖子

(B) slope [3] 〔slop〕 *n.* 斜坡（= *slant*）

(C) sidewalk [2] 〔'saɪd,wɔk〕 *n.* 人行道（= *pavement*）

(D) ***skyscraper*** [3] 〔'skaɪ,skrepɚ〕 *n.* 摩天大樓

* advance [2] 〔əd'væns〕 *n.* 進步
construction [4] 〔kən'strʌkʃən〕 *n.* 建築；建設
technique [3] 〔tɛk'nik〕 *n.* 技術　　allow [1] 〔ə'lau〕 *v.* 允許
narrow [2] 〔'næro〕 *adj.* 窄的；狹的　　width [2] 〔wɪdθ〕 *n.* 寬度；幅度
increase [2] 〔ɪn'kris〕 *v.* 增加　　height [2] 〔haɪt〕 *n.* 高度

12. (**D**) "Girl power" is a <u>slogan</u> that encourages and celebrates women's independence and confidence.
「女權」這<u>標語</u>鼓勵和歌頌女性的獨立和信心。

(A) sketch [4] 〔skɛtʃ〕 *n.* 素描

(B) snack [2] 〔snæk〕 *n.* 點心

(C) shampoo³ 〔 ʃæm'pu 〕 *n.* 洗髮精

(D) *slogan*⁴ 〔'slogən 〕 *n.* 口號;標語

＊encourage² 〔 ɪn'kɝɪdʒ 〕 *v.* 鼓勵

celebrate³ 〔'sɛlə,bret 〕 *v.* 慶祝;歌頌

independence² 〔,ɪndɪ'pɛndəns 〕 *n.* 獨立

confidence⁴ 〔'kɑnfədəns 〕 *n.* 信心

13. (**D**) The rules of badminton are <u>somewhat</u> similar to those for tennis, but with several modifications.

羽毛球的規則和網球<u>有點</u>相似,但有些改變。

(A) someday³ 〔'sʌm,de 〕 *adv.* (將來) 某天

(B) somehow³ 〔'sʌm,hau 〕 *adv.* 以某種方法

(C) somewhere² 〔'sʌm,hwɛr 〕 *adv.* 在某處

(D) *somewhat*³ 〔'sʌm,hwɑt 〕 *adv.* 有一點 (*= sort of = kind of*)

＊rule¹ 〔 rul 〕 *n.* 規則　　　badminton² 〔'bædmɪntən 〕 *n.* 羽毛球 (運動)

similar² 〔'sɪmələ 〕 *adj.* 相似的 < *to* >　　　tennis² 〔'tɛnɪs 〕 *n.* 網球

modification 〔,mɑdəfə'keʃən 〕 *n.* 變更

14. (**C**) Lifeguards ordered everyone out of the water after a <u>shark</u> was spotted in shallow water near the beach.

有<u>鯊魚</u>在鄰近海灘的淺水區被發現後,救生員命令所有人不要下水。

(A) shrimp² 〔 ʃrɪmp 〕 *n.* 蝦子　　(B) snail² 〔 snel 〕 *n.* 蝸牛

(C) *shark*¹ 〔 ʃɑrk 〕 *n.* 鯊魚

(D) spider² 〔'spaɪdə 〕 *n.* 蜘蛛

＊lifeguard³ 〔'laɪf,gɑrd 〕 *n.* 救生員　　　order¹ 〔'ɔrdə 〕 *v.* 命令

spot² 〔 spɑt 〕 *v.* 發現;看見　　　shallow³ 〔'ʃælo 〕 *adj.* 淺的

15. (**A**) The most remarkable feature of the palace is its <u>splendid</u> series of balconies. 這宮殿最顯著的特色就是一連串華麗的陽台。

(A) *splendid*⁴ 〔'splɛndɪd 〕 *adj.* 華麗的 (*= magnificent*)

(B) spiritual⁴ 〔'spɪrɪtʃʊəl 〕 *adj.* 精神上的

(C) solid³ 〔'sɑlɪd 〕 *adj.* 堅固的 (*= hard = firm*) ;固體的

(D) specific³ 〔 spɪ'sɪfɪk 〕 *adj.* 特定的 (*= particular*)

＊feature³ 〔'fitʃə 〕 *n.* 特色　　　palace³ 〔'pælɪs 〕 *n.* 宮殿

series⁵ 〔'sɪrɪz 〕 *n.* 一連串;連續　　　balcony² 〔'bælkənɪ 〕 *n.* 陽台

TEST 26

【命題範圍：「高中生必背 4500 字」
p.211-220，spoon～switch】

Directions: Choose the one word that best completes the sentence.

1. Male tigers mark their territories by _____ urine on trees.
   (A) spraying　　　　　　(B) spraining
   (C) stinging　　　　　　(D) starving　　　　　( )

2. Somehow, they managed to _____ 12 people into the minivan.
   (A) spread　　　　　　　(B) squeeze
   (C) stab　　　　　　　　(D) sprinkle　　　　　( )

3. The _____ in the courtyard was created by a sculptor from France.
   (A) stitch　　　　　　　(B) status
   (C) statue　　　　　　　(D) standard　　　　　( )

4. The hiking trail includes several _____ and strenuous routes.
   (A) steady　　　　　　　(B) stable
   (C) steep　　　　　　　　(D) stormy　　　　　( )

5. A cloud of _____ rose from the wet soil in the hot sun.
   (A) stool　　　　　　　　(B) stereo
   (C) stadium　　　　　　　(D) steam　　　　　( )

6. Spiders use their silk to make webs, which function as _____ nets to catch other bugs.
   (A) stiff　　　　　　　　(B) straight
   (C) strict　　　　　　　　(D) sticky　　　　　( )

7. In chess and similar board games, complex _____ may be deployed by experienced players.
   (A) stresses　　　　　　　(B) strategies
   (C) structures　　　　　　(D) substances　　　( )

8. She _____ the fabric until it ripped.
   (A) stretched   (B) struck
   (C) strove   (D) stripped   ( )

9. The investigators produced a _____ of their findings.
   (A) submarine   (B) summary
   (C) subway   (D) stroke   ( )

10. This new computer is far _____ to the old one.
    (A) suitable   (B) suspicious
    (C) superior   (D) swift   ( )

11. The doctor said Ben might need _____ to remove the tumor.
    (A) summit   (B) surgeon
    (C) surface   (D) surgery   ( )

12. Millions of people spend hours a day _____ the Internet.
    (A) swinging   (B) swearing
    (C) staring   (D) surfing   ( )

13. After we _____ our expenses for the month, we should have some
    money left over.
    (A) succeed   (B) suggest
    (C) subtract   (D) suffer   ( )

14. If a _____ number of dogs attacked a man at the same time, he
    would have little chance of escape.
    (A) sufficient   (B) successful
    (C) shallow   (D) stubborn   ( )

15. Fearing the suspect might attempt to flee the country, the judge
    ordered him to _____ his passport.
    (A) swallow   (B) surrender
    (C) survive   (D) survey   ( )

TEST　26　詳解

1. (**A**) Male tigers mark their territories by spraying urine on trees.
雄性老虎藉由在樹上撒尿來標示牠們的領土。

    (A) **spray**[3]〔spre〕 v. 噴灑

    (B) sprain[3]〔spren〕 v. 扭傷

    (C) sting[3]〔stɪŋ〕 v. 叮咬（ = bite ）；刺痛

    (D) starve[3]〔starv〕 v. 飢餓；餓死；使挨餓

    *male[2]〔mel〕 adj. 公的；雄的　　mark[2]〔mark〕 v. 做記號；標記
territory[3]〔'tɛrə,torɪ〕 n. 領土　　urine[6]〔'jʊrɪn〕 n. 尿

2. (**B**) Somehow, they managed to squeeze 12 people into the minivan.
他們設法把十二個人成功擠進一台休旅車。

    (A) spread[2]〔sprɛd〕 v. 散播

    (B) **squeeze**[3]〔skwiz〕 v. 擠壓（ = press ）；塞；擠

    (C) stab[3]〔stæb〕 v. 刺（ = pierce ）；戳

    (D) sprinkle[3]〔'sprɪŋkl̩〕 v. 撒；下小雨；灑（ = scatter = spray ）

    *somehow[3]〔'sʌm,haʊ〕 adv. 以某種方法
manage[3]〔'mænɪdʒ〕 v. 設法；能夠
minivan〔'mɪnɪ,væn〕 n. 小客車；休旅車

3. (**C**) The statue in the courtyard was created by a sculptor from France.
庭院的雕像是一位來自法國的雕刻家所創造的。

    (A) stitch[3]〔stɪtʃ〕 n. 一針；一縫

    (B) status[4]〔'stetəs〕 n. 狀況；地位（ = standing ）；身份（ = position ）

    (C) **statue**[3]〔'stætʃʊ〕 n. 雕像

    (D) standard[2]〔'stændəd〕 n. 標準（ = criterion ）

    *courtyard[5]〔'kɔrt,jɑrd〕 n. 庭院　　create[2]〔krɪ'et〕 v. 創造；設計
sculptor[5]〔'skʌptə〕 n. 雕刻家

4. (**C**) The hiking trail includes several steep and strenuous routes.
這登山步道有好幾個陡峭且費力的路線。

    (A) steady[3]〔'stɛdɪ〕 adj. 穩定的

    (B) stable[3]〔'stebl̩〕 adj. 穩定的（ = steady ）

    (C) **steep**[3]〔stip〕 adj. 陡峭的；急遽的

(D) stormy³〔'stɔrmɪ〕*adj.* 暴風雨的（= *turbulent*）；激烈的；多風波的

＊hiking³〔'haɪkɪŋ〕*n.* 遠足　　trail³〔trel〕*n.* 小路；小徑

include²〔ɪn'klud〕*v.* 包含　　strenuous〔'strɛnjʊəs〕*adj.* 費力的

route⁴〔rut〕*n.* 路；路線

5. (**D**) A cloud of <u>steam</u> rose from the wet soil in the hot sun.

一股<u>蒸汽</u>在炎熱的陽光下從濕潤的土壤升起。

(A) stool³〔stul〕*n.* 凳子

(B) stereo³〔'stɛrɪo〕*n.* 立體音響；鉛版印刷

(C) stadium³〔'stedɪəm〕*n.* 體育館

(D) **steam**²〔stim〕*n.* 蒸汽（= *vapor*）；水蒸氣

＊cloud¹〔klaʊd〕*n.* 雲；雲狀物

rose¹〔roz〕*v.* 上升【三態變化：rise–rose–risen】

soil¹〔sɔɪl〕*n.* 土壤

6. (**D**) Spiders use their silk to make webs, which function as <u>sticky</u> nets to catch other bugs.

蜘蛛用牠們的絲來築網，這些有<u>黏性的</u>網能捕捉其他的昆蟲。

(A) stiff³〔stɪf〕*adj.* 僵硬的

(B) straight²〔stret〕*adj.* 坦率的；直的（= *direct*）

(C) strict²〔strɪkt〕*adj.* 嚴格的

(D) **sticky**³〔'stɪkɪ〕*adj.* 濕熱的（= *humid*）；黏的（= *adhesive*）

＊spider²〔'spaɪdɚ〕*n.* 蜘蛛　　silk²〔sɪlk〕*n.* 絲

web³〔wɛb〕*n.* 網　　function²〔'fʌŋkʃən〕*v.* 起作用；有功效

net²〔nɛt〕*n.* 網　　bug¹〔bʌg〕*n.* 蟲；昆蟲

7. (**B**) In chess and similar board games, complex <u>strategies</u> may be deployed by experienced players.

在西洋棋和類似的桌遊，經驗豐富的玩家可能要部署複雜的<u>策略</u>。

(A) stress²〔strɛs〕*n.* 重音；強調；壓力

(B) **strategy**³〔'strætədʒɪ〕*n.* 策略（= *scheme*）；戰略

(C) structure³〔'strʌktʃɚ〕*n.* 結構；組織（= *organization*）

(D) substance³〔'sʌbstəns〕*n.* 物質（= *material*）；毒品；內容

＊chess²〔tʃɛs〕*n.* 西洋棋　　***board game*** 桌面遊戲

complex³〔'kɑmplɛks〕*adj.* 複雜的　　deploy〔dɪ'plɔɪ〕*v.* 部屬

experienced²〔ɪks'pɪrɪənst〕*adj.* 經驗豐富的

8. (**A**) She stretched the fabric until it ripped. 她拉扯那塊布直到它裂開。

　　(A) **stretch** [2] ﹝strɛtʃ﹞ *v.* 拉長；伸展

　　(B) strike [2] ﹝straɪk﹞ *v.* 打擊；（災難）侵襲

　　　　【三態變化：strike–struck–struck】

　　(C) strive [4] ﹝straɪv﹞ *v.* 努力【三態變化：strive–strove–striven】

　　(D) strip [5] ﹝strɪp﹞ *v.* 剝去（= *remove*）；剝奪；脫掉（= *undress*）

　　* fabric [5] ﹝'fæbrɪk﹞ *n.* 織物；布　　rip [5] ﹝rɪp﹞ *v.* 裂開

9. (**B**) The investigators produced a summary of their findings.
　　調查人員製作了一份他們研究發現的摘要。

　　(A) submarine [3] ﹝'sʌbmə,rin﹞ *n.* 潛水艇　　*adj.* 海底的；海中的

　　(B) **summary** [3] ﹝'sʌmərɪ﹞ *n.* 摘要（= *outline*）

　　(C) subway [2] ﹝'sʌb,we﹞ *n.* 地下鐵

　　(D) stroke [4] ﹝strok﹞ *n.* 打擊；中風；一筆；一劃

　　* investigator [6] ﹝ɪn'vɛstə,getə﹞ *n.* 調查者；研究者
　　produce [2] ﹝prə'djus﹞ *v.* 生產；製作；拿出
　　findings [1] ﹝'faɪndɪŋz﹞ *n. pl.* 研究發現

10. (**C**) This new computer is far superior to the old one.
　　這台新電腦遠遠比舊的好。

　　(A) suitable [3] ﹝'sutəbl̩﹞ *adj.* 適合的（= *appropriate*）

　　(B) suspicious [4] ﹝sə'spɪʃəs﹞ *adj.* 可疑的（= *questionable*）；懷疑的

　　(C) **superior** [3] ﹝sə'pɪrɪə﹞ *adj.* 較優秀的；較佳的（= *better*）< to >

　　(D) swift [3] ﹝swɪft﹞ *adj.* 快速的

　　* far [1] ﹝fɑr﹞ *adv.* 遠遠地；大大地

1. (**D**) The doctor said Ben might need surgery to remove the tumor.
　　醫生說班可能需要手術來移除腫瘤。

　　(A) summit [3] ﹝'sʌmɪt﹞ *n.* 顛峰；山頂（= *mountaintop*）

　　(B) surgeon [4] ﹝'sɝdʒən﹞ *n.* 外科醫生

　　(C) surface [2] ﹝'sɝfɪs﹞ *n.* 外觀；表面（= *covering*）

　　(D) **surgery** [4] ﹝'sɝdʒərɪ﹞ *n.* 手術

　　* remove [3] ﹝rɪ'muv﹞ *v.* 移除　　tumor [6] ﹝'tjumə﹞ *n.* 腫瘤

2. (**D**) Millions of people spend hours a day surfing the Internet.
　　一天有幾百萬的人花好幾個小時上網。

(A) swing² 〔 swɪŋ 〕 v. 搖擺 (= *sway*)

(B) swear³ 〔 swɛr 〕 v. 發誓 (= *vow*)；詛咒 (= *curse*)

(C) stare³ 〔 stɛr 〕 v. 凝視 (= *gaze*)；瞪眼看

(D) *surf*⁴ 〔 'slogən 〕 v. 衝浪；瀏覽 (= *browse*)

* *millions of* 幾百萬的

13. (**C**) After we <u>subtract</u> our expenses for the month, we should have some money left over. 我們把這個月的費用<u>扣除</u>後，應該還有剩下一些錢。

(A) succeed² 〔 sək'sid 〕 v. 成功 < *in* >；繼承 < *to* >；接著發生

(B) suggest³ 〔 səg'dʒɛst 〕 v. 暗示；建議 (= *advise*)；顯示 (= *indicate*)

(C) *subtract*² 〔 səb'trækt 〕 v. 扣除；減掉 (= *take away* = *deduct*)

(D) suffer³ 〔 'sʌfɚ 〕 v. 罹患；受苦 (= *be in pain*)

* expense³ 〔 ɪk'spɛns 〕 n. 花費；費用　　*leave over* 留下；剩餘

14. (**A**) If a <u>sufficient</u> number of dogs attacked a man at the same time, he would have little chance of escape.

如果同時攻擊男士的狗數量<u>夠多</u>的話，他不會有機會逃脫。

(A) *sufficient*³ 〔 sə'fɪʃənt 〕 *adj.* 足夠的 (= *enough* = *adequate*)

(B) successful² 〔 sək'sɛsfəl 〕 *adj.* 成功的 (= *triumphant*)

(C) shallow³ 〔 'ʃælo 〕 *adj.* 淺的；膚淺的

(D) stubborn³ 〔 'stʌbɚn 〕 *adj.* 頑固的 (= *obstinate*)

* attack² 〔 ə'tæk 〕 v. 攻擊　　*at the same time* 同時

chance¹ 〔 tʃæns 〕 n. 機會　　escape³ 〔 ə'skep 〕 v. 逃走；逃脫

15. (**B**) Fearing the suspect might attempt to flee the country, the judge ordered him to <u>surrender</u> his passport.

害怕該嫌疑犯可能會逃出國，法官命令他<u>交出</u>護照。

(A) swallow² 〔 'swɑlo 〕 v. 吞　　n. 燕子

(B) *surrender*⁴ 〔 sə'rɛndɚ 〕 v. 放棄；投降 (= *give in*)；交出

(C) survive² 〔 sə'vaɪv 〕 v. 生還 (= *remain alive*)；自…中生還

(D) survey³ 〔 sə've 〕 v. 調查

* fear¹ 〔 fɪr 〕 v. 害怕　　suspect³ 〔 'sʌspɛkt 〕 n. 嫌疑犯

attempt³ 〔 ə'tɛmpt 〕 v. 嘗試　　flee⁴ 〔 fli 〕 v. 逃離

judge² 〔 dʒʌdʒ 〕 n. 法官　　order¹ 〔 'ɔrdɚ 〕 v. 命令

passport³ 〔 'pæs,port 〕 n. 護照

TEST 27

【命題範圍：「高中生必背 4500 字」
p.221-230，sword～tremendous】

Directions: Choose the one word that best completes the sentence.

1. His girlfriend was not at all _____ to his marriage proposal.
   (A) systematic
   (B) talkative
   (C) sympathetic
   (D) technical ( )

2. The dove is a _____ of peace and hope.
   (A) target
   (B) talent
   (C) symbol
   (D) syllable ( )

3. She has a _____ to take things too literally.
   (A) temperature
   (B) tension
   (C) tendency
   (D) theme ( )

4. Most predators in the wild are violently protective of their _____.
   (A) terror
   (B) textbook
   (C) tablet
   (D) territory ( )

5. The rings of Saturn are visible with the use of a high-powered _____.
   (A) telegraph
   (B) telegram
   (C) telescope
   (D) temper ( )

6. He had a _____ loss of memory and struggled to remember the man's name.
   (A) tender
   (B) temporary
   (C) tense
   (D) terrific ( )

7. According to Jim's _____, the power should shut itself off if the water level rises to a certain height.
   (A) theory
   (B) sympathy
   (C) technique
   (D) symphony ( )

8. The funny poem _____ his imagination.
   - (A) tickled
   - (B) tolerated
   - (C) tended
   - (D) tamed   (　)

9. Taste buds are found on different areas of the _____.
   - (A) thread
   - (B) thumb
   - (C) tongue
   - (D) term   (　)

10. The land was cleared of _____ by illegal logging operators.
    - (A) treasure
    - (B) syrup
    - (C) timber
    - (D) sword   (　)

11. Thank you for calling when I was ill—it was very _____ of you.
    - (A) tiresome
    - (B) timid
    - (C) thoughtful
    - (D) tidy   (　)

12. It wasn't until her ex-boyfriend _____ to kill her that Lucy called the cops.
    - (A) tightened
    - (B) teased
    - (C) threatened
    - (D) terrified   (　)

13. A special air conditioner is used to cool the mine from 55°C down to a more _____ 28°C.
    - (A) tiny
    - (B) tolerable
    - (C) thankful
    - (D) thorough   (　)

14. Bobby has lost a _____ amount of weight since we last saw him, hasn't he?
    - (A) tolerant
    - (B) traditional
    - (C) tremendous
    - (D) tragic   (　)

15. There are certain words in Japanese that don't _____ to English, and vice versa.
    - (A) transport
    - (B) translate
    - (C) transform
    - (D) transfer   (　)

TEST 27 詳解

1. (**C**) His girlfriend was not at all <u>sympathetic</u> to his marriage proposal.
　　他的女朋友完全不<u>同意</u>他的求婚。
　　(A) systematic⁴ (ˌsɪstəˈmætɪk) *adj.* 有系統的
　　(B) talkative² (ˈtɔkətɪv) *adj.* 愛說話的
　　(C) *sympathetic*⁴ (ˌsɪmpəˈθɛtɪk) *adj.* 同情的；有同感的；同意的
　　　　be sympathetic to 同意
　　(D) technical³ (ˈtɛknɪkḷ) *adj.* 技術上的；專業的
　　* marriage² (ˈmærɪdʒ) *n.* 婚姻　　proposal³ (prəˈpozḷ) *n.* 提議；求婚

2. (**C**) The dove is a <u>symbol</u> of peace and hope. 鴿子是和平和希望的<u>象徵</u>。
　　(A) target² (ˈtɑrgɪt) *n.* 目標
　　(B) talent² (ˈtælənt) *n.* 才能
　　(C) *symbol*² (ˈsɪmbḷ) *n.* 象徵
　　(D) syllable⁴ (ˈsɪləbḷ) *n.* 音節
　　* dove¹ (dʌv) *n.* 鴿子　　peace² (pis) *n.* 和平

3. (**C**) She has a <u>tendency</u> to take things too literally.
　　她<u>傾向</u>於過分按照字面意義解釋事情。
　　(A) temperature² (ˈtɛmprətʃɚ) *n.* 溫度
　　(B) tension⁴ (ˈtɛnʃən) *n.* 緊張；緊張關係
　　(C) *tendency*⁴ (ˈtɛndənsɪ) *n.* 傾向
　　(D) theme⁴ (θim) *n.* 主題
　　* literally⁶ (ˈlɪtərəlɪ) *adv.* 字面上地；按照字面意義地
　　　take things too literally 過分按照字面意義解釋事情

4. (**D**) Most predators in the wild are violently protective of their <u>territory</u>.
　　大部分野生的掠食者會強烈保護牠們的<u>領土</u>。
　　(A) terror⁴ (ˈtɛrɚ) *n.* 驚恐；恐怖
　　(B) textbook² (ˈtɛkstˌbʊk) *n.* 教科書
　　(C) tablet³ (ˈtæblɪt) *n.* 藥片；平板電腦
　　(D) *territory*³ (ˈtɛrəˌtorɪ) *n.* 領土；領域

*predator〔'prɛdətɚ〕*n.* 掠食者　　wild²〔waɪld〕*n.* 野生狀態
violently³〔'vaɪələntlɪ〕*adv.* 暴力地；激烈地；強烈地
protective³〔prə'tɛktɪv〕*adj.* 保護的

5. (**C**) The rings of Saturn are visible with the use of a high-powered
<u>telescope</u>. 使用高倍率的<u>望遠鏡</u>就可以看見土星的環。

(A) telegraph⁴〔'tɛlə͵græf〕*n.* 電報
(B) telegram⁴〔'tɛlə͵græm〕*n.* 電報
(C) ***telescope***⁴〔'tɛlə͵skop〕*n.* 望遠鏡
(D) temper³〔'tɛmpɚ〕*n.* 脾氣

*ring¹〔rɪŋ〕*n.* 環　　Saturn〔'sætən〕*n.* 土星
visible³〔'vɪzəbḷ〕*adj.* 看得見的
power¹〔'pauɚ〕*n.* 力量；倍率　　***high-powered*** 高倍率的

6. (**B**) He had a <u>temporary</u> loss of memory and struggled to remember
the man's name. 他<u>暫時</u>失憶，很奮力地想要記起那人的名字。

(A) tender³〔'tɛndɚ〕*adj.* 溫柔的
(B) ***temporary***³〔'tɛmpə͵rɛrɪ〕*adj.* 暫時的
(C) tense⁴〔tɛns〕*adj.* 緊張的；拉緊的
(D) terrific²〔tə'rɪfɪk〕*adj.* 很棒的

*loss²〔lɔs〕*n.* 喪失；損失　　memory²〔'mɛmərɪ〕*n.* 記憶力
struggle²〔'strʌgḷ〕*v.* 掙扎；奮力

7. (**A**) According to Jim's <u>theory</u>, the power should shut itself off if the
water level rises to a certain height.
根據吉姆的<u>理論</u>，當水位上升到某個高度時會自動斷電。

(A) ***theory***³〔'θiərɪ〕*n.* 理論
(B) sympathy⁴〔'sɪmpəθɪ〕*n.* 同情；憐憫
(C) technique³〔tɛk'nik〕*n.* 技術；方法
(D) symphony⁴〔'sɪmfənɪ〕*n.* 交響曲

*shut¹〔ʃʌt〕*v.* 關閉　　level¹〔'lɛvḷ〕*n.* 高度；程度
water level 水位　　rise¹〔raɪz〕*v.* 上升
certain¹〔'sɝtn̩〕*adj.* 某個　　height²〔haɪt〕*n.* 高度

8. (**A**) The funny poem <u>tickled</u> his imagination.
　　　 這首好玩的詩<u>激發</u>了他的想像力。
　　　(A) ***tickle*** [3] [ˈtɪkl̩] *v.* 搔癢；刺激
　　　(B) tolerate [4] [ˈtɑləˌret] *v.* 容忍；忍受
　　　(C) tend [3] [tɛnd] *v.* 傾向於
　　　(D) tame [3] [tem] *v.* 馴服　*adj.* 溫馴的
　　　*funny [1] [ˈfʌnɪ] *adj.* 好笑的；好玩的　　poem [2] [ˈpo·ɪm] *n.* 詩
　　　imagination [3] [ɪˌmædʒəˈneʃən] *n.* 想像力

9. (**C**) Taste buds are found on different areas of the <u>tongue</u>.
　　　 味蕾位於<u>舌頭</u>的不同部位上。
　　　(A) thread [3] [θrɛd] *n.* 線
　　　(B) thumb [2] [θʌm] *n.* 大拇指【注意發音】
　　　(C) ***tongue*** [2] [tʌŋ] *n.* 舌頭；語言
　　　(D) term [2] [tɝm] *n.* 用語；名詞；期限
　　　*taste [1] [test] *n.* 味覺　　bud [3] [bʌd] *n.* 花蕾；花苞
　　　taste bud 味蕾

10. (**C**) The land was cleared of <u>timber</u> by illegal logging operators.
　　　 這片土地上的<u>木材</u>都被非法的伐木業者砍光了。
　　　(A) treasure [2] [ˈtrɛʒə] *n.* 寶藏
　　　(B) syrup [4] [ˈsɪrəp] *n.* 糖漿
　　　(C) ***timber*** [3] [ˈtɪmbə] *n.* 木材
　　　(D) sword [3] [sord] *n.* 劍
　　　*land [1] [lænd] *n.* 陸地；土地　　clear [1] [klɪr] *v.* 除去；開墾
　　　illegal [2] [ɪˈligl̩] *adj.* 非法的　　log [2] [lɑg] *n.* 圓木　*v.* 伐木
　　　operator [3] [ˈɑpəˌretə] *n.* 經營者；業者

11. (**C**) Thank you for calling when I was ill—it was very <u>thoughtful</u> of you.
　　　 謝謝你在我生病時打電話來——你真是<u>體貼</u>。
　　　(A) tiresome [4] [ˈtaɪrsəm] *adj.* 令人厭煩的；無聊的
　　　(B) timid [4] [ˈtɪmɪd] *adj.* 膽小的
　　　(C) ***thoughtful*** [4] [ˈθɔtfəl] *adj.* 體貼的
　　　(D) tidy [3] [ˈtaɪdɪ] *adj.* 整齊的

12. (**C**) It wasn't until her ex-boyfriend <u>threatened</u> to kill her that Lucy
called the cops. 直到前任男友<u>威脅</u>要殺死她時，露西才報了警。

(A) tighten³〔'taɪtn̩〕*v.* 變緊；變嚴格

(B) tease³〔tiz〕*v.* 嘲弄；取笑

(C) ***threaten***³〔'θrɛtn̩〕*v.* 威脅

(D) terrify⁴〔'tɛrə,faɪ〕*v.* 使害怕

*ex- 為表示「從前的」的字首

13. (**B**) A special air conditioner is used to cool the mine from 55°C down
to a more <u>tolerable</u> 28°C. 一台特殊的空調機，被用來使礦坑裡的溫
度從 55°C 降到較<u>可以忍受的</u> 28°C。

(A) tiny¹〔'taɪnɪ〕*adj.* 微小的

(B) ***tolerable***⁴〔'talərəbl̩〕*adj.* 可容忍的；可接受的

(C) thankful³〔'θæŋkfəl〕*adj.* 感激的

(D) thorough⁴〔'θɝo〕*adj.* 徹底的

air conditioner³ 空氣調節機；冷氣機

cool¹〔kul〕*adj.* 涼爽的　*v.* 使涼爽　　mine²〔maɪn〕*n.* 礦坑

14. (**C**) Bobby has lost a <u>tremendous</u> amount of weight since we last saw
him, hasn't he?
自從我們上次看到巴比到現在，他已經瘦了<u>好多</u>，不是嗎？

(A) tolerant⁴〔'talərənt〕*adj.* 寬容的

(B) traditional²〔trə'dɪʃənl̩〕*adj.* 傳統的；慣例的

(C) ***tremendous***⁴〔trɪ'mɛndəs〕*adj.* 巨大的
a tremendous amount of 大量的；很多

(D) tragic⁴〔'trædʒɪk〕*adj.* 悲劇的

15. (**B**) There are certain words in Japanese that don't <u>translate</u> to English,
and vice versa. 日文中有一些字沒辦法<u>翻譯</u>成英文，反之亦然。

(A) transport³〔træns'port〕*v.* 運輸

(B) ***translate***⁴〔'trænslet〕*v.* 翻譯

(C) transform⁴〔træns'fɔrm〕*v.* 轉變

(D) transfer⁴〔træns'fɝ〕*v.* 調職；轉移；轉學；轉車

*vice versa¹〔'vaɪsɪ'vɝsə〕*adv.* 反過來也一樣；反之亦然

TEST 28

【命題範圍：「高中生必背 4500 字」
p.231-240，trend～weekend】

Directions: *Choose the one word that best completes the sentence.*

1. Monsoons typically occur in _____ climates.
   (A) troublesome   (B) tribal
   (C) tropical   (D) tricky   (　)

2. There's nothing better than a _____ dinner on Thanksgiving Day.
   (A) turtle   (B) walnut
   (C) turkey   (D) vinegar   (　)

3. He has a very _____ ability to irritate people.
   (A) visible   (B) universal
   (C) various   (D) unique   (　)

4. The children are terribly _____ about their parents' divorce.
   (A) upset   (B) violent
   (C) urgent   (D) typical   (　)

5. The captain's _____ was salvaged from the shipwreck with all of its contents intact.
   (A) trunk   (B) trumpet
   (C) triumph   (D) triangle   (　)

6. In railroad terms, a bridge is the opposite of a _____. One goes over or around an obstacle; the other goes through or under it.
   (A) trend   (B) trial
   (C) tunnel   (D) tube   (　)

7. Stars don't really _____. The phenomenon is caused by the movement of air causing the light particles to bend.
   (A) upload   (B) twinkle
   (C) tumble   (D) twist   (　)

8. He brought home a bouquet of _____, her favorite flower.
   (A) tunes
   (B) tubs
   (C) tulips
   (D) twigs ( )

9. Dinosaurs _____ from the earth millions of years ago.
   (A) varied
   (B) volunteered
   (C) vanished
   (D) weaved ( )

10. The company was overwhelmed by the _____ of incoming orders.
    (A) vocabulary
    (B) virus
    (C) volume
    (D) virtue ( )

11. Tim's good looks are his most _____ asset.
    (A) vain
    (B) valuable
    (C) vast
    (D) vacant ( )

12. Smoking in the park is a _____ of the law.
    (A) universe
    (B) union
    (C) violation
    (D) victory ( )

13. Goodman's Hardware has a wide _____ of tools and supplies on sale.
    (A) variety
    (B) vitamin
    (C) valley
    (D) uniform ( )

14. The _____ looked across the courtroom, pointed at Jack Vincent and said, "That's him. He's the one who hit me."
    (A) vegetarian
    (B) victim
    (C) tutor
    (D) typist ( )

15. The students argue that the school has _____ their right to free speech.
    (A) voted
    (B) warned
    (C) violated
    (D) wakened ( )

高中生必背 4500 字測驗 *165*

TEST 28 詳解

1. (**C**) Monsoons typically occur in tropical climates.
季風通常發生在<u>熱帶</u>氣候。
   - (A) troublesome⁴〔ˈtrʌbl̩səm 〕*adj.* 麻煩的
   - (B) tribal⁴〔ˈtraɪbl̩ 〕*adj.* 部落的
   - (C) ***tropical***³〔ˈtrɑpɪkl̩ 〕*adj.* 熱帶的
   - (D) tricky³〔ˈtrɪkɪ 〕*adj.* 難處理的；棘手的
   - *monsoon〔mɑnˈsun 〕*n.* 季風　　typically³〔ˈtɪpɪkl̩ 〕*adv.* 通常
     occur²〔əˈkɝ 〕*v.* 發生　　climate²〔ˈklaɪmɪt 〕*n.* 氣候

2. (**C**) There's nothing better than a <u>turkey</u> dinner on Thanksgiving Day.
在感恩節時，沒有什麼比一頓<u>火雞</u>晚餐更棒了。
   - (A) turtle²〔ˈtɝtl̩ 〕*n.* 海龜
   - (B) walnut⁴〔ˈwɔlnət 〕*n.* 核桃
   - (C) ***turkey***²〔ˈtɝkɪ 〕*n.* 火雞；火雞肉
   - (D) vinegar³〔ˈvɪnɪɡɚ 〕*n.* 醋
   - *Thanksgiving〔ˌθæŋksˈɡɪvɪŋ 〕*n.* 感恩節

3. (**D**) He has a very <u>unique</u> ability to irritate people.
他激怒人的能力<u>獨一無二</u>。
   - (A) visible³〔ˈvɪzəbl̩ 〕*adj.* 看得見的
   - (B) universal⁴〔ˌjunəˈvɝsl̩ 〕*adj.* 普遍的；全世界的
   - (C) various³〔ˈvɛrɪəs 〕*adj.* 各種的；各式各樣的
   - (D) ***unique***⁴〔juˈnik 〕*adj.* 獨一無二的；獨特的
   - *ability²〔əˈbɪlətɪ 〕*n.* 能力　　irritate⁶〔ˈɪrəˌtet 〕*v.* 激怒

4. (**A**) The children are terribly <u>upset</u> about their parents' divorce.
孩子們對於他們父母親的離婚非常<u>難過</u>。
   - (A) ***upset***³〔ʌpˈsɛt 〕*adj.* 不高興的；難過的
   - (B) violent³〔ˈvaɪələnt 〕*adj.* 暴力的
   - (C) urgent⁴〔ˈɝdʒənt 〕*adj.* 迫切的；緊急的
   - (D) typical³〔ˈtɪpɪkl̩ 〕*adj.* 典型的；特有的
   - *terribly²〔ˈtɛrəblɪ 〕*adv.* 非常地　　divorce⁴〔dəˈvɔrs 〕*n.* 離婚

5. (**A**) The captain's <u>trunk</u> was salvaged from the shipwreck with all of its contents intact.

船長的<u>大皮箱</u>從沉船裡被打撈上來，裡面所有的東西都沒有受損。

(A) ***trunk***³ 〔 trʌŋk 〕 *n.* (汽車的) 行李箱；樹幹；大皮箱

(B) trumpet² 〔'trʌmpɪt 〕 *n.* 喇叭

(C) triumph⁴ 〔'traɪəmf 〕 *n.* 勝利

(D) triangle² 〔'traɪˌæŋgl̩ 〕 *n.* 三角形

*captain² 〔'kæptən 〕 *n.* 船長　　salvage 〔'sælvɪdʒ 〕 *v.* 打撈
shipwreck 〔'ʃɪpˌrɛk 〕 *n.* 船難；遇難船 (= *wreck*³)
contents⁴ 〔'kɑntɛnts 〕 *n., pl.* 內容物
intact⁶ 〔 ɪn'tækt 〕 *adj.* 完整的；未受損的

6. (**C**) In railroad terms, a bridge is the opposite of a <u>tunnel</u>. One goes over or around an obstacle; the other goes through or under it.

以鐵路用語來說，橋是<u>隧道</u>的相反。一個越過或繞過障礙物；
另一個則是穿過它或是從下面通過。

(A) trend³ 〔 trɛnd 〕 *n.* 趨勢

(B) trial² 〔'traɪəl 〕 *n.* 審判；試驗

(C) ***tunnel***² 〔'tʌnl̩ 〕 *n.* 隧道；地道

(D) tube² 〔 tjub 〕 *n.* 管子

*railroad¹ 〔'relˌrod 〕 *n.* 鐵路　　term² 〔 tɝm 〕 *n.* 名詞；用語
bridge¹ 〔 brɪdʒ 〕 *n.* 橋　　opposite³ 〔'ɑpəzɪt 〕 *n.* 相反
obstacle⁴ 〔'ɑbstəkl̩ 〕 *n.* 障礙　　through² 〔 θru 〕 *prep.* 穿過

7. (**B**) Stars don't really <u>twinkle</u>. The phenomenon is caused by the movement of air causing the light particles to bend. 星星並不是
<u>真正在閃爍</u>。這個現象是空氣流動導致光粒子轉向而造成的。

(A) upload⁴ 〔 ʌp'lod 〕 *v.* 上傳

(B) ***twinkle***⁴ 〔'twɪŋkl̩ 〕 *v.* 閃爍

(C) tumble³ 〔'tʌmbl̩ 〕 *v.* 跌倒

(D) twist³ 〔 twɪst 〕 *v.* 扭曲；扭傷

*phenomenon⁴ 〔 fə'nɑməˌnɑn 〕 *n.* 現象
movement¹ 〔'muvmənt 〕 *n.* 移動；流動　　light¹ 〔 laɪt 〕 *n.* 光
particle⁵ 〔'pɑrtɪkl̩ 〕 *n.* 微粒；粒子　　bend² 〔 bɛnd 〕 *v.* 彎曲；轉向

8. (**C**) He brought home a bouquet of <u>tulips</u>, her favorite flower.
他帶了一束<u>鬱金香</u>回家，那是她最喜歡的花。
(A) tune [3] 〔 tjun 〕 *n.* 曲子
(B) tub [3] 〔 tʌb 〕 *n.* 浴缸
(C) ***tulip*** [3] 〔'tulɪp 〕 *n.* 鬱金香
(D) twig [3] 〔 twɪg 〕 *n.* 小樹枝
*bouquet 〔 bu'ke 〕 *n.* 花束

9. (**C**) Dinosaurs <u>vanished</u> from the earth millions of years ago.
恐龍在數百萬年前從地球上<u>消失</u>。
(A) vary [3] 〔'vɛrɪ 〕 *v.* 改變；不同
(B) volunteer [4] 〔ˌvɑlən'tɪr 〕 *v.* 自願
(C) ***vanish*** [3] 〔'vænɪʃ 〕 *v.* 消失
(D) weave [3] 〔 wiv 〕 *v.* 編織
*dinosaur [2] 〔'daɪnəˌsɔr 〕 *n.* 恐龍　　earth [1] 〔 ɝθ 〕 *n.* 地球

10. (**C**) The company was overwhelmed by the <u>volume</u> of incoming orders.
這家公司無法承受進來的訂單<u>量</u>。
(A) vocabulary [2] 〔 və'kæbjəˌlɛrɪ 〕 *n.* 字彙
(B) virus [4] 〔'vaɪrəs 〕 *n.* 病毒
(C) ***volume*** [3] 〔'vɑljəm 〕 *n.* 音量；數量
(D) virtue [4] 〔'vɝtʃu 〕 *n.* 美德
*overwhelm [5] 〔ˌovɚ'hwɛlm 〕 *v.* 壓倒；使無法承受
incoming 〔'ɪnˌkʌmɪŋ 〕 *adj.* 進來的　　order [1] 〔'ɔrdɚ 〕 *n.* 訂單

11. (**B**) Tim's good looks are his most <u>valuable</u> asset.
提姆好看的容貌是他最<u>有價值的</u>資產。
(A) vain [4] 〔 ven 〕 *adj.* 無用的；徒勞無功的
(B) ***valuable*** [3] 〔'væljuəbl̩ 〕 *adj.* 珍貴的；有價值的
(C) vast [4] 〔 væst 〕 *adj.* 巨大的
(D) vacant [3] 〔'vekənt 〕 *adj.* 空的
*asset [5] 〔'æsɛt 〕 *n.* 資產　　looks [1] 〔 luks 〕 *n., pl.* 外表；容貌

12. (**C**) Smoking in the park is a <u>violation</u> of the law.　在公園吸煙<u>違反</u>法律。

(A) universe³〔'junə,vɝs〕*n.* 宇宙

(B) union³〔'junjən〕*n.* 聯盟；工會

(C) *violation*⁴〔,vaɪə'leʃən〕*n.* 違反；侵害

(D) victory²〔'vɪktrɪ , 'vɪktərɪ〕*n.* 勝利

13. (**A**) Goodman's Hardware has a wide <u>variety</u> of tools and supplies on sale. 古德曼五金行有<u>各式各樣的</u>工具和補給品在特賣。

    (A) *variety*³〔və'raɪətɪ〕*n.* 多樣性；種類

       a variety of 各種的；各式各樣的

    (B) vitamin³〔'vaɪtəmɪn〕*n.* 維他命

    (C) valley²〔'vælɪ〕*n.* 山谷

    (D) uniform²〔'junə,fɔrm〕*n.* 制服

    *hardware¹〔'hɑrd,wɛr〕*n.* 五金器具；硬體

     tool³〔tul〕*n.* 工具   supply³〔sə'plaɪ〕*n.* 供給品；補給品

14. (**B**) The <u>victim</u> looked across the courtroom, pointed at Jack Vincent and said, "That's him. He's the one who hit me." <u>被害人</u>越過法庭看過去，指著傑克・文森說：「就是他。他就是襲擊我的人。」

    (A) vegetarian⁴〔,vɛdʒə'tɛrɪən〕*n.* 素食主義者

    (B) *victim*³〔'vɪktɪm〕*n.* 受害者

    (C) tutor³〔'tjutɚ〕*n.* 家庭教師

    (D) typist⁴〔'taɪpɪst〕*n.* 打字員

    *across¹〔ə'krɔs〕*prep.* 橫越   courtroom³〔'kort,rum〕*n.* 法庭

     point³〔pɔɪnt〕*v.* 指；點

15. (**C**) The students argue that the school has <u>violated</u> their right to free speech. 學生們堅稱，學校<u>違反</u>了他們的言論自由權。

    (A) vote²〔vot〕*v.* 投票

    (B) warn³〔wɔrn〕*v.* 警告

    (C) *violate*⁴〔'vaɪə,let〕*v.* 違反

    (D) waken³〔'wekən〕*v.* 喚醒；叫醒

    *argue¹〔'ɑrgju〕*v.* 主張；堅稱   right³〔raɪt〕*n.* 權利

    speech³〔spitʃ〕*n.* 說話；言論

TEST 29

【命題範圍：「高中生必背 4500 字」
p.241-246，weekly～zoo】

Directions: Choose the one word that best completes the sentence.

1. He entered a contest to guess the _____ of a pig.

   (A) wheat   (B) wheel

   (C) wisdom   (D) weight   (   )

2. Employers must be concerned with the _____ of their workers.

   (A) width   (B) willow

   (C) wing   (D) welfare   (   )

3. She _____ in his ear that she wanted to leave.

   (A) whispered   (B) weighed

   (C) whipped   (D) widened   (   )

4. Wind _____ through cracks in the window frame.

   (A) wiped   (B) wondered

   (C) whistled   (D) withdrew   (   )

5. I wasn't _____ to accept every item on the list.

   (A) weekly   (B) willing

   (C) western   (D) whole   (   )

6. It's a pity to see so many _____ animals kept in cages.

   (A) wild   (B) windy

   (C) wide   (D) warm   (   )

7. The doctors bandaged his _____.

   (A) wreck   (B) wire

   (C) wound   (D) wood   (   )

8. There were no _____ to the crime.

   (A) wizards   (B) witches

   (C) winners   (D) witnesses   ( )

9. The blue _____ is the world's largest living animal.

   (A) wolf   (B) whale

   (C) worm   (D) zebra   ( )

10. He came to work wearing a badly _____ shirt.

   (A) yawned   (B) wept

   (C) yelled   (D) wrinkled   ( )

11. She sprained her _____ when playing volleyball.

   (A) yard   (B) youth

   (C) wrist   (D) zone   ( )

12. His favorite part of an egg is the creamy yellow _____.

   (A) wine   (B) yolk

   (C) yam   (D) yogurt   ( )

13. The night market has many _____ snacks.

   (A) yucky   (B) youthful

   (C) yummy   (D) yearly   ( )

14. _____ wants the last piece of cake is welcome to have it.

   (A) Whenever   (B) Whatever

   (C) Wherever   (D) Whoever   ( )

15. He has _____ interest in dating again after the death of his fiancée.

   (A) zero   (B) wit

   (C) west   (D) zipper   ( )

TEST 29 詳解

1. (**D**) He entered a contest to guess the <u>weight</u> of a pig.
   他參加一場比賽，要猜豬的<u>體重</u>。
   (A) wheat[3] 〔hwit〕 *n.* 小麥
   (B) wheel[2] 〔hwil〕 *n.* 輪子
   (C) wisdom[3] 〔'wɪzdəm〕 *n.* 智慧
   (D) *weight*[1] 〔wet〕 *n.* 重量；體重
   * enter[1] 〔'ɛntɚ〕 *v.* 參加　　contest[4] 〔'kɑntɛst〕 *n.* 比賽
     guess[1] 〔gɛs〕 *v.* 猜　　pig[1] 〔pɪg〕 *n.* 豬

2. (**D**) Employers must be concerned with the <u>welfare</u> of their workers.
   老闆必須關心員工的<u>福利</u>。
   (A) width[2] 〔wɪdθ〕 *n.* 寬度
   (B) willow[3] 〔'wɪlo〕 *n.* 柳樹
   (C) wing[2] 〔wɪŋ〕 *n.* 翅膀
   (D) *welfare*[4] 〔'wɛl,fɛr〕 *n.* 福利
   * employer[3] 〔ɪm'plɔɪɚ〕 *n.* 雇主；老闆　　*be concerned with* 關心
     worker[1] 〔'wɝkɚ〕 *n.* 工作者；工人

3. (**A**) She <u>whispered</u> in his ear that she wanted to leave.
   她在他耳邊<u>小聲說</u>她想要離開。
   (A) *whisper*[2] 〔'hwɪspɚ〕 *v.* 小聲說
   (B) weigh[1] 〔we〕 *v.* 重…
   (C) whip[3] 〔hwɪp〕 *v.* 鞭打
   (D) widen[2] 〔'waɪdn̩〕 *v.* 使變寬
   * *whisper in* one's *ear* 對某人講悄悄話（ = *speak in* one's *ear* ）

4. (**C**) Wind <u>whistled</u> through cracks in the window frame.
   風颼颼作響地穿過窗框的縫隙。
   (A) wipe[3] 〔waɪp〕 *v.* 擦
   (B) wonder[2] 〔'wʌndɚ〕 *v.* 想知道　*n.* 驚奇；奇觀

(C) *whistle*³〔'hwɪsl̩〕*v.* 吹口哨;(風)颼颼作響 *n.* 哨子

(D) withdraw⁴〔wɪð'drɔ〕*v.* 撤退;提(款)

*crack⁴〔kræk〕*n.* 裂縫   frame⁴〔frem〕*n.* 框;窗框

5.(**B**) I wasn't <u>willing</u> to accept every item on the list.
並不是清單上的所有項目,我都願意接受。

(A) weekly⁴〔'wiklɪ〕*adj.* 每週的 *n.* 週刊

(B) *willing*²〔'wɪlɪŋ〕*adj.* 願意的

(C) western²〔'wɛstɚn〕*adj.* 西方的

(D) whole¹〔hol〕*adj.* 整個的

*accept²〔ək'sɛpt〕*v.* 接受   item²〔'aɪtəm〕*n.* 項目
list¹〔lɪst〕*n.* 清單

6.(**A**) It's a pity to see so many <u>wild</u> animals kept in cages.
看到這麼多<u>野生</u>動物被關在籠子裡,真令人遺憾。

(A) *wild*²〔waɪld〕*adj.* 野生的;瘋狂的

(B) windy²〔'wɪndɪ〕*adj.* 多風的

(C) wide¹〔waɪd〕*adj.* 寬的

(D) warm¹〔wɔrm〕*adj.* 溫暖的

*pity³〔'pɪtɪ〕*n.* 可惜的事;遺憾的事
keep¹〔kip〕*v.* 拘留;拘禁   cage¹〔kedʒ〕*n.* 籠子

7.(**C**) The doctors bandaged his <u>wound</u>.
醫生用繃帶包紮他的<u>傷口</u>。

(A) wreck³〔rɛk〕*n.* 遇難的船;殘骸

(B) wire²〔waɪr〕*n.* 電線;鐵絲

(C) *wound*²〔wund〕*n.* 傷口

(D) wood¹〔wʊd〕*n.* 木頭

*bandage³〔'bændɪdʒ〕*v.* 用繃帶包紮;給…包上繃帶

8.(**D**) There were no <u>witnesses</u> to the crime.
沒有<u>目擊者</u>看到犯罪的經過。

(A) wizard [4] (ˈwɪzəd) n. 巫師

(B) witch [4] (wɪtʃ) n. 巫婆

(C) winner [2] (ˈwɪnə) n. 優勝者

(D) *witness* [4] (ˈwɪtnɪs) n. 證人；目擊者

　*crime [2] (kraɪm) n. 罪；犯罪

9. (**B**) The blue <u>whale</u> is the world's largest living animal.
　　藍鯨是全世界現存最大型的動物。

(A) wolf [2] (wulf) n. 狼

(B) *whale* [2] (hwel) n. 鯨魚　　*blue whale* 藍鯨

(C) worm [1] (wɜm) n. 蟲

(D) zebra [2] (ˈzibrə) n. 斑馬

　*living [2] (ˈlɪvɪŋ) adj. 活的；現存的

10. (**D**) He came to work wearing a badly <u>wrinkled</u> shirt.
　　他穿了一件非常皺的襯衫來上班。

(A) yawn [3] (jɔn) v. 打呵欠

(B) weep [3] (wip) v. 哭泣

(C) yell [3] (jɛl) v. 大叫

(D) *wrinkle* [4] (ˈrɪŋkḷ) v. 使起皺紋　 n. 皺紋
　　wrinkled [4] adj. 皺的

　*badly [1] (ˈbædlɪ) adv. 非常

11. (**C**) She sprained her <u>wrist</u> when playing volleyball.
　　她打排球時扭傷了手腕。

(A) yard [2] (jɑrd) n. 院子；碼

(B) youth [2] (juθ) n. 年輕

(C) *wrist* [3] (rɪst) n. 手腕

(D) zone [3] (zon) n. 地區

　*sprain [3] (spren) v. 扭傷
　volleyball [2] (ˈvɑlɪˌbɔl) n. 排球

12. (**B**) His favorite part of an egg is the creamy yellow <u>yolk</u>.
一顆蛋當中，他最喜歡的部分是柔滑的黃色<u>蛋黃</u>。

    (A) wine¹〔waɪn〕*n.* 酒；葡萄酒

    (B) ***yolk***³〔jok〕*n.* 蛋黃

    (C) yam¹〔jæm〕*n.* 蕃薯

    (D) yogurt⁴〔'jogət〕*n.* 優格

    *favorite²〔'fevərɪt〕*adj.* 最喜愛的   creamy²〔'krimɪ〕*adj.* 柔滑的

13. (**C**) The night market has many <u>yummy</u> snacks.
夜市有很多<u>好吃的</u>小吃。

    (A) yucky¹〔'jʌkɪ〕*adj.* 討厭的；令人厭惡的

    (B) youthful⁴〔'juθfəl〕*adj.* 年輕的

    (C) ***yummy***¹〔'jʌmɪ〕*adj.* 好吃的

    (D) yearly⁴〔'jɪrlɪ〕*adj.* 每年的；一年一次的

    *market¹〔'markɪt〕*n.* 市場   ***night market*** 夜市

    snack²〔snæk〕*n.* 點心；小吃

14. (**D**) <u>Whoever</u> wants the last piece of cake is welcome to have it.
<u>凡是</u>想要最後一塊蛋糕<u>的人</u>，都歡迎取用。

    (A) whenever²〔hwɛn'ɛvə〕*conj.* 無論何時

    (B) whatever²〔hwat'ɛvə〕*pron.* 無論什麼

    (C) wherever²〔hwɛr'ɛvə〕*conj.* 無論何處

    (D) ***whoever***²〔hu'ɛvə〕*pron.* 無論是誰；凡是…的人

15. (**A**) He has <u>zero</u> interest in dating again after the death of his fiancée.
在他的未婚妻過世之後，他對再次約會<u>完全沒有</u>興趣。

    (A) ***zero***¹〔'zɪro〕*n.* 零   *adj.* 一點也沒有的；全無的

    (B) wit⁴〔wɪt〕*n.* 機智

    (C) west¹〔wɛst〕*n.* 西方

    (D) zipper³〔'zɪpə〕*n.* 拉鍊

    *interest¹〔'ɪntrɪst〕*n.* 興趣   ***have interest in*** 對…有興趣

    date¹〔det〕*v.* 約會   fiancée〔fi'anse〕*n.* 未婚妻

TEST 30

【命題範圍：「高中生必背 4500 字」
p.201-246，shall～zoo】

Directions: Choose the one word that best completes the sentence.

1. He stared at the blank _____ of paper.
   (A) sheet　　　　　　　　(B) shame
   (C) shore　　　　　　　　(D) shell　　　　　　　(　)

2. His promises are of no _____ to us anymore.
   (A) sportsmanship　　　　(B) significance
   (C) silence　　　　　　　(D) substance　　　　　(　)

3. She _____ to sweat heavily when under stress.
   (A) suits　　　　　　　　(B) stretches
   (C) tends　　　　　　　　(D) spares　　　　　　(　)

4. The house needs a _____ cleaning from top to bottom.
   (A) typical　　　　　　　(B) stingy
   (C) thorough　　　　　　(D) superior　　　　　(　)

5. No one would _____ that James stole the money.
   (A) suspect　　　　　　　(B) switch
   (C) surround　　　　　　(D) swallow　　　　　(　)

6. If you look closely, you can see craters on the _____ of the moon.
   (A) syrup　　　　　　　　(B) surface
   (C) stocking　　　　　　(D) stomach　　　　　(　)

7. Although he often considered _____, he never had the guts to go through with it.
   (A) strength　　　　　　(B) survival
   (C) symbol　　　　　　　(D) suicide　　　　　　(　)

8. The _____ measured the man's waist and shoulders.

   (A) tailor   (B) survivor

   (C) teenager   (D) technician   ( )

9. He took off his wet clothes and _____ the water out.

   (A) suggested   (B) squeezed

   (C) struggled   (D) subtracted   ( )

10. If you don't eat the bread tonight, it will be _____ in the morning.

   (A) temporary   (B) stale

   (C) skillful   (D) suitable   ( )

11. She _____ the sidewalk outside her house every morning.

   (A) transfers   (B) sweeps

   (C) swells   (D) sways   ( )

12. They installed _____ panels on the roof of the building.

   (A) singular   (B) sincere

   (C) strict   (D) solar   ( )

13. The carpenter cut the wood into several small _____.

   (A) trunks   (B) squares

   (C) syllables   (D) systems   ( )

14. The restaurant staff did a _____ job of serving guests at the party.

   (A) suspicious   (B) spicy

   (C) tame   (D) splendid   ( )

15. The crowd erupted in applause when the singer appeared on _____.

   (A) slope   (B) string

   (C) stage   (D) slice   ( )

TEST 30 詳解

1. (**A**) He stared at the blank <u>sheet</u> of paper.
   他盯著那張空白的紙看。
   - (A) *sheet*[1] 〔 ʃit 〕*n.* 一張 (紙) ；床單
   - (B) shame[3] 〔 ʃem 〕*n.* 羞恥；可惜的事
   - (C) shore[1] 〔 ʃor 〕*n.* 海岸
   - (D) shell[2] 〔 ʃɛl 〕*n.* 貝殼；甲殼

   *stare[3] 〔 stɛr 〕*v.* 凝視；瞪眼看 < *at* >
   blank[2] 〔 blæŋk 〕*adj.* 空白的

2. (**B**) His promises are of no <u>significance</u> to us anymore.
   他的承諾對我們不再有任何的意義。
   - (A) sportsmanship[4] 〔'sportsmən͵ʃɪp 〕*n.* 運動家精神
   - (B) *significance*[4] 〔 sɪg'nɪfəkəns 〕*n.* 意義；重要性
   - (C) silence[2] 〔'saɪləns 〕*n.* 沈默
   - (D) substance[3] 〔'sʌbstəns 〕*n.* 物質

   *promise[2] 〔'prɑmɪs 〕*n.* 承諾；保證　　*not…anymore* 不再…

3. (**C**) She <u>tends</u> to sweat heavily when under stress.
   她在有壓力時，會流很多汗。
   - (A) suit[2] 〔 sut 〕*v.* 適合　*n.* 西裝
   - (B) stretch[2] 〔 strɛtʃ 〕*v.* 拉長；伸展
   - (C) *tend*[3] 〔 tɛnd 〕*v.* 易於；傾向於　　*tend to V.* 易於…；傾向於…
   - (D) spare[4] 〔 spɛr 〕*v.* 騰出 (時間) ；吝惜　*adj.* 空閒的

   *sweat[3] 〔 swɛt 〕*v.* 流汗　　heavily[1] 〔'hɛvɪlɪ 〕*adv.* 大量地
   stress[2] 〔 strɛs 〕*n.* 壓力

4. (**C**) The house needs a <u>thorough</u> cleaning from top to bottom.
   這間房子需要全部徹底的打掃。
   - (A) typical[3] 〔'tɪpɪkl̩ 〕*adj.* 典型的
   - (B) stingy[4] 〔'stɪndʒɪ 〕*adj.* 吝嗇的

(C) ***thorough*** [4] (ˋθɝo) *adj.* 徹底的

(D) superior [3] (səˋpɪrɪɚ) *adj.* 較優秀的

*bottom [1] (ˋbɑtəm) *n.* 底部　　***from top to bottom*** 全部地；完全地

5. (**A**) No one would <u>suspect</u> that James stole the money.
沒有人會懷疑詹姆士偷了錢。

(A) ***suspect*** [3] (səˋspɛkt) *v.* 懷疑

(B) switch [3] (swɪtʃ) *v.* 交換　　*n.* 開關

(C) surround [3] (səˋraʊnd) *v.* 圍繞；環繞

(D) swallow [2] (ˋswɑlo) *v.* 吞　　*n.* 燕子

6. (**B**) If you look closely, you can see craters on the <u>surface</u> of the moon.
如果你仔細看，就可以看到月球的<u>表面</u>有火山口。

(A) syrup [4] (ˋsɪrəp) *n.* 糖漿

(B) ***surface*** [2] (ˋsɝfɪs) *n.* 表面

(C) stocking [3] (ˋstɑkɪŋ) *n.* 長襪

(D) stomach [2] (ˋstʌmək) *n.* 胃

*closely [1] (ˋkloslɪ) *adv.* 仔細地　　crater [5] (ˋkretɚ) *n.* 火山口
moon [1] (mun) *n.* 月亮；月球

7. (**D**) Although he often considered <u>suicide</u>, he never had the guts to go through with it. 雖然他常考慮<u>自殺</u>，但他從未有勇氣實行。

(A) strength [3] (strɛŋθ) *n.* 力量；長處

(B) survival [3] (səˋvaɪvl̩) *n.* 生還；存活

(C) symbol [2] (ˋsɪmbl̩) *n.* 象徵

(D) ***suicide*** [3] (ˋsuə‚saɪd) *n.* 自殺

*consider [2] (kənˋsɪdɚ) *v.* 考慮　　guts [5] (gʌts) *n. pl.* 勇氣
go through with 完成；實行

8. (**A**) The <u>tailor</u> measured the man's waist and shoulders.
<u>裁縫師</u>測量那個男人的腰和肩膀。

(A) ***tailor*** [3] (ˋtelɚ) *n.* 裁縫師

(B) survivor [3] (səˋvaɪvɚ) *n.* 生還者

(C) teenager [2] 〔'tin‚edʒɚ 〕 *n.* 青少年

(D) technician [4] 〔 tɛk'nɪʃən 〕 *n.* 技術人員

*measure [2,4] 〔'mɛʒɚ 〕 *v.* 測量　　waist [2] 〔 west 〕 *n.* 腰

shoulder [1] 〔'ʃoldɚ 〕 *n.* 肩膀

9. (**B**) He took off his wet clothes and <u>squeezed</u> the water out.

他脫下濕衣服，<u>擰乾</u>了水。

(A) suggest [3] 〔 səg'dʒɛst 〕 *v.* 建議

(B) ***squeeze*** [3] 〔 skwiz 〕 *v.* 擠壓；擰出

(C) struggle [2] 〔'strʌgḷ 〕 *v.* 掙扎

(D) subtract [2] 〔 səb'trækt 〕 *v.* 減去；減掉

****take off*** 脫掉　　wet [2] 〔 wɛt 〕 *adj.* 濕的

clothes [2] 〔 kloz 〕 *n. pl.* 衣服

10. (**B**) If you don't eat the bread tonight, it will be <u>stale</u> in the morning.

如果你今天晚上不把麵包吃掉，早上就會<u>不新鮮</u>。

(A) temporary [3] 〔'tɛmpə‚rɛrɪ 〕 *adj.* 暫時的

(B) ***stale*** [3] 〔 stel 〕 *adj.* (餅乾、麵包) 不新鮮的

(C) skillful [2] 〔'skɪlfəl 〕 *adj.* 熟練的；擅長的

(D) suitable [3] 〔'sutəbḷ 〕 *adj.* 適合的

11. (**B**) She <u>sweeps</u> the sidewalk outside her house every morning.

她每天早上都會<u>掃</u>她家外面的人行道。

(A) transfer [4] 〔 træns'fɝ 〕 *v.* 調職；轉移；轉學；轉車

(B) ***sweep*** [2] 〔 swip 〕 *v.* 掃

(C) swell [3] 〔 swɛl 〕 *v.* 膨脹；腫起來

(D) sway [4] 〔 swe 〕 *v.* 搖擺

*sidewalk [2] 〔'saɪd‚wɔk 〕 *n.* 人行道

outside [1] 〔'aʊt‚saɪd 〕 *prep.* 在⋯的外面

2. (**D**) They installed <u>solar</u> panels on the roof of the building.

他們在建築物的屋頂上安裝<u>太陽能</u>面板。

(A) singular [4] 〔'sɪŋgjələ 〕 *adj.* 單數的

(B) sincere [3] 〔 sɪn'sɪr 〕 *adj.* 眞誠的

(C) strict [2] 〔 strɪkt 〕 *adj.* 嚴格的

(D) *solar* [4] 〔'solə 〕 *adj.* 太陽的；利用太陽能的

* install [4] 〔 ɪn'stɔl 〕 *v.* 安裝　　　panel [4] 〔'pænḷ 〕 *n.* 面板

roof [1] 〔 ruf 〕 *n.* 屋頂　　　building [1] 〔'bɪldɪŋ 〕 *n.* 建築物

13. (**B**) The carpenter cut the wood into several small <u>squares</u>.
那位木匠將木頭切成好幾個小<u>正方形</u>。

(A) trunk [3] 〔 trʌŋk 〕 *n.* 後車廂；樹幹

(B) *square* [2] 〔 skwɛr 〕 *n.* 正方形　　*adj.* 平方的

(C) syllable [4] 〔'sɪləbḷ 〕 *n.* 音節

(D) system [3] 〔'sɪstəm 〕 *n.* 系統

* carpenter [3] 〔'kɑrpəntə 〕 *n.* 木匠　　　wood [1] 〔 wʊd 〕 *n.* 木頭

14. (**D**) The restaurant staff did a <u>splendid</u> job of serving guests at the party.
餐廳的職員在宴會中對客人提供<u>非常好的</u>服務。

(A) suspicious [4] 〔 sə'spɪʃəs 〕 *adj.* 可疑的；懷疑的

(B) spicy [4] 〔'spaɪsɪ 〕 *adj.* 辣的

(C) tame [3] 〔 tem 〕 *adj.* 溫馴的；順從的　　*v.* 馴服

(D) *splendid* [4] 〔'splɛndɪd 〕 *adj.* 壯麗的；非常好的

* staff [3] 〔 stæf 〕 *n.* 職員【集合名詞】　　　guest [1] 〔 gɛst 〕 *n.* 客人

15. (**C**) The crowd erupted in applause when the singer appeared on <u>stage</u>.
當那位歌手出現在<u>舞台</u>上時，群眾爆發出熱烈的掌聲。

(A) slope [3] 〔 slop 〕 *n.* 斜坡

(B) string [2] 〔 strɪŋ 〕 *n.* 細繩；一連串

(C) *stage* [2] 〔 stedʒ 〕 *n.* 舞台　　***on stage*** 在舞台上

(D) slice [3] 〔 slaɪs 〕 *n.* （一）片

* crowd [2] 〔 kraʊd 〕 *n.* 群眾　　　erupt [5] 〔 ɪ'rʌpt 〕 *v.* 爆發

erupt in 突然爆發　　　applause [5] 〔 ə'plɔz 〕 *n.* 鼓掌

appear [1] 〔 ə'pɪr 〕 *v.* 出現

高三同學要如何準備「升大學考試」

　　考前該如何準備「學測」呢？「劉毅英文」的同學很簡單，只要熟讀每次的模考試題就行了。每一份試題都在7000字範圍內，就不必再背7000字了，從後面往前複習，越後面越重要，一定要把最後10份試題唸得滾瓜爛熟。根據以往的經驗，詞彙題絕對不會超出7000字範圍。每年題型變化不大，只要針對下面幾個大題準備即可。

準備「詞彙題」最佳資料：

背了再背，背到滾瓜爛熟，讓背單字變成樂趣。

考前不斷地做模擬試題就對了！

你做的題目愈多，分數就愈高。不要忘記，每次參加模考前，都要背單字、背自己所喜歡的作文。考壞不難過，勇往直前，必可得高分！

練習「模擬試題」，可參考「學習出版公司」最新出版的「7000字學測試題詳解」。我們試題的特色是：
①以「高中常用7000字」為範圍。②經過外籍專家多次校對，不會學錯。③每份試題都有詳細解答，對錯答案均有明確交待。

「克漏字」如何答題

　　第二大題綜合測驗（即「克漏字」），不是考句意，就是考簡單的文法。當四個選項都不相同時，就是考句意，就沒有文法的問題；當四個選項單字相同、字群排列不同時，就是考文法，此時就要注意到文法的分析，大多是考連接詞、分詞構句、時態等。「克漏字」是考生最弱的一環，你難，別人也難，只要考前利用這種答題技巧，勤加練習，就容易勝過別人。

準備「綜合測驗」（克漏字）可參考「學習出版公司」最新出版的「7000字克漏字詳解」。

本書特色：

1. 取材自大規模考試，英雄所見略同。
2. 不超出7000字範圍，不會做白工。
3. 每個句子都有文法分析。一目了然。
4. 對錯答案都有明確交待，列出生字，不用查字典。
5. 經過「劉毅英文」同學實際考過，效果極佳。

「文意選填」答題技巧

　　在做「文意選填」的時候，一定要冷靜。你要記住，一個空格一個答案，如果你不知道該選哪個才好，不妨先把詞性正確的選項挑出來，如介詞後面一定是名詞，選項裡面只有兩個名詞，再用刪去法，把不可能的選項刪掉。也要特別注意時間的掌控，已經用過的選項就劃掉，以免重複考慮，浪費時間。

準備「文意選填」，可參考「學習出版公司」最新出版的「7000字文意選填詳解」。

特色與「7000字克漏字詳解」相同，不超出7000字的範圍，有詳細解答。

「閱讀測驗」的答題祕訣

① 尋找關鍵字——整篇文章中,最重要就是第一句和最後一句,第一句稱為主題句,最後一句稱為結尾句。每段的第一句和最後一句,第二重要,是該段落的主題句和結尾句。從「主題句」和「結尾句」中,找出相同的關鍵字,就是文章的重點。因為美國人從小被訓練,寫作文要注重主題句,他們給學生一個題目後,要求主題句和結尾句都必須有關鍵字。

② 先看題目、劃線、找出答案、標題號——考試的時候,先把閱讀測驗題目瀏覽一遍,在文章中掃瞄和題幹中相同的關鍵字,把和題目相關的句子,用線畫起來,便可一目了然。通常一句話只會考一題,你畫了線以後,再標上題號,接下來,你找其他題目的答案,就會更快了。

③ 碰到難的單字不要害怕,往往在文章的其他地方,會出現同義字,因為寫文章的人不喜歡重覆,所以才會有難的單字。

④ 如果閱測內容已經知道,像時事等,你就可以直接做答了。

準備「閱讀測驗」,可參考「學習出版公司」最新出版的「7000字閱讀測驗詳解」,本書不超出7000字範圍,每個句子都有文法分析,對錯答案都有明確交待,單字註明級數,不需要再查字典。

「中翻英」如何準備

可參考劉毅老師的「英文翻譯句型講座實況DVD」,以及「文法句型180」和「翻譯句型800」。考前不停地練習中翻英,翻完之後,要給外籍老師改。翻譯題做得越多,越熟練。

「英文作文」怎樣寫才能得高分？

① 字體要寫整齊，最好是印刷體，工工整整，不要塗改。

② 文章不可離題，尤其是每段的第一句和最後一句，最好要有題目所說的關鍵字。

③ 不要全部用簡單句，句子最好要有各種變化，單句、複句、合句、形容詞片語、分詞構句等，混合使用。

④ 不要忘記多使用轉承語，像 *at present*（現在），*generally speaking*（一般說來），*in other words*（換句話說），*in particular*（特別地），*all in all*（總而言之）等。

⑤ 拿到考題，最好先寫作文，很多同學考試時，作文來不及寫，吃虧很大。但是，如果看到作文題目不會寫，就先寫測驗題，這個時候，可將題目中作文可使用的單字、成語圈起來，寫作文時就有東西寫了。但千萬記住，絕對不可以抄考卷中的句子，一旦被發現，就會以零分計算。

⑥ 試卷有規定標題，就要寫標題。記住，每段一開始，要內縮5或7個字母。

⑦ 可多引用諺語或名言，並注意標點符號的使用。文章中有各種標點符號，會使文章變得更美。

⑧ 整體的美觀也很重要，段落的最後一行字數不能太少，也不能太多。段落的字數要平均分配，不能第一段只有一、兩句，第二段一大堆。第一段可以比第二段少一點。

準備「英文作文」，可參考「學習出版公司」出版的：

1. 用會話背7000字① 書+CD一片 / 280元

將「高中常用7000字」融入日常生活會話，極短句，控制在5個字以內。以三句一組，容易背，背短句，比背單字還快，每句話都用得到，可以主動和外國人說。背完後，會說話、會寫作，更會考試。

2. 一分鐘背9個單字 書+CD一片 / 280元

顛覆傳統，一次背9個單字，把9個單字當作1個單字背，不斷熟背，變成直覺，就能終生不忘記，唯有不忘記，才能累積。利用相同字首、字尾編排，整理出規則，會唸就會拼，背單字變得超簡單。準確地鎖定「高中常用7000字」，用不到的、不考的字，不用浪費時間背。

3. 時速破百單字快速記憶 書 250元

7000字背誦法寶，用五種方法，以「一口氣」方法呈現，把7000字串聯起來，以發音為主軸，3字一組，9字一回，變成長期記憶。鎖定7000字，不超出7000字範圍。

4. 如何寫英文作文 書 250元

從頭到尾把英文作文該怎麼寫，敘述得一清二楚。從標題、主題句、推展句，到結尾句，非常完整。有最完整的轉承語，背了就有寫作文的衝動。

5. 7000字克漏字詳解 書 250元

保證7000字範圍，做克漏字測驗等於複習「高中常用7000字」。句子分析，一看就懂，對錯答案都有明確交代，翻譯、註釋樣樣齊全，不需要再查字典。Test 1～Test 5還有錄音QR碼，可跟著美籍老師唸，培養語感。

6. 7000字文意選填詳解　書 250元

「文意選填」是近年大學入試的新題型。本書取材自名校老師命題，每回測驗都在「劉毅英文」實際考過，效果極佳。有句子分析、翻譯及註釋，一看就懂。保證在7000字範圍內，每個單字都標明級數。

7. 7000字閱讀測驗詳解　書 250元

符合大學入學考試的命題原則，具知識性、趣味性、教育性，和生活性。有翻譯及註釋，每個單字都註明級數。由淺至深編排，因為不必查字典，像是看小說一樣，越做越想做。保證在7000字範圍內，不會碰到考試不考、以後又用不到的單字。

8. 7000字學測試題詳解　書 250元

精選6份完整的試題，按照大學入學考試新題型命題。每份試題附有翻譯和註釋，單字有標明級數，對錯答案都有明確交待。把這6份試題當作課本一樣熟讀，再做其他試題就簡單了。

9. 高中常用7000字解析【豪華版】　書 390元

取材自大學入學考試中心新修編的「高中英文參考詞彙表」研究計劃報告，收錄的均是教育部公布的重要字彙，讓同學背得正確，迅速掌握方向，並有效用於考場上。重要字彙皆有例句，提供讀者八種不同的學習方式，包含記憶技巧、同反義字、常考片語、典型考題等。

10. 高中7000字測驗題庫　書 180元

取材自大規模考試，每條題目都有詳細解答。做詞彙題能增加閱讀能力，只要詞彙題滿分，其他克漏字、文意選填、閱讀測驗、翻譯、作文，稍加努力，就能完全征服。

11.
文法寶典　書990元

文法是語言的歸納，不完全的文法規則，反而會造成學習的障礙。這套書是提供讀者查閱的，深入淺出，會讓學生很高興，有了「文法寶典」，什麼文法難題都可以迎刃而解。

12.
一口氣背文法　書+CD 280元

文法規則無限多，沒人記得下來，只要背216句，就學完文法，利用背的句子可說出來，還可寫作文。郭雅惠博士說：我很感恩，因為您發明的「一口氣背文法」，憑著那216句＋您的DVD＋我課前的準備，就可上課。

13.
全真英文法450題詳解　書280元

文法題目出起來可不簡單，不小心就會出現二個答案，中國人出題造句，受到中文的影響，很容易出錯。這本書選擇大陸、日本和台灣各大規模考試，大型考試出題者比較慎重，再請三位美籍老師校對，對錯答案都有明確交代。

14.
一口氣考試英語　書+CD 280元

單教試題，題目無法應用在日常生活當中，同學學起來很枯燥，把試題變成會話，就精彩了。試題往往有教育性，用這些題目來編會話，是最佳的選擇。同學一面準備考試，一面學會話，進步速度才快

15.
一口氣背同義字寫作文…① 書+MP3 280元

英文有17萬多字，沒有人背得下來，背了同義字，對寫作文有幫助，每個Unit先背九句平常用得到的會話，如：Unit 1 The Way to Success（成功之道），先背 九個核心關鍵句。

16.

一口氣背7000字①~⑯合集　書 990元

大考中心公佈的「高中英文常考字彙表」共6,369個字，也就是俗稱的「高中7000字」，我們按照「一口氣英語」的方式，三字一組來背，可快速增加單字。

17.

全真克漏字282題詳解　書 280元

本書取材自大陸和日本大學入學試題，經過美籍權威教授Laura E. Stewart和本公司編輯Christian Adams仔細校對。書中每篇克漏字都有句子分析，對錯答案都有明確交代。另有劉毅老師親授「克漏字講座DVD」，同步學習，效果加倍。

18.

翻譯句型800　書 180元

將複雜的英文文法濃縮成800個句子，同學可看著中文唸出英文，第二遍可看著中文默寫英文，也可在每一回Test中抽出一句練習。利用練習翻譯的機會，對閱讀能力、英文作文等也有幫助，一石多鳥。

19.

如何寫看圖英作文①　書 180元

四張連環圖：採用「一口氣英語」方式，每一張圖片三句為一組，四張共12句，剛好120字左右。同學只要想到一張圖寫三句話，就會覺得輕鬆很多。兩張圖為一段，就可寫出漂亮的文章。

20.

如何寫看圖英作文②　書 180元

一張圖片：以「一口氣英語」的方式，三句為一組，四組十二句，再以「人事時地物」為出發點，說明過去發生什麼事，現在情況如何，未來可能發生的情形，再說明你的看法即可。